The Global Police State

The Global Police State

William I. Robinson

PLUTO PRESS

First published 2020 by Pluto Press
345 Archway Road, London N6 5AA

www.plutobooks.com

British Library Cataloguing in Publication Data
A catalogue record for this book is available from the British Library

ISBN 978 0 7453 4163 7 Hardback
ISBN 978 0 7453 4164 4 Paperback
ISBN 978 1 7868 0665 9 PDF eBook
ISBN 978 1 7868 0667 3 Kindle eBook
ISBN 978 1 7868 0666 6 EPUB eBook

This book is printed on paper suitable for recycling and made from fully managed
and sustained forest sources. Logging, pulping and manufacturing processes are
expected to conform to the environmental standards of the country of origin.

Typeset by Stanford DTP Services, Northampton, England

Simultaneously printed in the United Kingdom and United States of America

Contents

A Brief Acknowledgment
of Collective Authorship

An acknowledgment is a recognition of the collective nature of creative works. Intellectual labor is no different than any other form of work: it is collective, part of the social labor process. A proper acknowledgment here would involve three levels in reference to the more immediate collective labor behind this study. First and foremost are those who have contributed directly by providing feedback and other forms of encouragement. Second are those who have contributed to my ideas or helped in one way or another in recent years during which I have been researching and writing on the themes taken up in the present work, in particular, on capitalist crisis and global police state. Third are the many people who over the decades have contributed to my own intellectual and political development and to the output of my publications. This latter category involves literally hundreds of people, a list too vast to take up here. Many among these friends, comrades, and colleagues have been mentioned in the acknowledgements sections of previous books and articles. At present, all I can do is mention some of the people who either contributed more immediately to the current work through support and comments or whom I may have inadvertently left out in earlier acknowledgements. In alphabetical order, these are: Victor Acuña, Paul Almeida, Myrna Alonso, Yousef Baker, Mario Barrera, Patrick Bond, Chris Chase-Dunn, Wilma Dunaway, Bill Fletcher Jr., Nathan Garrido, Felipe Gonzalez, the Great Transition Initiative and its director, Paul Raskin, Jerry Harris, Hiroko Inoue, Rosemary Lee, Peter McLaren, Steven Miller, Marcela Orozco, Peter Phillips, Salvador Rangel, Juan Manuel Sandoval, Xuan Santos, Oscar Soto, Martin Vega, and the late Immanuel Wallerstein. Apologies for anyone I may have inadvertently left out. A very special thanks to my wife, Venus Leung, who read over and commented on the entire manuscript, and who has supported me throughout the project, to two anonymous reviewers at Pluto Press, to my publisher at Pluto, David Castle, and to my copy-editor, Jeanne Brady.

Acronyms

ABS	Asset-Backed Securities
ALEC	American Legislative Exchange Council
CCA	Corrections Corporation of America
CIA	Central Intelligence Agency
CIT	Computer and Information Technology
DHS	Department of Homeland Security
GDP	Gross Domestic Product
ICE	Immigration and Customs Enforcement
ILO	International Labor Organization
IMF	International Monetary Fund
MDG	Millennial Development Goals
MENA	Middle East and North Africa
NSA	National Security Agency
NATO	North Atlantic Treaty Organization
OECD	Organization of Economic Cooperation and Development
PMF	Private Military Firm
RMA	Revolution in Military Affairs
TCC	Transnational Capitalist Class
TNC	Transnational Corporation
TNS	Transnational State
WEF	World Economic Forum
WSF	World Social Forum

Introduction
"George Orwell Got It Wrong"

In her novel *Everything is Known*, Liza Elliott describes a future dystopia where five global mega-corporations, dubbed Affiliations, rule the planet. "Infested with the inescapable surveillance industry, the five global Affiliations manipulated Big Data to commodify and commercialize all human activity for profit." The Affiliations had subordinated states to their domination: "George Orwell got it wrong. Big Brother did not come from a totalitarian state, but from a totalitarian non-state." Big Data was "a relentless cybernetic grandmaster who with sneaky eyes and listening ears spied on everything: your clothes, your friends, recording every word you spoke or wrote. It kept account of all this and more to amass the info power it needed to control the market, the heartbeat of the money economy." The world's population had become divided into three segregated social clusters: the members of the Core, the Peripherals, and the Outliers who comprised a majority of humanity:

> Outliers were the discarded people. If they could not function in the Affiliation run world, they were cast off. Their lives, such as they happened, were their own fault. There would never be sympathy. They scrounged out a life with the dregs, the overruns, and the un-sellable excesses from the opulent Core and stark Periphery. Some worked unpredictable marginal field-labor jobs while others scrounged in the leftovers, the scraps, and the trash.[1]

The world Elliott describes could well be, with not much of a stretch, a portrait of the one we live in. The unprecedented concentration of capital at the global level has cemented the financial power of a transnational corporate elite that uses its economic power to wield political influence and control states. In 2018, just 17 global financial conglomerates collectively managed $41.1 trillion, more than half the GDP of the entire planet. That same year, the richest 1 percent of humanity, led by 36 million millionaires and 2,400 billionaires, controlled more than half of the world's wealth while the bottom 80 percent had to make do with just 4.5 percent of this wealth. It is this mass of downcast humanity that make up Elliott's Peripherals and Outliers, what in the pages to follow are referred to as "surplus humanity."

Yet the technical infrastructure of the twenty-first century is producing the resources in which a political and economic system very different from the global capitalism in which we live could be achieved. Through popular political control of the new technologies, as Srnicek and Williams remind us, we could collectively transform our world for the better:

> Machines are accomplishing tasks that were unimaginable a decade ago. The internet and social media are giving a voice to billions who previously went unheard, bringing global participative democracy closer than ever to existence. Open-source designs, copyleft creativity, and 3D printing all portend a world where the scarcity of many products might be overcome. New forms of computer simulation could rejuvenate economic planning and give us the ability to direct economies rationally in unprecedented ways. The newest wave of automation is creating the possibility for huge swathes of boring and demeaning work to be permanently eliminated. Clean energy technologies make possible virtually limitless and environmentally sustainable forms of power production. And new medical technologies not only enable a longer, healthier life, but also make possible new experiments with gender and sexual identity. Many of the classic demands of the left—for less work, for an end to scarcity, for economic democracy, for the production of socially useful goods, and for the liberation of humanity—are materially more achievable than at any other point in history.[2]

If we are to free ourselves through these new technologies of the Fourth Industrial Revolution, however, we would first need to overthrow the oppressive and archaic social relations of global capitalism. At a time when both fascism and socialism again appear to be on the agenda around the world, it behooves us study the system of global capitalism, less as an intellectual exercise in itself than in order to struggle against its depredations with a view towards replacing it with one that can avert catastrophe and meet the material and spiritual needs of humanity. Rather than serving to liberate humanity, the new technologies are being applied at this time by the agents of this system to bring about a global police state.

While I am hardly the first to talk about a police state, I mean in this book considerably more than what we typically associate with a police state—police and military repression, authoritarian government, the suppression of civil liberties and human rights. Certainly we see this, and more, around the world. In this study, however, I want to develop the concept of global police state to identify more broadly the emerging character of the global economy and society as a repressive totality whose logic is as much economic and cultural as it is political. By global police state I refer to three interrelated developments.

First is the ever more omnipresent systems of mass social control, repression, and warfare promoted by the ruling groups to contain the real and the potential rebellion of the global working class and surplus humanity. Savage global inequalities are politically explosive and to the extent that the system is simply unable to incorporate surplus humanity it turns to ever more violent forms of containment. The methods of control include sealing out the surplus population through border and other containment walls, deportation regimes, mass incarceration and spatial apartheid, alongside omnipresent new systems of state and private surveillance and criminalization of the poor and working classes. They also include the deadly new modalities of policing and repression made possible by applications of digitalization and Fourth Industrial Revolution technologies. The global police state brings all of global society into what in Pentagon jargon is called "battlespace," concentrated in the world's megacities that are now home to more than half of humanity.

Second is how the global economy is itself based more and more on the development and deployment of these systems of warfare, social control, and repression simply as a means of making profit and continuing to accumulate capital in the face of stagnation—what I term *militarized accumulation*, or *accumulation by repression*. If it is evident that unprecedented global inequalities can only be sustained by ubiquitous systems of social control and repression, it has become equally evident that quite apart from political considerations, the ruling groups have acquired a vested interest in war, conflict, and repression as a means of accumulation. As war and state-sponsored violence become increasingly privatized, the interests of a broad array of capitalist groups shift the political, social, and ideological climate towards generating and sustaining social conflict—such as in the Middle East—and in expanding systems of warfare, repression, surveillance, and social control. We are now living in a veritable global war economy.

And third is the increasing move towards political systems that can be characterized as twenty-first-century fascism, or even in a broader sense, as totalitarian. The increasing influence around the world of neo-fascist, authoritarian, and rightwing populist parties and movements, symbolized above all by Trumpism in the United States, has sparked a flurry of debate on whether fascism is again on the rise. There has been a sharp polarization around the world between insurgent left and popular forces, on the one hand, and an insurgent far Right, on the other, at whose fringe are openly fascist tendencies. A project of twenty-first-century fascism is on the ascent in the civil societies of many countries around the world. The project has made significant advances in recent years in its competition to win state power, and in some cases, it has gained a foothold in the capitalist state. At the same time, a neo-fascist culture appears to be emerging through militarism, misogyny, extreme masculinization, and racism. Such a culture generates a climate conducive to mass violence, often directed against the racially oppressed, ethnically persecuted, women, and poor, vulnerable communities. But a fascist outcome is not inevitable. Whether or not a fascist project manages to congeal is entirely contingent on how the struggle among social and political forces unfolds in the coming years.

This global police state is emerging at a time when world capitalism descends into a crisis that is unprecedented, given its magnitude, its global reach, the extent of ecological degradation and social deterioration, and the sheer scale of the means of violence that is now deployed around the world. In the first instance, global police state is a story of control and repression of the poor and working classes. There are growing movements against the many expressions of global police state—mass incarceration, police violence, U.S.-led wars around the world, the persecution of immigrants and refugees, the repression of environmental justice activists. Yet often these movements are based on moral appeal to social justice, which by itself begets, at best, mild reform. If these movements are to attack the global police state in its jugular vein, they must identify global capitalism as the driver of the systems of social control and repression that they are combating. This book attempts to do just that. It sets out to identify the contemporary dynamics of capitalist transformation and the novel forms that are emerging. This concept of global police state allows us to specify how the economic dimensions of global capitalist transformation intersect in new ways with political, ideological, and military dimensions of this transformation.

Methodologically speaking, the causal sequence in this story starts with a critique of global capitalism and its crisis, and especially a new round of transformations in world capitalism in recent decades. Chapter 1, "Global

Capitalism and Its Crisis," summarizes my theory of globalization as a new epoch in the ongoing and open-ended evolution of the world capitalist system. I then show how a global police state is coming about as a response to a crisis that is driven by the contradictions internal to the system. The focus is on the underlying structural level of the crisis, what is known as overaccumulation, a concept I introduce in Chapter 1 and expand on in Chapter 2. The chapter ends by examining the financialization and digitalization of global capitalism, arguing that these processes, far from resolving the crisis, are bound to aggravate it.

From this starting point, we trace the social, political, and cultural-ideological conditions that fertilize a global police state, as laid out in the next three chapters. These chapters combine theory and analysis with an abundance of empirical, often shocking, data on the global police state. We will see in Chapter 2, "Savage Inequalities: The Imperative of Social Control," that the concentration of economic power in the hands of the transnational capitalist class generates a concentration of its political power that can only be considered a dictatorship of transnational capital. It is the revolt of the oppressed and exploited populations around the world that compels this transnational capitalist class to impose increasingly coercive and repressive forms of rule. The global police state is centrally aimed at *coercive exclusion* of surplus humanity. The chapter identifies the underlying process of capitalist accumulation that has led to the exclusion of several billion people and made work in the capitalist economy more and more tenuous. It also explores how cognitive labor is becoming precarious in a process of digitalization that may displace millions more and result in laborless production. The emerging megacities of the world are the battlegrounds where the excluded and the oppressed face off against the global police state.

Chapter 3, "Militarized Accumulation and Accumulation by Repression," shows how transnational capital is more and more dependent on a global war economy that in turn relies on perpetual state-organized war making, social control, and repression. The circuits of militarized accumulation coercively open up opportunities for capital accumulation worldwide. The generation of conflicts and the repression of social movements and vulnerable populations around the world become a strategy that conjoins profit making with political objectives and may even trump those objectives as the driver of militarization and repression. The events of September 11, 2001 marked the start of an era of a permanent global war in which warfare, intelligence, repression, and surveillance are more and more the privatized domain of transnational capital. Criminalization of surplus humanity activates state-sanctioned repression that opens up new profit-making opportunities for the transnational capitalist class. The chapter concludes with a look at social cleansing and militarized accumulation around the world.

In Chapter 4, "The Battle for the Future," I discuss the threat of twenty-first-century fascism and the global reform project to save capitalism from itself. From there, I contemplate the prospects for a renewal of emancipatory projects around the world and the challenge of revitalizing a Left that could help bring about an ecological socialist future. Once we have exposed the brutal world of global capitalist inequality and exploitation, the most urgent matter becomes how can we can move forward toward greater social justice. But it is not one that I take up at any length in the conclusion. This is in part because I myself do not have the answers; those must come through collective struggle itself. And it is in part because my contribution in this work is to uncover the beast of global police state through analysis and theoretical insight combined with eye-opening empirical exposition.

To that end, I offer a "big picture" of the emerging global police state in a short book that is eminently readable. The pages to follow may startle many readers and make them angry. I trust the work will serve as a warning of the dystopic future that is upon us. More importantly, by exposing the nature and dynamics of this out-of-control system, I hope it will contribute to the struggles to bring about an alternative future based on human freedom and liberation. We do face a crisis of *humanity*. The destruction under global capitalism of the social fabric worldwide and the extreme alienation of labor, our very *species being*, raises fundamental questions about what it means to be human and how to recover our humanity. It is in the nature of our species to work together to assure our collective existence. But the capitalist system that throws up a global police state turns such cooperation into a process of destruction for masses of humanity as we are made to compete with one another to survive. Crises of values, identity, meaning, and community ensue. If we are to recover our humanity we must—contra capital—re-embed ourselves in relations of reciprocity and mutual well-being.

Finally, a caveat is necessary. I have strived to make the study readable to a politically engaged public and social justice activists yet satisfying to scholars from diverse fields. Keeping it short and assuring that it is accessible means that inevitably there are generalizations that do not apply everywhere and that some nuance must be forsaken. It will be left for those readers intellectually or politically motivated by this study to further pursue the matters it raises. Those who want to delve deeper into the academic literature and theoretical debates that have helped inform my study can follow up on the extensive references that I have placed in the endnotes.

Los Angeles
October 2019

1

Global Capitalism and its Crisis

"The difficulty lies not so much in developing new ideas as in escaping from the old ones."

John Maynard Keynes

All social orders exist in a perpetual state of development, transformation, and eventual demise. Capitalism is no exception. It is the most dynamic system that humanity has ever seen, and also the most destructive. Certainly, the inner workings of the capitalist system have remained constant over the centuries. These include the relentless drives to endlessly accumulate capital (to maximize profit) and to expand outwardly. These drives led over the centuries to ongoing waves of colonialism and imperialism as the system expanded out of its original heartland in Western Europe and came to engulf the entire planet. What *has* continuously changed over the centuries are the social formations and technologies through which capitalism operates and the institutions and sets of class relations that organize the system. But now world capitalism is in the midst of a severe crisis. Will the system survive? Will humanity survive the ravages of this crisis? Capitalism has proved remarkably resilient even as it has faced one crisis after another in its centuries-long existence, defying predictions of its imminent demise and emerging renewed after each major crisis. Indeed, in response to global crisis, the system is at this time undergoing a new round of transformations, involving the construction of a global police state. At a time when both fascism and socialism have reappeared on the global agenda, it is urgent that we study these transformations.

World capitalism has gone through several historical stages, or epochs, in its ongoing and open-ended evolution. Constructing what social scientists refer to as a "periodization" allows us to make sense out of the process of historic development and transformation of a system; it means not that earlier stages disappear but that they become superseded by transformation from within. The first stage in world capitalism, symbolized by the bloody conquest of the Americas starting in 1492, is known as the

8

epoch of *mercantilism and primitive accumulation*, what Marx referred to as the "rosy dawn of the era of capitalist production." It was marked by the creation of a world market, the colonial system, the emergence of a trans-Atlantic economy, and the intensification of trade between West and East. The second, *competitive or classical capitalism*, was marked by the Industrial Revolution, the rise of the bourgeoisie, and the forging of the modern nation-state, keynoted by the American Revolution of 1776 and the French Revolution of 1789. The mercantile epoch ran from the symbolic dates of 1492 to 1789, while the age of classical capitalism gave way in the late nineteenth century to the third stage, that of *national corporate ("monopoly") capitalism*. This stage brought a new wave of imperialist conquest, the consolidation of the world market, and the rise of powerful national financial and industrial corporations.

Globalization marks a shift towards a qualitatively new epoch in world capitalism, that of *global capitalism*. Let us here review my theory of global capitalism as I have laid it out elsewhere.[1] The turning point in the epochal shift came during the world crisis of the 1970s, about which I will have more to say below. Capitalism was able to transcend that crisis by "going global," leveraging globalization processes into a vast new restructuring and integration of the world economy. This new transnational phase is marked by a number of qualitative shifts in the system and by novel articulations of social power worldwide. The hallmark of the new epoch is the rise of truly *transnational capital* and a new globally integrated production and financial system into which all nations and much of humanity have been integrated. To be sure, capitalism has always been a *world* system—it was never simply national or regional. It expanded from the onset, ultimately engulfing the entire world, and depending throughout its existence on a web of worldwide trade relations. National development has always been conditioned by the larger worldwide system of trade and finance and on the international division of labor that colonialism brought about.

But this began to change in the latter decades of the twentieth century. Surveying the world economy at century's end, the British historian Eric Hobsbawm observed:

The world economy in the Golden Age [1945–73] remained *international* rather than *transnational*. Countries traded with each other to an ever greater extent ... [T]hough the industrial economies increasingly bought and sold each others' production, the bulk of their economic activity remained home-centered. Nevertheless, an increasingly *trans-*

national economy began to emerge, especially from the 1960s on, that is to say, a system of economic activity for which state territories and state frontiers are not the basic framework, but merely complicating factors … and which sets limits to what even the economies of the very large and powerful states can do. Some time in the early 1970s such a transnational economy became an effective global force.[2]

This new transnational phase entails a shift from a *world economy* to a *global economy*. In the world economy, countries and regions were linked to each other via trade and financial flows in an integrated international market. In the new global economy, nations are linked to each more organically through the transnationalization of the production process, of finance, and of the circuits of capital accumulation. By circuit of accumulation I mean the process by which the production of a good or a service is first planned and financed (by capitalists), followed by attaining and then mixing together the component parts (labor, land, raw materials, buildings and machinery, etc.) in production sequences, and then by the marketing of the final product. At the end of this process, the capitalist recovers his initial capital outlay as well as profit and has thus "accumulated" capital. This is what Karl Marx referred to as the "circuit of capital." In earlier epochs much of the circuit was "self-contained" within a single country.

Technological developments, above all the introduction of computer and information technologies (CIT), alongside the revolution in transportation and novel organizational and managerial strategies, allowed capital to achieve global mobility. Capitalists set about in the late twentieth century to reorganize production worldwide in order to maximize profit-making opportunities and to gain further advance over the global working and popular classes. Having achieved this newfound *global reach*, capitalists could now freely search for the cheapest labor, lowest taxes, and laxest regulatory environments as they forged a new global economy. They put in place a globally integrated yet spatially fragmented production and financial system organized through vast networks of subcontracting and outsourcing that span the planet. As national production systems fragmented, they became integrated externally into the new globalized circuits of accumulation.

Previously, to take an oft-cited example, auto companies in the United States produced cars from start to finish, with the exception of the procurement abroad of some raw materials, and then exported them to other countries. The circuit of accumulation was national, save for the final export and foreign payment. Now, instead, the process of producing a car has been decentralized and fragmented into dozens of different phases that are scattered across many countries around the world. Often individual parts are manufactured in several different countries, assembly may be stretched out over others, and management may be coordinated from a central computer terminal unconnected to actual production sites or to the corporation's country of domicile.[3]

The global economy that emerged out of this restructuring is epitomized by the rise of the global assembly line and the spread of modern-day sweatshops in free-trade zones around the world, as well as a digitalized global financial system through which money moves seamlessly and instantaneously across the globe, and by a global capitalist culture of corporate brands, consumerism, and a narcissistic individualism. More recently, services have also experienced transnationalization involving the decentralized provision across borders of services, including digital services and ecommerce, along with the further privatization of health care, telecommunications, and other service industries. With this globally integrated economy comes a more organic integration of social life worldwide. Even the most remote communities are now linked into the new circuits of global economy and society through vast decentralized networks of production and distribution, as well as by global communications and other integrative technologies and cultural flows increasingly fostering these networks.

The Transnational Capitalist Class and Transnational State Apparatuses

But global capitalism is not faceless. A transnational capitalist class (henceforth, TCC) emerged as the manifest agent of global capitalism, about which much has been written in recent years.[4] The leading sectors of national capitalist classes have experienced integration with one another across borders in a process of transnational class formation. Its interests lie in promoting global rather than national markets and circuits of accumulation, in competition with local and national capitalist groups whose fate is more closely bound up with their particular nation-states. This TCC is the *hegemonic fraction of capital on a world scale*. It is made up of the owners and managers of the giant transnational corporations, or TNCs, and the financial institutions that drive the global economy.

These transnational corporate conglomerates have ceased to be corporations of a particular country and have increasingly come to represent transnational capital. The TNCs have internalized markets within their networks across national and regional frontiers, making themselves independent of their states of origin and their territories. The TCC may have originally emerged out of the "Atlantic ruling class," or among North American and European capitalists. But by the second decade of the twenty-first century, it had become a truly global ruling class, with contingents from most countries and every continent, even if still skewed disproportionately towards the traditional Western core of world capitalism and now China.[5] As we shall see, the TCC and the global corporate conglomerates they control have become progressively invested in a global police state.

How does the TCC organize itself to pursue its interests around the world? How do the class and social relations of global capitalism become institutionalized? What is the system's political authority structure? Despite the rhetoric of market fundamentalism, the capitalist system cannot be sustained through market relations alone. Capitalism requires the state in order to function. There emerged two broad approaches to understanding the capitalist state in the 1960s and 1970s, the heyday of theorizing on exactly how the capitalist class is able to assure that the state represents its interests and reproduces capitalism. One approach held that the state was "instrumentalized" directly by the dominant groups in order to shape policies in their interests, for instance, by placing their agents in government positions, by lobbying, or by financing election campaigns. The other held that dominant groups did not necessarily instrumentalize the state directly but rather the very structure of capitalist society forced the state to implement policies that advanced the interests of these dominant groups.

In this latter view, the state is structurally dependent on capital; for instance, it requires capital to invest in the economy in order to generate employment and revenue and must therefore implement policies that assure a favorable investment climate for capitalists. It is clear that both these processes are at play in global capitalism. The TCC directly instrumentalizes states around the world and at the same time every country and the whole global economy is structurally dependent on transnational capital. States have to generate the conditions for transnational capital accumulation, and this means not only assuring a favorable climate for making profit but also repressing any threat to the rule of capital. It is important to see this relationship of the state to transnational capital. Many resistance and social justice movements target governments as the visible heads of the global police state yet fail to see transnational capital behind the state, entrenched in civil society, which, as we shall see, is the most potent site of the global police state.

But it is clear that in this age of globalization national governments do not exercise the transnational political authority that global capitalism requires. The TCC has attempted to convert the structural power of the global economy into supranational political authority and to exercise its class power around the world through transnational state (TNS) apparatuses. TNS apparatuses should not be confused with a global government, which does not and may never exist. Methodologically speaking, the TNS is not a thing; it is an analytical abstraction that helps us make sense of contemporary developments. This TNS is constituted as a loose network made up of trans- and supranational organizations together with national states that have been captured by transnationally oriented policy makers and state managers. TNS apparatuses function to organize the conditions around the world for transnational accumulation—that is, to open up resources and labor around the world to transnational corporate plunder. They form an institutional network around the world through which the TCC and its political agents attempt to create and reproduce the conditions for global capital accumulation. But this does not mean that the nation-state disappears. To the contrary, as I will discuss later, one of the most explosive contradictions of global capitalism is the contradictory mandate that national governments have. They must promote the conditions for global capital accumulation in their territories and at the same time they must secure their legitimation through "the nation."

It is difficult to understate the extent to which capital has become transnationally integrated, concentrated, and centralized in the TCC. One oft-cited 2011 report by the Swiss Federal Institute of Technology undertook an analysis of the share ownerships of 43,000 transnational corporations. It identified among these a core of 1,318 TNCs with interlocking ownerships. Each of these core TNCs, in turn, had ties to two or more other companies and on average they were connected to 20. Although they represented only 20 percent of global operating revenues, these 1,318 TNCs appeared to collectively own through their shares the majority of the world's largest blue chip and manufacturing firms, representing a further 60 percent of global revenues—for a total of 80 percent of the world's revenue.[6] But when the research team dug further they found that these 1,318 TNCs tracked back to a "super entity" of 147 even more tightly knit companies, representing just 1 percent of the global corporate stock, that controlled 40 percent of the total wealth of the network. Not surprisingly, the top 50 of these corporations were global financial institutions. If the TCC is the hegemonic fraction of capital on a world scale, it is clear that *transnational finance capital* is hegemonic within the TCC. The worldwide mesh of transnational finance capital has its tentacles in every nook and cranny of the global economy and shapes the lives of every person on the planet. As we shall see, it is deeply enmeshed with the global police state.

In his masterful 2018 study *Giants: The Global Power Elite*, sociologist Peter Phillips provides a stunning portrait of the extent to which the TCC has centralized and concentrated global economic control worldwide. In the tradition of power elite studies, he exposes an inner core of 389 individuals drawn from the upper echelons of the TCC who stand at the very apex of the global power structure and who have brought about the transnational inter-penetration of what were in an earlier era national power networks. We see a cementing now at the global level of political and economic power in this transnational elite through an unprecedented concentration of financial capital and through the political influence that this economic control wields over states and TNS institutions. In short, in 2018 just 17 global financial conglomerates collectively managed $41.1 trillion dollars "in a self-invested network of interlocking capital that spans the globe."[7] Moreover, these 17 were cross-invested in each other to such an extent that it appeared as simply a mass of interlocking global financial capital. The figure of $41.1 trillion is actually misleadingly low because, as the study shows, it does not include the value of capital stock that these conglomerates hold in all branches of the global corporate structure. This amalgamated mass of transnational finance capital is deeply invested in media, industry, commerce, and the global military-industrial-security complex.[8]

This enormous concentration of economic power translates into the centralization of worldwide policy-making influence in the TCC. Phillips notes that the top echelons of the TCC and the global power elite take an active part in global policy-planning institutions of the TNS. They serve as advisors to the International Monetary Fund, the World Bank, the World Trade Organization, the International Bank of Settlements, the Group of 7 and the Group of 20 rich country clubs; they take up key positions in national governments, especially in ministries of finance and the treasury, central banks, trade, and foreign affairs, and also often ministries of defense, among other government cabinet-level officials and advisory roles to heads of state. The global power elite also works out policies to manage and protect global capital and enforce debt collection worldwide in many private policy-making forums. These include the World Economic Forum, the Trilateral Commission, the Group of 30, the Atlantic Council, and the Bilderberg group. At the same time, members of the TCC and their political agents impose these policies through the placement of their individuals within individual states and TNS institutions. This relationship of economic (class) power to state power is one in which the TCC issues commands to government officials. As one member of the global elite put it, these officials are "pilots flying our airplane." In Phillips's words, the global power elite "doesn't produce recommendations but rather instructions which they expect to be followed."[9]

While competition abounds among the giant global corporate conglomerates, the top echelons of the TCC form a class-conscious and well-organized politicized leadership for the TCC as a whole. The lesser known Group of 30 (G-30), founded in 1978, brings together top bankers, financiers, policymakers and academics of the transnational elite. The members of the Group, who themselves hold official positions in states and TNS institutions, issues periodic reports to governments and TNS institutions around the world. The G-30 and other such private associations of the politicized inner circle of the TCC and the intellectuals in their service are places where

> ... TCC power elites can speak openly on global capital and security issues, moving toward a consensus of understanding on needed policies and their implementation. These meetings offer TCC power elite individuals opportunities to personally interact with each other face-to-face in private, off-the-record settings that allow for personal intimacies, trust, and friendships to emerge. These interactions are the foundation of TCC class-consciousness and social awareness of common interests. The central activity of the TCC power elite is the management and protection of global capital. With this understanding, a wide variety of policy issues emerge for implementation by transnational entities, security institutions (military/police and intelligence agencies), and ideological organizations (media and public relations firms).[10]

In sum, the astonishing centralization and concentration of worldwide economic management, control, and decision-making power in a handful of ever more powerful TNCs suggests that the global economy is acquiring the character of a planned oligopoly, with centralized planning taking place within the inner network of TNC nodes, TNS apparatuses, and the global elite forums that Phillips and others have documented. In particular, the TCC has gained enormous structural power over states and political processes in its pursuit of global corporate interests. If a shockingly small group exercises control over the fate of humanity, the broad processes associated with global capitalism involve as well more expansive and novel relations of inequality, domination, and exploitation in global society, including the increasing importance of transnational social and class inequalities relative to North–South inequalities, or to inequalities that are geographically or territorially conceived. North–South inequalities measured in the traditional way as inequalities in per-capita GDP among countries are actually growing and remain a crucial part of the story, but their causal explanation lies with the underlying transnational class relations of global capitalism. These class relations of inequality, domination, and exploitation are played out through a global police state.

The Crisis of Humanity

Globalization did reactivate accumulation on a world scale in the late twentieth and early twenty-first centuries following a period of crisis and stagnation of the 1970s. The expansion of transnational capital from the 1980s into the first decade of the new century involved hyper-accumulation through new technologies, especially CIT, through neo-liberal policies (more on these below), and through new modalities of mobilizing and exploiting the global labor force—including a massive new round of primitive accumulation that uprooted and displaced hundreds of millions of people. "Primitive accumulation" refers to the process whereby masses of people are separated, often violently, from the means of production, especially land and other forms of community property, as these means of production come under control of capitalists and leave people with no way to survive other than to sell their mental and physical labor to capitalists and to the institutions of the capitalist system. The very first wave of primitive accumulation took place in the English countryside in earlier centuries, in a process known as *enclosures*. Through colonialism and imperialism, hundreds of millions around the world were violently dispossessed in past centuries in ongoing waves of primitive accumulation that brought more and more of humanity under the domination of capital. As I will discuss later, globalization involved a massive new round of primitive accumulation around the world, throwing hundreds of millions more into the ranks of surplus humanity subject to the control of an expanding global police state.

But the globalization boom of the late twentieth and early twenty-first centuries was short-lived. The global financial meltdown of 2008 marked the onset of a new structural crisis of global capitalism, one that opens the possibility for systemic change. Karl Marx was the first to identify crisis as immanent to capitalism and there is a vast literature on capitalist crisis.[11] Here I identify three types of crisis. Cyclical crises, or recessions, occur about every ten years in the capitalist system and typically last some 18 months. These comprise the so-called "business cycle." There were recessions in the early 1980s, the early 1990s, and the early 2000s. "Structural crises," so called because the only way out of crisis is to restructure the system, occur approximately every 40–50 years. A new wave of colonialism and imperialism resolved (that is, displaced) the first recorded structural crisis of the 1870s and 1880s. The next structural crisis, the Great Depression of the 1930s, was resolved through a new type of redistributive capitalism, referred to as the "class compromise" of Fordism-Keynesianism, social democracy, New Deal capitalism, and so on (more on this below). As we have seen, capital responded to the next structural crisis, that of the 1970s, by going global.

Each of these major episodes of structural crisis have presented this potential for systemic change. Historically, each has involved the breakdown of state legitimacy, escalating class and social struggles, and military conflicts. In the past, structural crises have led to a restructuring that includes new institutional arrangements, class relations, and accumulation activities that eventually resulted in a restabilization of the system and renewed capitalist expansion. Yet a new period of far-reaching restructuring through digitalization appears to be under way at this time. Before we return to this new wave of restructuring, let us focus on the nature of the current crisis, which shares aspects of earlier system-wide structural crises of the 1880s, the 1930s, and the 1970s. Yet there are several interrelated dimensions to the current crisis that I believe sets it apart from these earlier ones and suggest that a simple restructuring of the system will not lead to its restabilization—that is, our very survival requires now a revolution against global capitalism.

Above all is the existential crisis posed by the ecological limits to the reproduction of the system. We have already passed tipping points in climate change, the nitrogen cycle, and diversity loss. For the first time ever, human conduct is intersecting with and fundamentally altering the earth system in such a way that threatens to bring about a sixth mass extinction.[12] While capitalism cannot be held solely responsible for the ecological crisis, it is difficult to image that the environmental catastrophe can be resolved within the capitalist system given capital's implacable impulse to accumulate and its accelerated commodification of nature. The ecological dimensions of global crisis have been brought to the forefront of the global agenda by the worldwide environmental justice movement. Communities around the world have come under the escalating repression of a global police state as they face off against transnational corporate plunder of their environment and demand environmental justice and action by governments to avert the climate catastrophe. And climate change refugees, who are likely to run into the hundreds of millions in the years ahead, are vilified by racist and neo-fascist forces and repressed by a global police state.

This accelerated commodification of nature points to another underlying dimension of the current crisis. We are reaching limits to the extensive expansion of capitalism, in the sense that there are no longer any new territories of significance to integrate into world capitalism and new spaces to commodify are drying up. The capitalist system is by its nature expansionary. In each earlier structural crisis, the system went through a new round of extensive expansion—that is, incorporating new territories and populations into it—from waves of colonial conquest in earlier centuries, to the integration in the late twentieth and early twenty-first centuries of the former socialist bloc countries, China, India and other areas that had been marginally outside the system. There are no longer any new territories to integrate into world capitalism. At the same time, the privatization of education, health, utilities, basic services, and public lands are turning those spaces in global society that were outside of capital's direct control into "spaces of capital," so that intensive expansion—that is, the commodification of what were non-commodified resources and activities—is reaching depths never before seen. Commodification refers to the process of turning people, the things that people produce, and nature into things that are privately owned, have a monetary value, and that can be bought and sold. Capitalism by its nature must constantly expand intensively by commodifying more and more of the world. What is there left to commodify? Where can the system now expand? New spaces have to be violently cracked open and the peoples in these spaces must be repressed by a global police state. But what does exhaustion of spaces for extensive and intensive expansion imply for the reproduction of the system?

The sheer magnitude of the means of violence and social control is unprecedented, as well as the magnitude and concentrated—and increasingly privatized—control over these means of violence along with the means of global communication and the production and circulation of symbols, images, and knowledge. As I will discuss in more detail in Chapters 2 and 3, computerized wars, drone warfare, robot soldiers, bunker-buster bombs, satellite surveillance, cyberwar, spatial control technology, and so forth, have changed the face of warfare, and more generally, of systems of social control and repression. We have arrived at the panoptical surveillance society, a point brought home by revelations of the defector from the U.S. National Security Agency (NSA), Edward Snowden, that the NSA monitored virtually every communication on the planet. It is no exaggeration to say that we are now in the age of thought control by those who control global flows of communication, information, and symbolic production. But most frightening is the production and deployment of a new generation of nuclear weapons and the threat of "limited" nuclear war.[13] If global crisis leads to a new world war, the destruction would simply be unprecedented. Combined with ecological meltdown, it is difficult to see how humanity could survive such a conflagration.

Global capitalism lends itself to escalating *inter*-national tensions with the potential to spill over into major interstate conflict. But we should not explain these tensions through the outdated nation-state/interstate mode of analysis that attributes such tensions to national rivalry and competition among national capitalist classes for international economic control. Rather, these tensions derive, above all, from an acute political contradiction in global capitalism that I already alluded to above: economic globalization takes places within a nation-state-based system of political authority. Nation-states face a contradiction between the need to promote transnational capital accumulation in their territories and their need to achieve political legitimacy. In the age of capitalist globalization, governments must attract to the national territory transnational corporate and financial investment, which requires providing capital with all the incentives associated with neo-liberalism—downward pressure on wages, deregulation, low or no taxes, privatization, fiscal austerity, and on so— that aggravate inequality, impoverishment, and insecurity for working and popular classes. As a result, states around the world have been experiencing spiraling crises of legitimacy. To put it in more technical terms, there is a contradiction between the accumulation function and the legitimacy function of nation-states.

This situation generates bewildering, unstable, and seemingly contradictory politics. It helps explain the rise of far-right and neo-fascist forces that espouse rhetoric of nationalism and protectionism even as they promote neo-liberalism, such as the Trump government in the United States, and has confused some into believing that "deglobalization" is under way as we move backward to an earlier era of national protectionism. In fact, the "old protectionism" of the twentieth century aimed to protect national products and the national capitalist groups that produced them with tariffs and subsidies. The new protectionism—if we could call it that, as the term is extremely misleading and leads to much confusion—aims to create the conditions to attract transnational capital to national territories. Despite its protectionist rhetoric, for instance, the Trump White House called not for locking out foreign investors but for transnational investors from around the world to invest in the United States, enticed by a regressive tax reform, unprecedented deregulation, and some limited tariff walls that would benefit groups from anywhere in the world that establish operations behind them. "America is open for business," Trump declared at the 2018 meeting of the global elite gathered for the annual conclave of the World Economic Forum (WEF) in Davos, Switzerland: "Now is the perfect time to bring your business, your jobs and your investments to the United States."[14] And the biggest single beneficiary of steel tariffs that Trump imposed in 2018 on imported steel was ArcelorMittal, the Indian-based company that owns majority shares in U.S. Steel.[15] Moreover, as we will see later, TCC contingents from countries around the world that appear to be in geo-political competition are not just heavily invested in global police state but they are cross- and mutually invested in it.

More to the point here, economic globalization as it has unfolded within the interstate system generates mounting international and geo-political tensions to the extent that the crisis exacerbates the problem of legitimacy and destabilizes national political systems and elite control. Inter-national tensions must be seen as derivative of the contradiction between the expansion of transnational capital within the framework of the nation-state/inter-state system, in which global capitalism pits nationally constrained workers against one another and sets up the conditions for the TCC to manipulate the crises of state legitimacy and the international tensions generated by this contradiction. The political tensions generated by this contradiction can and do take on the appearance of geo-political competition.[16] Will the centrifugal pressures produced by this contradiction undercut the centripetal pressures brought about by economic globalization? Will these centrifugal pressures break out into open, large-scale inter-state warfare?[17] Will geo-political tensions "overdetermine" the corporate interests of the TCC?

We need here to extend the analysis of transnational politics and the TNS in order to understand this dimension of global crisis, especially so considering that it is central to the story of global police state. Transnational elites have been clamoring for more effective TNS institutions, in part, in order to resolve this disjuncture between economic globalization and the nation-state system of political authority. However, the fragmentary and highly emergent nature of TNS apparatuses makes the effort problematic given both the dispersal of formal political authority across many nation-states and the loose nature of TNS apparatuses with no center or formal constitution. The more "enlightened" elite representatives of the TCC are now searching for ways to develop a more powerful TNS, one that could impose regulation on the global market and certain controls on unbridled global accumulation. They are seeking transnational mechanisms of "governance" that would allow the global ruling class to rein in the anarchy of the system in the interests of saving global capitalism from itself and from radical challenges from below—from both an insurgent Left and extreme Right.

More than in any other forum, the politicized strata of the transnational elite comes together in the activities of the WEF, a "network of networks" for the TCC and the transnational elite that holds its famed annual meeting in Davos. Indeed, it is not for nothing that "Davos Man" has been used to describe the new global ruling class. WEF founder and Executive Chairman Klaus Schwab called in 2008 for renovated forms of "global leadership" by the TCC:

Whether it is poverty in Africa or the Haze over Southeast Asia, an increasing number of problems require bilateral, regional or global solutions and, in many cases, the mobilization of more resources than any single government can marshal ... The limits of political power are increasingly evident. The lack of global leadership is glaring, not least because the existing global governance institutions are hampered by archaic conventions and procedures devised, in some instances, at the end of World War II. Sovereign power still rests with national governments, but authentic and effective global leadership has yet to emerge. Meanwhile, public governance at the local, national, regional, and international levels has weakened. Even the best leaders cannot operate successfully in a failed system.[18]

But if the transnational elite wants a stronger TNS in order to cement the TCC's rule and stabilize the system, it has not been able to resolve the contradictory mandate it has accorded to the TNS. On the one hand, the TNS sets out to promote the conditions for capitalist globalization; on the other, it tries to resolve the myriad problems globalization creates: economic crisis, poverty, environmental degradation, chronic political instability, and military conflict. The TNS has had great difficulty addressing these issues because of the dispersal of formal political authority across many nation-states. To reiterate, TNS apparatuses are fragmentary; there is no center or formal constitution, and there is certainly no transnational enforcement capacity. These TNS apparatuses have not been able to substitute for a leading nation-state—what the international relations literature refers to as a "hegemon"—with enough power and authority to organize and stabilize the system, much less to impose regulations on transnational capital.

The politicized strata of the TCC and transnationally oriented elites and organic intellectuals, including those who staff TNS institutions, attempt to define the long-term interests of the system and to develop policies, projects, and ideologies to secure these interests. Since the specific interests of the various components of the global power bloc are divergent, it is the TNSs' role to *unify* and *organize* the various classes and fractions to uphold their long-term political interests against the threat of the exploited and oppressed classes around the world. But the inability of the TNS to impose coherence and regulation on transnational accumulation and to stabilize the system is also due to the vulnerability of the TCC as a class group in terms of its own internal disunity and fractionation, and its blind pursuit of immediate accumulation—that is, of its immediate and particular profit-seeking interests over the long-term or general interests of the class.

There is of course a profound social dimension of global crisis. In these times of unprecedented worldwide inequalities, capitalist crisis breaks apart the social fabric and devastates communities everywhere. Billions of people around the world face struggles to survive from one day to the next, with no guarantee that they will succeed in this struggle (indeed, many are not and many more won't). In academic terms we could call this a crisis of social reproduction, but this phrase does nothing to capture the depths of misery that poverty, disease, un- and underemployment, food insecurity, social exclusion, racist, xenophobic, and other forms of social violence into which billions are thrust on a daily basis, or to the persecution that they face as migrants, refugees, surplus labor, and so on. The next two chapters will take up these matters. However, let us point out that the social crisis is decidedly *not* a crisis for capital, and may even help it to reproduce its rule, until or unless it leads to mass rebellion that threatens the ruling groups' control.

Overaccumulation: Capitalism's Achilles Heel

The turn towards a global police state is structurally rooted in perhaps *the* fundamental contradiction of capitalism: *overaccumulation*. The trajectory of global capital accumulation in recent years has been shaped by overaccumulation, which is interwoven with other dimensions of global crisis discussed above. What is meant by overaccumulation? Internal to the dynamic of capital accumulation is a tendency for the rate of profit to fall because as capitalists compete with one another, strive to control labor, and to reduce labor costs, they raise productivity through organizational and technological innovations in the production process. This means that ever less labor is required to produce ever more wealth. Yet labor is the source of all surplus value—that is, of profits. Overaccumulation refers to how enormous amounts of capital are accumulated, yet this capital cannot be reinvested profitably and becomes stagnant, or in Marx's words, "the capitalist would have won nothing by his own exertions but the obligation to supply more in the same labor time, in a word, more difficult conditions for the augmentation of the value of his capital."[19]

In the next chapter I will expand on this analysis of overaccumulation. Let us note here that overaccumulation is expressed—or *appears* at the level of the market—as a problem of "overproduction" or "underconsumption." Marx analyzed in *Capital* how social polarization and inequality are inherent to the capitalist system since capitalists own the means of producing wealth and therefore appropriate as profits as much wealth as possible that society collectively produces. But such inequalities end up undermining the stability of the system since the mass of working people cannot purchase the wealth that pours out of the capitalist economy to the extent that capitalists and the well-off retain more and more of total income relative to that which goes to labor. The gap grows between what is (or could be) produced and what the market can absorb. If capitalists

cannot actually sell (or "unload") the products of their plantations, factories, and offices, then they cannot make ("realize") profit. This is what in
critical political economy constitutes the underlying internal contradiction
of capitalism, or the overaccumulation problem. Capitalists accumulate
huge amounts of surplus but—to reiterate—do not find outlets to continue
to profitably invest that surplus. Hence, if left unchecked, the expanding
social polarization that is endemic to capitalism results in crisis: in stagnation, recessions, depressions, social upheavals, and war.

Globalization has greatly exacerbated overaccumulation. To make
sense of this, we must take the story back to the early twentieth century.
The particular form of capitalism, or social order, that took shape in
the decades following the 1930s Great Depression, what we will call
Fordism-Keynesianism, involved high growth rates, a rise in living standards
for substantial sectors of the working class, and a decrease in inequalities
in the developed core of world capitalism. Why "Fordism-Keynesianism"?
It was the U.S. industrialist Henry Ford who first recognized that the
new system of mass, standardized production ("Fordism") could not be
sustained without introducing mass, standardized consumption. This
meant establishing a stable employment arrangement—or capital-labor
relation—for a significant portion of the working classes and wages high
enough for the working class to actually consume the goods and services
that their labor produced, in exchange for workers' obedience to capital. In
turn, the British economist John Keynes analyzed that the Great Depression owed to insufficient demand as a result of the concentration of wealth.
The state needed, in Keynes's view, to intervene in the economy in order
to regulate the market (especially financial markets) and to boost demand
through state spending on public projects such as infrastructure and social
services as well as through the establishment of minimum wages, unemployment insurance, pensions, and so forth.[20]

These Fordist-Keynesian arrangements came about not by the good will
of capitalists but because of the mass struggles of working and popular
classes from the late 1800s into the 1930s, including worker, populist, and
socialist movements, the Bolshevik revolution, and the anti-colonial and
national liberation struggles in the Third World. The period of post-World
War II prosperity in the core countries owed a great deal to this combination of Fordist production and regulated capital-labor relations and
Keynesian monetary, budgetary, and regulatory policies (along with the
pillage of the colonial world, which allowed wealth to flow back to core
countries, where it was redistributed). State intervention in the capital-

ist market and a component of redistribution came to define economic policy in the mid-twentieth century in the then-First World, as well as in the then-Third World in the wake of decolonization. This redistributive nation-state capitalism evolved, therefore, from capital's accommodation to mass upheavals from below in the wake of the crisis of the two World Wars and the Great Depression. State regulation of the market, redistributive policies, and working-class power acted as what we call "countervailing tendencies" to the tendency towards overaccumulation—that is, they helped offset overaccumulation.

But when the next great crisis hit, that of the 1970s, emergent transnational capital went global as a strategy of the TCC to reconstitute its social power by breaking free of nation-state constraints to accumulation, to do away with the Fordist-Keynesian arrangement, and to beat back the tide of revolution in the Third World. The post-WWII "class compromise" had served capital well for several decades. Corporate profits rose sharply from 1945 to 1968, and then declined until the early 1980s, when it again rose very rapidly, this time as a result of globalization.[21] The corporate class and its agents identified the mass struggles and demands of popular and working classes and state regulation as fetters to its freedom to make profits and accumulate wealth as the rate of profit declined in the 1970s. As the TCC congealed, it forged what became known as the "Washington Consensus," or the agreement around sweeping worldwide economic restructuring through neo-liberalism to put in place a new transnational corporate order and to go on the offensive in its class warfare against working and popular classes. Warren Buffet, one of the richest men in the world who made his multi-billion-dollar fortune in the age of late twentieth-century globalization, was quite frank about this. "There's been class warfare going on for the last 20 years," he declared in 2011, "and my class has won."[22]

Restructuring through capitalist globalization involved tearing down any and every obstacle to the free flow of global capital, assuring unimpeded access to the planet's resources, and continuously opening up new spaces for expansion. The process has involved the deregulation of markets and lifting regulations on the operation of transnational capital, including the passage of open investment regimes and free trade agreements—that is, conditions that allowed free rein to transnational capital around the world. It also involved the sweeping privatization of public assets, social austerity, and the reduction and even elimination of social protection systems such as welfare, and other measures that dismantled nation-states' controls over transnational capital and promoted global economic integration. The global economy experienced a boom in the late twentieth century as the former socialist countries entered the global market and as capital, liberated from nation-state constraints, unleashed a vast new round of accumulation worldwide. The TCC unloaded surpluses and resumed profit making in the emerging globally integrated production and financial system through the acquisition of privatized assets, the extension of mining and agro-industrial investment on the heels of the displacement of hundreds of millions from the countryside, and a new wave of industrial expansion assisted by the revolution in CIT. Public policy became reconfigured through austerity, bailouts, corporate subsidies, government debt, and the global bond market as governments transferred wealth directly and indirectly from working people to the TCC.

The globalization boom of the late twentieth and early twenty-first centuries was also fueled by the rise of new high-consumption market segments around the world, themselves a product of escalating social polarization and inequality. The apologists of global capitalism tout the rise of several hundred million new middle-class consumers in China, India, and elsewhere in the former Third World. Yet the underside to these newly affluent layers brought into the global market is the escalation in those countries of inequality and immiseration for the majorities left out of the global cornucopia.[23] In the United States, the top 5 percent of households in terms of income were responsible for about 27 percent of total consumer spending in 1992, whereas it rose to 38 percent by 2012.[24] Already by 2005, a team of stock market analysts at Citigroup warned that the United States was becoming a "plutocracy" in which growth was driven by small high-income clusters. They advised wealthy investors to avoid purchasing stock in industries producing for mass consumption and to instead invest in companies producing luxury goods and services for the rich.[25] Consumer spending beyond the elite, as we will see below, has been buoyed by mounting and unsustainable debt.

Globalization thus enhanced the structural power of transnational capital over states and popular classes worldwide. Popular and working classes became less effective in defending wages in the face of capital's newfound global mobility. And states saw the erosion of their ability to capture and redistribute surpluses given the privatization of public assets, ever more regressive tax systems and prospects for corporate tax evasion, mounting debt to transnational finance capital, inter-state competition to attract transnational capital, and the ability of the TCC to transfer money instantaneously around the world through new digital financial circuits. Behind this alleged "loss of state sovereignty," capitalist globalization changed the correlation of class forces worldwide in favor of the TCC. Transnational capital has been able to exercise a newfound structural power over states and territorially bound working and popular classes. "Corporations around the world simultaneously benefitted from the broad-based decline in labor's bargaining power, increased globalization, lower anti-trust enforcement, technology allowing for greater scale and lower marginal cost, and lower corporate taxes, interest rates, and tariffs," candidly noted one global investment management firm. "These factors have produced the most pro-corporate environment in history globally."[26]

But by liberating capital from redistribution at the nation-state level as a countervailing tendency to that of social polarization, globalization unleashed a dizzying spiral of social polarization and unprecedented global inequalities that, far from diminishing, have escalated at an astonishing rate since the 2008 Great Recession. In 2015, according to the international development agency Oxfam, just 1 percent of humanity owned over half of the world's wealth and the top 20 percent own 94.5 of that wealth, while the remaining 80 percent had to make do with just 4.5 percent.[27] By escalating this polarization and inequality, globalization fueled the chronic problem of overaccumulation. The extreme concentration of the planet's wealth in the hands of the few and the accelerated impoverishment and dispossession of the majority meant that the TCC had increasing difficulty in finding productive outlets to unload enormous amounts of surplus it has accumulated. By the late 1990s, stagnation once again set in and the system faced renewed crisis as privatizations dried up, the conquered and reconquered regions were brought into the system, global markets became saturated, and new technologies reached the limits of fixed capital expansion.

A series of lesser jolts to the global economy, from the Mexico peso crisis of 1995, to the Asian financial meltdown of 1997–99 and its spread to several other regions, and then the dot-com busts and global recession of 2000–01, were preludes to the 2008 collapse of the global financial system. The Great Recession of 2008 marked the onset of a new structural crisis of overaccumulation. Given such extreme polarization of income and wealth, the global market cannot absorb the output of the global economy. Corporations recorded record profits during the second decade of the new century at the same time that corporate investment declined.[28] In 2017, the largest U.S.-based companies were sitting on an outstanding $1.01 trillion in uninvested cash,[29] while worldwide corporate cash reserves topped $12 trillion, more than the foreign exchange reserves of the world's central governments.[30] Transnational corporations could not find opportunities to profitably reinvest their profits.[31] As uninvested capital accumulates, enormous pressures build up to find outlets for unloading the surplus. Capitalist groups pressure states to create new opportunities for profit making. By the twenty-first century, the TCC turned to several mechanisms in order to sustain global accumulation in the face of overaccumulation, among them, financial speculation; the plunder of public finances; debt-driven growth, and state-organized militarized accumulation.

The Predatory and Parasitic World of Transnational Finance Capital

Deregulation of the financial industry and the creation of a globally integrated financial system in recent decades allowed the TCC to unload trillions of dollars into speculation. The sequence of speculative waves in the global casino since the 1980s included real estate investments in the emerging global property market that inflated property values in one locality after another, wild stock market speculation leading to periodic booms and busts, most notable the bursting of the dot-com bubble in 2001, the phenomenal escalation of hedge-fund flows, currency speculation, and every imaginable derivative (see below). U.S. treasury bailouts of the Wall Street-based banks following the 2008 collapse which was triggered by speculation in the housing market went to bail out individual and institutional investors from around the world, while the U.S. debt was itself financed by these same investors from all over the world. According to a 2011 report by the U.S. government's General Accounting Office, the U.S. Federal Reserve undertook a whopping $16 trillion in secret bailouts between 2007 and 2010 to banks and corporations from around the world.[32] But then the banks and institutional investors simply recycled trillions of dollars it received in bailout money into new speculative activities in global commodities markets, in cryptocurrencies, and in land around the world, fueling a new global "land grab" (see next chapter). As opportunity dries up for speculative investment in one sector, the TCC simply turns to another sector to unload its surplus.

This bewildering world of transnational finance capital compels us think in new ways about global capitalism, its crisis, and the prospects for resisting it. One key innovation in this "revolution in finance" was the development of asset-backed securitization, often abbreviated as ABS. Made possible by digitalization and the growing global integration of markets and finance, ABS essentially involves turning debt into a commodity that can be bought and sold by investors and then speculated on. Any current *or future* stream of earnings (dividends, interest, mortgages, credit card payments, state and private bond maturities, commodity deliveries, and so forth) is transformed by ABS into an easily tradable capital asset. It emerged in the early 1970s but did not take off until the late 1990s, when it expanded from its origins in the United States to the whole global economy in the context of rapid globalization. Through securitization, individual debts are packaged together into a so-called "debt instrument." In other words, thousands or even millions of mortgages, student loans, and credit card and other debts—including government debt—are "bundled" together by a financial institution into "packages," converting illiquid individual debts into mobile marketable securities to be bought and sold by individual and institutional investors from around the world. In the past, for instance, if a family took out a mortgage with a bank, that bank held the mortgage for years or decades as the family gradually paid it back, with interest of course. The idea that the bank could sell the mortgage to other financial institutions was unheard of. With ABS, however, the initial mortgage lender may and almost always does "sell" the mortgage to a financial institution, sometimes within hours or days of the mortgage being issued. Millions of these mortgages are then "bundled," sold and resold as speculative investments.

In simplified terms, this revolution in finance, led by ABS, has involved the rise over the past few decades of all sorts of financial innovations through securitization—a vast and bewildering array of derivatives, from swaps, futures markets, hedge funds, institutional investment funds, mortgage-backed securities, collateralized debt obligations, Ponzi schemes, pyramiding of assets, and many more.[33] These innovations make possible a global casino, or transnational financial circuits based on speculation and the ongoing expansion of fictitious capital, which refers to money thrown into circulation without any base in commodities or in production. Just as capital takes over and appropriates all spheres through the drumbeat march of commodification, the circuits of financial accumulation steadily take over in the capitalist system since money capital is universally convertible to any other commodity form of capital. Of course, this notion of "making money from money" is an illusion. The phenomenal growth of these "financial instruments" represents not the creation of new value (wealth), which can only be created by labor, but the expansion of fictitious capital. On the one hand, the income streams generated by financial speculation in these "financial instruments" merely redistributes to financial speculators in the realm of circulation the values created in production (in the factories, plantations, mines, and service centers) of the global economy.[34] On the other hand, a major portion of the income generated by financial speculation is fictitious, meaning (here in simplified form) that it exists on paper but does not correspond to real wealth in the world, such as food, clothing, houses, and so on. The accumulation of fictitious capital through speculation may offset the crisis temporally into the future or spatially to new digital geographies and new population groups, but in the long run only exacerbates the underlying problem of overaccumulation. It was precisely the conversion of millions of mortgages into ABS and the wild speculation in this market that triggered (but did not cause) the 2008 financial collapse. Cascading defaults in the credit card, student loan, or other such markets would likely trigger new financial crises as would government debt defaults.

The rise to hegemony of transnational finance capital is a major historical development of the globalization epoch. With the deregulation and liberalization of financial markets worldwide in the 1980s and 1990s and the introduction of CIT, national financial systems have merged into an increasingly integrated global financial system—a monstrous global complex that allows for hitherto unknown concentrations of social power, including the ability to dictate to states and to other circuits of accumulation. The officers, directors, and owners of financial corporations (banks, insurance companies, securities firms, etc.) are usually at the center of interlocking directorates in the corporate economy. However, the concept of finance capital does not refer exclusively to individuals or institutions in the financial sector; it refers to the preponderant weight of the financial sector to the capitalist economy overall. The financial sector is now at the very center of just about every circuit of accumulation worldwide, as well as at the core of financial speculation in the global casino. "The financial economy today is pervasive, that is, it spreads across the entire economic cycle, co-existing with it, so to speak, from start to finish," Marazzi has observed. "This means that we are in a historic period in which finance is *cosubstantial* with the very production of goods and services."[35] What concerns us here is that transnational finance capital, as we shall see, is wedded to the global police state.

Meanwhile, the TCC has also turned to raiding and sacking public finance, which has been reconfigured through austerity, bailouts, corporate subsidies, government debt, and the global bond market as governments transfer wealth directly and indirectly from working people to the TCC. The global bond market—an indicator of total government debt world-wide—more than doubled between 2003 and 2017, when it surpassed $100 trillion.[36] Governments issue bonds to investors in order to close government budget deficits and also to subsidize private accumulation so as to keep the economy going. They then have to pay back these bonds (with interest) by extracting taxes from current and future wages of the working class. Already by the late twentieth century, state income brought in by bonds often just went right back to creditors. Thus, the reconfiguration of state finances amounts over time to a transfer of wealth from global labor to transnational capital, a claim by transnational capital on future wages, and a shift in the burden of the crisis to the working and popular classes. To put this another way, capitalist state finance has been reconfigured to reduce or even eliminate the state's role in social reproduction and to expand its role in facilitating transnational capital accumulation.

In this perverse world of predatory transnational finance, capital government debt and deficits themselves thus become new sources of financial speculation that help offset—momentarily—overaccumulation crisis. Governments facing insolvency in the wake of the Great Recession turned to bond emissions in order to stay afloat, which allowed transnational investors to unload surplus into these sovereign debt markets that they themselves helped to create. Just as with ABS, gone are the times that such bonds are bought and held to maturity. They are bought and sold by individual and institutional investors in frenzied 24-hour world-wide trading and bet on continuously through such mechanisms as credit default swaps that shift their values and make bond markets a high-stakes gamble of volatility and risk for investors. The toxic mixture of public finance and private transnational finance capital in this age of global capitalism constitutes a new battlefield in which the global rich are waging a war against the global poor and working classes. This becomes a critical part of the story of the global police state as resistance to this financial pillage mounts around the world. The structural violence of transnational finance capital is at the core of massive new rounds of dispossession world-wide, while the actual dispossession is then enforced by the direct violence of the courts, state and private military, police and paramilitary repression (see the next two chapters). At the same time, financial control becomes crucial to the story of heightened disciplinary pressure over these classes, who are subject to new and often draconian forms of coercion by creditors and states.[37] Financialization is a key lever in the transition from social welfare to social control states. As we shall see in the next two chapters, the poor are increasingly targeted by transnational finance capital for financial extraction—essentially swindling through debt and dependence—in processes that in turn allow the state to criminalize them, whence this criminalization opens up vast new opportunities for militarized accumulation and accumulation by repression.

Yet financial pillage cannot resolve the crisis of overaccumulation and ends up aggravating it in the long run, as the transfer of wealth from workers to the TCC further constricts the market. Growth in recent decades, and especially since 2008, has been driven by mounting public and private debt, including government, corporate, and consumer debt. In the United States, which has long been the "market of last resort" for the global economy, household debt was higher in 2017 than it has been for almost all of post-war history. U.S. households owed nearly $13 trillion in student loans, credit card debt, auto loans, and mortgages,[38] in what Soederberg calls "credit-led accumulation."[39] Of this total, U.S. credit card debt reached an all-time high of $1.02 trillion in 2017 as credit-card delinquencies rose steadily.[40] In just about every member country of the Organization for Economic Cooperation and Development (OECD), the ratio of income to household debt remains historically high and has steadily worsened since 2008.[41] In China, where the ratio of household debt to GDP more than doubled from 2011 to 2017, fear has mounted over consumer debt default, as household mortgage and credit-card debt ballooned.[42] The same goes for India, Brazil, South Africa, and other countries in the former Third World.[43] As noted, the global bond market—an indicator of total government debt worldwide—surpassed $100 trillion in 2017, while total global debt reached a staggering $215 trillion in 2016.[44]

As financial pillage and debt mount, the gap between the productive economy and "fictitious capital" grows ever wider as financial speculation spirals out of control. Doug Henwood reports that in 1986 the principal in interest rate swaps was $400 billion, with another $100 billion in currency swaps. Just four years later, by the end of 1990, the figures were $2.3 trillion and $578 billion, respectively, to which had been added another $561 billion in caps, floors, collars, and "swaptions." By 1997, these combined figures had reached a staggering $24 trillion.[45] And to put the relation between stock and derivative markets into perspective, by late 2008, the size of the world stock market was estimated at about $37 trillion, while the total world derivatives market had climbed to an unfathomable $791 trillion, eleven times the size of the entire world economy.[46] Fast-forward to 2017, and gross world product or the total value of goods and services produced worldwide, stood at some $75 trillion,[47] whereas currency speculation alone amounted to $5.3 trillion a day[48] that year and the global derivatives market was estimated at a mind-boggling $1.2 quadrillion.[49]

The implications here is that as we progressed into the twenty-first century, the massive concentrations of transnational finance capital were destabilizing the system and global capitalism ran up against the limits of financial fixes. The result is ever greater underlying instability in the global economy. Instability and crises appear no longer as the exceptions but as the norm. The more farsighted among transnational elites have expressed growing concern over this fragility in the global economy and the specter of chronic long-term stagnation. Former World Bank and U.S. Treasury official Larry Summers warned in 2016 of "secular stagnation" in the global economy, which has "entered unexplored, dangerous territory."[50] Yet these elites are not prepared to address the larger backdrops to global economic malaise—namely capitalism's intractable problem of overaccumulation. In sum, financial speculation, pillaging the state, and debt-driven growth cannot resolve the crisis of overaccumulation. They are crisis-management "fixes" that merely postpone a day of reckoning. Although the global economy largely recovered from the 2008 Great Recession, the worst economic crisis since the 1930s, the underlying structural conditions that triggered the financial collapse remained in place. As growth plodded forward in the second decade of the twenty-first century, the TCC appeared to hedge its bets on a new round of capitalist expansion and profit making based on a more thorough digitalization of the global economy and on a global police state.

The Digitalization of Global Capitalism

Karl Marx and Frederick Engels famously declared in *The Communist Manifesto* that "all that is solid melts into air," under the dizzying pace of change wrought by capitalism. Not since the Industrial Revolution of the eighteenth century has the world experienced such rapid and profound changes as that ushered in by globalization. But now it appears that the system is at the brink of another round of restructuring and transformation based on digitalization and Fourth Industrial Revolution technologies. Technological change is generally associated with cycles of capitalist crisis and social and political turmoil. The rise of the digital economy responds to earlier cycles of capitalist development and crisis, especially the downturn of the 1970s that led first to globalization, then the boom of the 1990s, followed by the dot-com bust, global recession in 2000–01, and then the global financial collapse of 2008 and its aftermath. Each one of these represents key turning points in digitalization. CIT introduced from the 1980s and on allowed globalization to take off, while the dot-com expansion of the following decade commercialized the Internet and laid the infrastructural basis for the digital economy.

The technological revolution associated with the rise of CIT in the 1980s was itself a response on the part of capitalists to the crisis of over-accumulation, declining rates of profit, and well-organized working classes and social movements in the 1960s and the 1970s. CIT, together with the revolution in transportation (intermodal transport, refrigeration, etc.) and novel organizational and managerial strategies, provided the technological basis for the global economy, described by sociologist Manuel Castells in his trilogy, *The Network Society*, as "an economy with the capacity to work as a unit in real time, or to choose time, on a planetary scale."[51] These technologies allowed capital to go global and also allowed it to reorganize the workplace, reduce dependence on masses of concentrated and well-organized workers, and instead outsource workers and impose flexibility, and thus forging a more favorable capital-labor relation (see next chapter).

But a second generation of digital-based technologies is now leading to a new round of worldwide economic and social restructuring. Digital technology is acquiring systemic importance, in the sense that, just as the original introduction of CIT and the Internet in the late twentieth century profoundly transformed world capitalism, ongoing digitalization now promises to have another transformative impact on the structures of the global economy, society, and polity. At the heart of a new round of restructuring is a digital economy based on more advanced information technology, on the collection, processing, and analysis of data, and on the application of digitalization to every aspect of global society, including war and repression. The tech sector—which includes computer and electronic product manufacturing, telecommunications, data processing, hosting, and other information services, platforms, and computer systems design and related services—is now at the cutting edge of capitalist globalization and is driving the digitalization of the entire global economy.

The first generation of capitalist globalization from the 1980s on involved the creation of a globally integrated production and financial system, whereas more recently, digitalization and the rise of "platforms" have facilitated a very rapid transnationalization of services (electronic off-shoring, unlike the overseas relocation of production facilities, is virtually frictionless and does not add transportation and other ancillary costs such as customs charges). Platforms refer to digital infrastructures that enable two or more groups to interact. As the dependence of economic activity on platforms spreads, the tech sector becomes ever more strategic to global capitalism. Trade in CIT goods in 2015 exceeded $2 trillion, according to United Nations data, while CIT services exports rose by 40 percent between 2010 and 2015. In that year, production of CIT goods and services repre-sented 6.5 percent of global GDP and 100 million people were employed in the CIT service sector. Moreover, global e-commerce sales reached $25 trillion, as 380 million people made purchases on overseas websites.[52] From 2009 to 2019, the volume of data crossing borders rose 64 times.[53] By 2017, services accounted for some 70 percent of the total gross world product[54] and included communications, informatics, digital and platform technology, e-commerce, financial services, professional and technical work, and a host of other non-tangible products such as film and music. Digitalization and the transnationalization of services—linked in turn to worldwide financialization as discussed above—have moved to the center of the global capitalist agenda. The press and social media have coined a plethora of catchphrases to refer to the rise of the digital economy: the "platform economy," "the sharing economy," "the on-demand economy," "the gig economy," "the app economy," and so on.

A special 2019 report in *The Economist* magazine on "The Future of Global Commerce" gave a sense of the transformations under way in the global economy through digitalization, data and transnational services:

Trade in the 20th century morphed three times, from boats laden with metals, meat and wool, to ships full of cars and transistor radios, to containers of components that feed into supply chains. Now the big opportunity is services. The flow of ideas can pack an economic punch; over 40% of productivity growth in emerging economies in 2004–14 came from knowledge flows. But Richard Baldwin, an economist, predicts a 'globotics revolution,' with remote workers abroad becoming more embedded in companies' operations. Indian outsourcing firms are shifting from running functions, such as Western payroll systems, to more creative projects, such as configuring new Walmart supermarkets. In November TCS, India's biggest firm, bought W12, a digital-design studio in London. Cross-border e-commerce is growing too. Alibaba expects its Chinese customers to spend at least $40 billion abroad in 2023. Netflix and Facebook together have over a billion cross-border customers.[55]

Digitalization in turn is leading to a new wave of technological development that has brought us to the verge of the "Fourth Industrial Revolution," based on robotics, 3D printing, the Internet of Things, artificial intelligence (AI) and machine learning, bio- and nanotechnology, quantum and cloud computing, new forms of energy storage, and autonomous vehicles.[56] There is now a fusion of technologies across physical, digital, and biological worlds (as in bioprinting, which refers to the use of 3D printing with materials that incorporate living cells). While the tech sector that drives forward this new revolution constitutes only a small portion of the gross world product, digitalization encompasses the entire global economy, from manufacturing and finance to services, and in both the formal and informal sectors. Corporations are now dependent on digital communications and data for all aspects of their business. "Tech firms," notes Foulis, "are becoming the conduit through which people interact with the world. The tech sector becomes a layer that sits across the entire economy."[57]

The shift in technology has made it possible to collect huge amounts of data. "With a long decline in manufacturing profitability," observes political scientist Nick Srnicek in his study *Platform Capitalism*, "capitalism has turned to data as one way to maintain economic growth and vitality in the face of a sluggish production sector." The platform has emerged as a new business model, in Srnicek's words, "capable of extracting and controlling immense amounts of data."[58] The technology needed for turning simple activities into recorded data became increasingly cheap, notes Srnicek, while the move to digital-based communications greatly simplified recording, opening up massive new expanses of potential data. "Just like oil," observes Srnicek, "data are a material to be extracted, refined, and used in a variety of ways."[59] Material commodities contain an increasing amount of knowledge embodied in them that is driven by data. Data has increasingly become a central resource for businesses if they are to remain competitive, and has become central to all of the processes associated with the global economy, from controlling and outsourcing workers, the flexibility of production processes, global financial flows, the coordination of global chains of supply, subcontracting and outsourcing, record keeping, marketing and sales, and to war and repression. As we will see with great clarity and an abundance of evidence in Chapter 3, Silicon Valley has become wedded to the global police state. As data mining and analysis has become more and more expansive, it opens up vast new potential for social control and becomes a central element in the development of a global police state.

In the wake of the 2008 Great Recession, the tech sector and big data became a major new outlet for surplus accumulated capital in the face of stagnation. Previously, from 1995 to 2000, the value of tech company shares in the NASDAQ quintupled in the lead-up to the dot-com bust of 2001.[60] But before long, institutional investors, especially speculative hedge and mutual funds, resumed pouring billions of dollars into the tech sector. Investment in the IT sector jumped from $17 billion in the 1970s to $175 billion in 1990, then to $496 billion in 2000, on the eve of the bursting of the turn-of-the-century dot-com bubble, but then climbed up again to new heights after 2008, surpassing $800 billion, as 2018 drew to a close.[61] In 2008, the tech sector accounted for 20 percent of all new investment across the whole economy in the United States.[62] As we shall see, finance and the IT sector seem to be fusing with and playing central roles in a global police state. A handful of U.S.- and Chinese-based tech companies that generate, extract, and process data have absorbed enormous amounts of cash from financiers desperate for new investment opportunities. In 2017, Apple held $262 billion in reserves, Microsoft held $133 billion, Alphabet (Google's parent company) held $95 billion, Cisco held $58 billion, Oracle held $66 billion, and so on.[63] Chinese-based giant Alibaba that year held $32 billion in reserve and Tencent held $52 billion,[64] although both companies also used earnings to engage in major worldwide acquisitions.

Can digitalization resolve the long-term problems of overaccumulation and stagnation? It is certainly plausible that digitalization will unleash a new round of capitalist expansion. It would be foolish to predict that the structural crisis in which the system appears to be mired is a "terminal crisis." Capitalism may be running up against ecological limits to its reproduction, but a collapse, if not averted, may be drawn out over decades or longer. Yet the enormous cash reserves and profits accumulated in the tech sector do not represent the production of new value so much as the appropriation by digital capitalists of the lion's share of surplus value through rents. As intermediaries, platforms intercede in the circuits of production and circulation of values through control over digitalized data production, extraction, and analysis, and cream off major chunks of this value in the form of "intellectual property." This helps us understand just how hypertrophied the leading digital and platform companies have become.

In 2018, the top tech companies worldwide registered a market capitalization of trillions of dollars. Although figures are never stable, Apple was in first place with an astounding capitalization of nearly $1 trillion, followed by Microsoft ($855 billion), Samsung ($765 billion), Alphabet ($757 billion), Alibaba ($457 billion), Berkshire Hathaway (which has major shares in Apple, IBM, and other tech companies, $433 billion), Amazon ($402 billion), Facebook ($435 billion), and Tencent ($357 billion).[65] By comparison, the nearest industrial company, Exxon Mobile, had a market capitalization that year of $344 billion.[66] As every area of the economy becomes increasingly integrated with a digital layer, the companies that control the digital infrastructure become immensely powerful and are able to reap a growing portion of total corporate profits in what appears, in significant part, to be rents. Vampire-like, financialization and digitalization suck up more and more value from the global economy. Nearly all of Google's and Apple's revenue comes from advertising, while Uber and Airbnb, which own no vehicles or housing units, skim value off the labor and resources of drivers, home owners, and their customers.

Yet it is questionable if the next round of transformation, driven by digitalization and Fourth Industrial Revolution technologies, can stave off crisis. In the short term, digitalization may expand opportunities for accumulation and allow for a new round of fixed capital expansion. Yet a general digitalization of global capitalism accelerates the predominance of relative surplus value over absolute surplus value. Surplus value refers to the value that is appropriated by capitalists above and beyond the value created by workers that is paid to them as wages. That is, a portion of the wealth created by labor is appropriated by capital as surplus value or profits. Surplus value can be increased in two ways. In simplified terms, the first is by increasing the level of productivity of workers by augmenting the technological content, or the fixed capital component (machinery, technology), of the production process relative to the labor component—this is what in Marxist political economy is referred to as "constant capital" (or machinery and technology) and "variable capital" (labor), respectively. The second is by increasing the amount of time each worker labors while holding wages constant and/or by lowing wages. General digitalization allows the TCC to develop new modalities for organizing the extraction of relative surplus value from workers as it appropriates the "general knowledge" of society.

Crises provide capital with the opportunity to restructure and to accelerate the process of forcing greater productivity out of fewer workers—a process that may increase exponentially through digitalization. Apologists for the current ruling order claim that the digital economy will bring high-skilled, high-paid jobs and resolve problems of social polarization and stagnation. But as we shall see in the next chapter, the evidence suggests that digitalization may deskill or completely eliminate many jobs and exacerbate inequality and social polarization many times over. Ultimately, digitalization to the extent that it replaces labor with technology pushes costs down toward zero. In fact, while the absolute volume of transnational corporate profits has snowballed, the rate of profit declined from an average of 10 percent in 2005–07 to 6 percent in 2017,[67] which suggests that this is perhaps a more powerful indicator of accumulation crisis than is the idle mass of uninvested surplus mentioned above. All of the contradictions of capitalism become intensified. The rate of profit decreases. The realization problem is aggravated. Hence the emerging digital economy is unlikely to resolve the problem of overaccumulation. Where can the TCC turn to continue to unload ever-rising amounts of surplus accumulated capital? Can war and a global police state resolve the system's dilemma?

2

Savage Inequalities:
The Imperative of Social Control

One thing I've been hearing from a lot of very wealthy people these days, since the [U.S.] election [in 2016 of Donald Trump], is that they all have escape plans. Rich people are buying up ranches in New Zealand and creating bunkers in the Bahamas, or wherever they're going, thinking that they're somehow going to be able to avoid the apocalypse when it comes. There's actually a business that operates in New York. It's a boat that will come, you can apparently pre-buy tickets, if there's some political crisis or some danger moment, and they'll come and pick you up and whisk you up the Hudson.

Interview with Rana Foroohar, associate editor of
Financial Times and CNN economic analyst[1]

Speaking at a "Business of Luxury Summit" in Monaco in 2015, the billionaire owner of the luxury jewelry company Cartier, Johann Rupert, told the audience that the prospect of robots replacing workers and the poor rising up "keeps me awake at night." Equally as frightening, he went on to say, is that in the face of imminent social upheaval the middle classes would no longer want to buy luxury goods for fear of exposing their wealth.[2] The TCC to which Rupert belongs has good reason to be frightened. The data on global inequality has by now been widely disseminated. Capitalist globalization, as we saw in the previous chapter, has resulted in unprecedented social polarization worldwide. The extent of global inequalities, and the rate of their acceleration, seem to defy the imagination. To reiterate the findings of the 2016 Oxfam report, in 2015, just 1 percent of humanity owned over half of the world's wealth and the top 20 percent own 94.5 of that wealth, while the remaining 80 percent had to make do with just 4.5 percent.[3]

But this polarization continues to intensify at a rate that appears to be exponential. Between 2017 and 2018, a new billionaire was created every two days and the world's 26 richest people owned as much as the poorest 50 percent, according to Oxfam's 2019 report. The wealth of the more than 2,200 billionaires across the globe increased by $900 billion in 2018. In that year, the 12 percent increase in wealth of the very richest contrasted with a fall of 11 percent in the wealth of the poorest half of the world's population.[4] In other words, there was in that year a direct transfer of $900 billion in wealth from the poorest half of humanity to the richest billionaires on the planet. Meanwhile, the British House of Commons released a report in 2018 which warned that the richest 1 percent of humanity are on course to control as much as two-thirds of the world's wealth by 2030.[5] And a report that same year by the Swiss bank UBS observed that "the fortunes of today's super-wealthy have risen at a far greater rate than at the turn of the twentieth century, when families such as the Rothschilds, Rockefellers and Vanderbilts controlled vast wealth."[6]

If such savage inequalities keep the TCC up at night, they impose untold hardships on billions of people who face daily struggles for survival and uncertain futures. Yet they also reflect a crisis of global capitalism that is *as much political* as it is structural. Although the global economy resumed growth and capital re-imposed its discipline in the years following the Great Recession, the 2008 fiasco was a political turning point in the breakdown of capitalist hegemony. Extreme inequality requires extreme violence and repression, that lend themselves to a global police state and projects of twenty-first-century fascism. As we saw in the previous chapter, capitalist globalization has undermined redistributive policies that came into being following the Great Depression of the 1930s, themselves the result of widespread social and class struggles from below that forced such redistribution on capitalist states. The more global inequalities expand, the more constricted is the world market and the more the system faces a structural crisis of overaccumulation. Yet such extreme levels of social polarization also present to dominant groups an escalating challenge of social control. It is this imperative of social control that in the first instance brings forth a global police state.

Expansion of the Global Working Class:
The Precariat and Surplus Humanity

As we saw previously, globalization brought about a change in power relations worldwide between capital and labor. The newfound relative power of global capital over global labor revolves around a new capital-labor relation. The essence of capitalism is production undertaken through a particular form of social interaction, the capital-labor relation, or capitalist production relations, in order to exchange what is produced, commodities, in a market for profit. For capitalist production to take place, there needs to be a class of people that have no means of production of their own—that is, the working class. This class enters into relation with a class of people, the capitalist class, who have come into possession of these means of production and in turn require a supply of labor in order to work these means of production so that commodities can be produced and sold for a profit. Capital and labor (capitalists and workers) only exist in relation to each other; they are antagonistic ends of the same pole. "Capital presupposes wage labor; wage labor presupposes capital," observes Marx. "They reciprocally condition the existence of each other; they reciprocally bring forth each other."[7]

At the core of the capitalist production process is this capital-labor relation, which refers to the relationship between workers and capitalists (or more precisely, the *form* of that relationship) as they come together in the process of producing goods that people want or need, along with the social processes, institutions, and norms that reproduce these relations. While capital and labor are locked into each other—only exist in relation to each other—the particular way that they come together is historically determined by many factors, but perhaps above all by the terms of the class struggle between capitalists and workers, or more broadly, the social struggles among the ruling groups and the popular masses of people.[8] The dynamics internal to capitalism and its cycles of expansion and crisis lead to the clash of social forces and ongoing restructuring that shape capital-labor relations in distinct ways in particular historical periods.

Capitalist globalization has brought about a new economic model known as *flexible accumulation*. It involves novel managerial forms such as the vertical disintegration of production, "just in time" and small-batch production, vast chains of subcontracting and outsourcing that span the globe and formal and informal transnational business alliances, that together with the application of digital technology make possible new subdivisions and specializations in production.[9] But at the core of flexible accumulation—what most interests us here—are new capital-labor relations around the world. The restructuring of the labor process associated with post-Fordist flexible accumulation has involved the fragmentation and cheapening of labor through widespread casualization or informalization of work. These arrangements involve alternative systems of labor control and diverse contingent categories of labor, captured in the term now most often used, *precarious labor*. Precarious labor involves all sorts of unstable, contingent categories of work, such as temporary and part-time work, casual, seasonal and on-call work, non-unionized contract and piece-meal work.[10]

Labor markets worldwide have been deregulated as workers in the global economy under these flexible arrangements are increasingly treated as a subcontracted component rather than a fixture internal to employer organizations—reduced to mere inputs just as another raw material—stockpiled, thrown into the accumulation process when needed, discarded when no longer needed. As workers become disposable under these arrangements, they not only lose employment stability but also the social protections that were often associated with regulated labor, such as minimum wage guarantees, unemployment insurance, access to social welfare assistance, health insurance, paid holidays, and so on. These arrangements have involved the ongoing withdrawal of the state from protection of labor and the erosion of reciprocal obligations on the part of the state and capital to labor, or even any notion that social reproduction of the worker is a part of the labor contract. These reciprocal obligations are replaced by a one-sided domination by capital. These new capital-labor relations are a result of the TCC's class struggle against the global working and popular classes whose collective power has been weakened by capitalist globalization.

As workers become "flexible" they join the ranks of a new global "pre-cariat" of proletarians who labor under these unstable, precarious work arrangements. While the concept of a precariat has been popularized by Standing's 2011 study, *The Precariat: The New Dangerous Class*,[11] the pre-cariat should be seen not as a separate class, as Standing insists, but as a condition—precariousness—imposed on increasing numbers of the global working class in the face of capitalist globalization and the transition underway for several decades now from Fordist to flexible accumulation. The precariat—to the extent that the concept is useful—is part of the global working class; it is the face of the working class. While precari-ousness has been the condition of most people brought into the capitalist economy over the centuries, precariatization now appears to be conjoined with expanding proletarianization and institutionalized in capital-labor relations worldwide, and includes white- and blue-collar work, service work, and professional and managerial work (see below). The fragmen-tation of labor markets has been made possible, in part, by digitalization, which as we saw previously has facilitated spatial decentralization, reorganization of the labor process, and new modalities of value extraction.

If globalization has given capital enhanced power over labor with which to impose these new capital-labor relations, the other crucial factor is the dramatic expansion of the global working class. Proletarianization worldwide has accelerated through new waves of primitive accumulation as billions of people have been uprooted, wrenched from their communities, and thrown into a global labor market that is increasingly saturated and deregulated. Primitive accumulation refers to the process whereby people are violently separated from the means of production (e.g., from the land) and left with no other way to survive than to sell their labor to those who violently appropriate the means of production, the capitalist class. Marx famously described the history of primitive accumulation in the final passage of Volume I of *Capital*:

> The accumulation of capital presupposes surplus-value; surplus-value presupposes capitalistic production; capitalistic production presupposes the preexistence of considerable masses of capital and of labor-power in the hands of producers of commodities. The whole movement, therefore, seems to turn in a vicious circle, out of which we can only get supposing a primitive accumulation preceding capitalistic production. In actual history, it is notorious that conquest, enslavement, robbery, murder, and force, play the great part. The methods of primitive accumulation are anything but idyllic. This history is written in the annals of mankind in letters of blood and fire. The discovery of gold and silver in America, the extirpation, enslavement and entombment in mines of the indigenous population of that continent, the beginnings of the conquest and plunder of India, and the conversion of Africa into a preserve for the commercial hunting of blackskins, are all things which characterize the rosy dawn of the era of capitalist production. These idyllic proceedings are the chief momenta of primitive accumulation. On their heels treads the commercial wars of the European nations, with the globe for a theater. These methods depend in part on brute force, that is, on the colonial system. Force is the midwife of every old society pregnant with a new one. It is itself an economic power. If money, according to one Biblical passage, comes into the world with a congenital bloodstain on one cheek, capital comes dripping from head to foot, from every pore, with blood and dirt.[12]

But the history of primitive accumulation did not end with the enclosures in England and the colonial system that set in motion world capitalism. The process has never ceased over the centuries and has been accelerated by capitalist globalization. The global wage labor force doubled from some 1.5 billion in 1980 to some three billion in 2006, as workers from China, India, and the former Soviet bloc entered the global labor pool,[13] and then increased by another 500 million by 2018, the largest size of the global labor force in recorded history.[14] Hundreds of millions, perhaps billions of people, have been displaced from the Third World countryside through new rounds of primitive accumulation brought about by neo-liberal policies as well as social cleansing, and organized violence such as the "war on drugs" and the "war on terror," both of which have served as instruments of primitive accumulation and for the violent restructuring and integration of countries and regions into the new global economy.[15] Banks, institutional investors, and corporate agribusiness began vast new land grabs around the world in the 2000s in what amounts to a new round of global enclosures. In China, several hundred million peasants have been uprooted from their land in recent decades as the country has integrated into global capitalism. Throughout the former Third World, agricultural policies and trade and investment liberalization imposed by the financial agencies of the transnational state (TNS) along with state repression and the private violence of landlords have resulted in the expulsion of millions of farmers from the countryside and the appropriation of their lands by transnational corporate agribusiness. In India, several hundred thousand farmers committed suicide in recent years after losing their land to creditors. In Mexico, several million families lost their land in the wake of the North American Free Trade Agreement signed with the United States and Canada in 1994, becoming internal and transnational migrants. A similar story has taken place in sub-Saharan Africa and Central and South America.[16]

Those uprooted from traditional livelihoods are increasingly concentrated in the vast slums, *favelas*, and shantytowns of the mega-cities of the world. The global economy appears as a world bound together by flows of telecommunications, finance, and trade among a network of megacities. "A watershed in human history, comparable to the Neolithic or Industrial revolutions" has taken place, notes Mike Davis in *Planet of Slums*. "For the first time the urban population of the earth will outnumber the rural."[17] By 2030, 41 cities will have more than 10 million inhabitants, up from 31 in 2016, and 66 percent of the world's population will live in an urban area by 2050.[18] Amin estimated in the early 2000s that the popular classes (by which he means the working classes, whether employed or unemployed, laboring in the formal or the informal economy) accounted for some three-quarters of the world's urban population, and that the precarious subcategory represented two-thirds of the popular classes on a world scale. "The main social transformation that characterizes the second half of the twentieth century can be summarized in a single statistic: the proportion of the precarious popular classes rose from less than one-quarter to more than one-half of the global urban population, and this phenomenon of pauperization has reappeared on a significant scale in the developed centers themselves," he observed. "This destabilized urban population has increased in a half-century from less than a quarter of a billion to more than a billion-and-a-half individuals, registering a growth rate which surpasses those that characterize economic expansion, population growth, or the process of urbanization itself."[19]

New rounds of primitive accumulation have generated a vast army of internal and transnational migrants who have swelled the ranks of the precariat and the structurally marginalized. In 2015, there were 232 million international migrants and 740 million internal migrants, according to the International Organization on Migration.[20] Some of the uprooted millions are super-exploited through incorporation into the global factories, farms, and offices as precarious labor, while others are marginalized and converted into surplus humanity, relegated to marginal existence on a planet of slums. The ILO reported that 1.53 billion workers around the world were in such "vulnerable" employment arrangements in 2009, representing more than 50 percent of the global workforce,[21] and that in 2018 a majority of the 3.5 billion workers in the world "experienced a lack of material well-being, economic security, equality opportunities or scope for human development."[22] As digitalization now drives a new round of worldwide restructuring, it promises to extend the precariatization of workers who have employment and also to expand the ranks of surplus humanity excluded from the labor market. The ILO also reported that in the late twentieth century some one-third of the global labor force had been made superfluous and locked out of the global economy.[23] Even the CIA felt compelled to warn in 2002 that "by the late 1990s a staggering one billion workers representing one-third of the world's labor force, most of them in the South, were either unemployed or underemployed."[24]

Hence the global working class brings together those exploited more intensively through precarious employment with those that have been excluded. Digitalization, in addition to generating precarious forms of employment, is expected to exponentially increase the surplus labor population. The processes by which surplus labor is generated have accelerated under globalization. The "end of work," the "jobless future," and the "rise of robots" that replace human workers is a commonplace topic among academics, journalists, and politicians.[25] Millions of people expelled from formal employment have managed to scratch out a living through Uber and other "platform companies" as informal and "self-employed" workers. But in 2016, Uber announced that it would replace one million drivers with autonomously driven vehicles.[26] In that year, plans were also underway to automate the trucking industry.[27] Foxconn, the Taiwanese-based conglomerate that assembles iPads and other electronic devices, announced in 2012 following a wave of strikes by its workers in China that it would replace one million workers with robots. A few years later, Walmart introduced robots to carry out inventory and janitorial work in its U.S. stores.[28] As digital technologies are introduced, they raise productivity and the system sheds more and more workers. One U.S. National Bureau of Economic Research report found that each new robot introduced in a locale results in a loss of 3–5.6 jobs.[29] In 1990, the top three carmakers in Detroit had a market capitalization of $36 billion and 1.2 million employees. In 2014, the top three firms in Silicon Valley, with a market capitalization of over $1 trillion had only 137,000 employees.[30]

The two dimensions of the global working class—those marginalized and made surplus, and those brought into the labor process and exploited—are not separate groups. They are two categories of the global working class that are conjoined; they form a unity in their antagonistic relationship to transnational capital. Surplus humanity is of no *direct* use to transnational capital; they are not subject to primary exploitation. However, in the larger picture, in addition to secondary forms of exploitation, surplus labor is crucial to global capitalism insofar as it places downward pressure on wages everywhere and allows transnational capital to impose heightened discipline over those who remain active in the labor market and even makes possible in some cases new systems of twenty-first-century slavery, including the enslavement of women for the thriving global sex trade.[31] "The overwork of the employed part of the working-class swells the ranks of the reserve," notes Marx, "whilst conversely the greater pressure that the latter by its competition exerts on the former, forces these to submit to over-work and to subjugation under the dictates of capital." He goes on:

But if a surplus population of workers is a necessary product of accumulation or the development of wealth on a capitalist basis, this surplus population also becomes, conversely, the lever of capital accumulation, indeed it becomes the condition for the existence of the capitalist mode of production. It forms a disposable industrial reserve army, which belongs to capital just as absolutely as if the latter had bred it at its own costs. Independently of the limits of the actual increase of population, it creates a mass of human material always ready for exploitation by capital in the interests of capital's own changing valorization requirements.[32]

However, the restructuring of world capitalism through globalization has given rise to a new global army of superfluous labor that goes well beyond the traditional reserve army of labor to which Marx refers. Let us revisit overaccumulation crisis and link it to this expansion of surplus labor worldwide. Capitalist competition and class struggle push capital to reduce costs and/or increase productivity by increasing the organic composition of capital, which leads to the tendency for the rate of profit to fall.[33] As discussed in the previous chapter, this tendency, the "most fundamental law" of political economy, is expressed as overaccumulation crisis. It is worth quoting Marx at length with regard to how capitalist production of necessity, constantly reproduces an "industrial reserve army" or "surplus population" because the creation and expansion of this surplus population is the central background factor to understanding unprecedented inequality worldwide, the expansion of surplus humanity through a new round of global capitalist restructuring based on digitalization, and the looming global crisis:

It is capitalistic accumulation itself that constantly produces, and produces in direct ratio of its own energy and extent, a relatively redundant population of laborers, i.e., a population of greater extent than suffices for the average needs of the self-expansion of capital, and therefore a surplus population. The laboring population therefore produces, along with the accumulation of capital produced by it, the means by which itself is made relatively superfluous, is turned into a relative surplus population; and it does this to an always increasing extent ... This increase is effected by the simple process that constantly "sets free" a part of the laborers; by methods which lessen the number of laborers employed in proportion to the increased production. The whole form of the movement of modern industry depends, therefore, upon the constant transformation of a part of the laboring population into unemployed or half-employed hands ... But the greater this reserve army in proportion to the active labor-army, the greater is the mass of a consolidated surplus-population, whose misery is in inverse ratio to its torment of labor. The more extensive, finally, the lazarus-layers of the working-class, and the industrial reserve army, the greater is official pauperism. *This is the absolute general law of capitalist accumulation.*[34]

The constantly replenished reserve army of labor to the pulse of capital accumulation is thus for Marx a consequence of "the general law of capitalist accumulation." Marx goes on to identify three forms of surplus labor: floating, latent, and stagnant. The first two were seen as those who weave in and out of the production process in accordance with the cycles of capital accumulation and changes in the division of labor. The third, however, is a group that has been pushed structurally outside of the production process—that is, a group which is of no *direct* use to capital over entire historical epochs. Marx tended to denigrate those in this latter category as lumpenproletariat. But given that digitalization, to the extent that it replaces labor with technology, has the potential to drastically reduce the need for labor ("variable capital" in Marx's lexicon) and to push costs towards zero, it may be, absent countervailing pressures, that the expansion of the ranks of surplus humanity worldwide is a permanent structural phenomenon of global capitalism rather than a transitory dislocation pending absorption into new circuits of accumulation.

The concept of the lumpenproletariat has an important etiology in the history of capitalism. Marx first discussed the lumpenproletariat in derogatory terms as a *déclassé* and degenerated element among the proletariat—prostitutes, vagabonds, petty criminals—an underclass without a class consciousness and prone to serving as "a bribed tool of reactionary intrigue." In *The Eighteenth Brumaire of Louis Napoleon*, he describes the lumpenproletariat as "vagabonds, discharged soldiers, discharged jailbirds, escaped galley slaves, swindlers, mountebanks, lazzaroni, pickpockets, tricksters, gamblers, pimps, brothel keepers, porters, literati, organ grinders, ragpickers, knife grinders, tinkers, beggars—in short, the whole indefinite, disintegrated mass, thrown hither and thither" by capitalism.[35] However, some of the negative connotations of the lumpenproletariat fell away in the mid-twentieth century as it became clear that racism, colonialism, and imperialism thrust hundreds of millions of their victims into the ranks of the displaced, the unemployed, and the excluded. The lumpenproletariat condition now appeared as a structural (and sometimes legal) location of marginality and informality in the world capitalist system with a contingent political agency. In *The Wretched of the Earth*, Franz Fanon referred to the lumpenproletariat as displaced peasants who constituted a potentially revolutionary force against the colonial system, although he warned that it is unpredictable and could as well turn into hired soldiers of the colonialists.[36] In the United States, the Black Panthers sought to organize the black lumpenproletariat as a mass social base, although this strategy was not without its limitations and its critics.[37]

But now, in this age of capitalist globalization, surplus humanity may be an analytically as well as politically superior concept to make sense of that mass of humanity thrown into the margins of the system. While there is certainly a delinquent element among the mass of humanity that has been "thrown hither and thither" by the destabilization of global capital, surplus humanity appears to be a structural category thrown up by an accelerated restructuring and a more advanced stage of global capital accumulation. Surplus humanity includes those who suffer from long-term structural un- and underemployment, the mass of people who eke out a living (or don't even manage to do so) in the informal economy of the slums of the world's megacities, as well as international refugees, those internally displaced by wars, repression, and natural disasters, migrant workers who may be forced underground and unable to enter the formal labor market, among others who exist in what Bradley and Lee call the "non-places of the world." In this regard, surplus humanity exists in conjunction with the precariat and may weave in and out of more formal yet precarious employment. "It is clear that 200 years after the birth of Marx, the composition of the lumpenproletariat has changed from 'vagabonds, criminals, prostitutes', pariahs and untouchables, to precarious workers, a working poor, to contract staff, day staff, zero-hour contract staff, and more desperately to the underclass or permanent underclass," observe Bradley and Lee. I concur with their political assessment: "Marx's distinction between the revolutionary laboring poor and the reactionary lumpenproletariat no longer holds under the global conditions of contemporary exploitation."[38] *Lumpenprecariat* captures the idea of a global working class that brings the precariat together with surplus humanity.[39]

The expanding ranks of the lumpenprecariat worldwide opens up a world of possibilities with regard to common interests and experiences even if organizing the global working class, or its self-organization, is made problematic by its atomization and individualized consciousness associated with the fragmentation of labor. And we should be mindful that there is still a "traditional"industrial working class that has stepped up its struggles in recent years.[40] Yet the lumpenprecariat condition changes the terms of its struggles and the challenges of regenerating working-class conscious-ness and a collective action capacity. Certainly, any emancipatory project in order for it to succeed would have to bring together surplus humanity and their struggles in the margins and at points of social reproduction with those formally inserted into the circuits of global capital under precari-ous work arrangements. As Aronowitz reminds us, following Marx, "the central criterion for class formation is the capacity of a social formation or a constellation of them for self-organization and self-representation"[41]— that is, to forge some sense of a shared identity and a community.

Sadistic Capitalism: Turning Poverty and Exclusion into Sources of Accumulation

The expansion of the precariat and surplus humanity presents a double challenge to the TCC. This mass of humanity must be controlled and any pretense at rebellion repressed. At the same time, capitalists seek ways to take advantage of its condition to develop new methods of accumulation, apart from the profitability of repression itself, as we will explore in the next chapter. Surplus humanity toils in all sorts of survival strategies in the informal world of a planet of slums that may be exploited by capital. More than two billion people across the globe work in the informal sector.[42] This informal sector has always been functionally linked to the formal sector in a myriad of ways, including as a bastion of social reproduction and for the provision of services to the formal sector.[43] Yet under globalization, the lines between formality and informality become ever more blurred. As Swidler notes, capital is increasingly reliant on methods of extracting surplus labor other than the wage relation, among them, social reproduc-tion in the family and the community, piece work, unpaid labor such as internships and prison labor, and shadow work.[44] Predatory finance, in par-ticular, has opened up new opportunities for capital to exploit workers and the poor outside of the formal wage relation. The increasing dependence of the poor on a wide range of credit arrangements across the globe is a novel mechanism of what Soederberg calls secondary exploitation, made possible by financialization and backed by the repressive instruments of the global police state.

The TCC, as Soederberg shows,[45] is now able to earn vast profits through the poverty and indebtedness of workers and surplus humanity. Primary exploitation refers to the exploitation that takes place in the capital-labor relation at the point of production of wealth, where capitalists directly appropriate from labor surplus value that is the source of profits. Surplus humanity cannot be directly exploited, that is, subject to primary exploitation. But unless they are to quietly die of starvation, they must enter into the market in the sphere of circulation to obtain their basic necessities, by hook or by crook. It is here, in the sphere of circulation, that secondary exploitation takes place. Secondary exploitation refers to the additional transfer of value (wealth) from workers (whether employed or unemployed) to capital, beyond that transferred in the sphere of production, even though this value was originally produced through primary exploitation. For instance, renters must transfer wealth to landlords, who play no part in the production of that wealth, for the temporary use of a house or apartment. In fact, corporate landlordism in many countries is becoming an important new outlet for surplus accumulated capital. In the United States, institutional investors, including hedge funds, private equity firms, and global banks, have spent tens of billions of dollars snatching up properties and converting them into rentals since the 2008 crisis, which resulted in foreclosure for millions of family homes.[46]

But above all, secondary exploitation takes place through the contraction of debt that must be paid back with interest. We saw previously that there has been an expansion of consumer credit among the working classes and surplus humanity who must incur rising levels of debt in order to secure basic necessities if their wages are insufficient to cover these necessities or if they are unable to contract secure employment. What Soederberg terms "credit-led accumulation" is a dominant strategy employed by capitalists since the 1990s "to absorb the tensions of overaccumulation" through "the creation and extension of credit money to low-income workers in exchange for high rates of interest as well as commissions and fees."[47] At the same time, this debt peonage becomes a powerful disciplinary mechanism forcing the poor and surplus humanity to find employment at any price and under the most onerous of conditions. The cycle of rising debt and more oppressive discipline is enforced by the "debtfare state" through a host of punitive legal measures for the collection of debt, such as changes to bankruptcy laws making it difficult if not impossible to discharge debt, allowing usury, abolishing consumer protection laws, authorizing the seizure of assets, and criminalization of debtors (this latter will be discussed in the next chapter).

This poverty industry preys in particular on the most vulnerable within the precariat, such as immigrants, racially oppressed communities, single mothers, the handicapped, informal sector workers, and the un- and under-employed, for whom "debt has become the last hope for avoiding, reducing, or at least delaying the pain of marginalization."[48] In the United States, there has been a very rapid dependence on credit-card debt for subsistence as banks pursue a predatory strategy of credit-led accumulation that preys on low-wage workers and impoverished communities. Between 1989 and 2001, credit-card debt among low-income families grew by 184 percent, as 40 percent of households came to rely on credit cards to pay for basic necessities because earnings were insufficient to cover these necessities, or because of a slide into under- and unemployment.[49] The financial industry even created a category—in its own words—of "unbanked" people, including undocumented immigrants.[50] While mortgage and car-loan debts are secured (asset backed), pay day loans, student and credit-card debt, rent-to-own facilities, and microfinance loans to the poor in Mexico, Bangladesh, or South Africa, are unsecured. However, exorbitant interest rates, origination fees, late fees, and other fee-based charges make the poverty industry immensely profitable even when debtors do not have steady employment and when debts are not repaid.[51] "The credit system develops the motive of capitalist production into the purest and most colossal system of gambling and swindling," notes Marx. It exhibits "this dual character of swindler and prophet."[52]

Meanwhile, microfinance has proliferated in many countries in the former Third World. "Financial inclusion" became a new buzzword from the 1990s and on for extending credit-based accumulation around the world and entrapping surplus humanity into the circuits of transnational finance capital. The transnational elite touted "microcredit" as a major step forward in poverty alleviation, a claim all too often echoed by development scholars and liberals and even leftists working in international non-governmental organizations. "Beneath the gloss," however, as Soederberg observes, "the target of the class-based project involved shifting the dependency of 2.5 billion surplus workers from informal lenders to formal (legally recognized) commercial lenders."[53] The global financial corporations that came to dominate the microfinance industry turned "poverty credit" into a major new opportunity for credit-led accumulation as borrowers came more and more to rely on these private credit markets for basic subsistence.

If capital turns poverty and inequality into profit, in some cases, it has managed to turn suffering and deprivation generated by global capitalism into a source of aesthetic pleasure, leisure, and entertainment—that is, to sell it to the affluent as a glamorized spectacle. In what can only be called sadistic capitalism, for instance, the South Africa Emoya Luxury Hotel and Spa company advertised in 2015 an opportunity to tourists to stay "in our unique Shanty Town ... and experience traditional township living within a safe private game reserve environment." A cluster of simulated shanties outside of Bloemfontein that the company has constructed "is ideal for team building, braais, bachelors [parties], theme parties and an experience of a lifetime," read the ad. The luxury accommodations, made to appear from the outside as shacks, featured paraffin lamps, candles, a battery-operated radio, an outside toilet, a drum and fireplace for cooking, as well as under-floor heating, air conditioning, and wireless Internet access. A well-dressed, young white couple is pictured embracing in a field with the corrugated tin shanties in the background. The only thing missing in this fantasy world of sanitized space and glamorized poverty was the people themselves living in poverty.[54]

In the larger picture, the global police state in this regard is coercive not just in regard to the direct repression it unleashes, such as in police and paramilitary violence against protesters, the persecution of immigrants, mass incarceration, or waging wars. It is also an instrument of structural violence wielded to transfer wealth to the TCC and to impose oppressive discipline on the global working class and surplus humanity. We saw in the previous chapter how the TCC has turned to financial speculation, the plunder of public finance, and debt-driven growth in the face of overaccumulation pressures. In providing an outlet for overaccumulated capital, the contraction of public and private debt is enormously profitable for the TCC. The commodification of debt has generated new modalities of exploiting precarious labor and surplus humanity while at the same time it has become a powerful tool for disciplining the global working class. Government deficits must be financed and debt paid to bond investors by transferring wealth from workers through social austerity measures such as cutbacks in social welfare, income and value-added sales tax, regressive income tax, cuts in public employment, escalating fees for public services, defunding public health, education, and old age pensions, the privatization of public assets, and so on. In 2013, according to one study, some 5.8

billion people, or 80 percent of the global population, were affected by such austerity measures.[55] As we will see further in the next chapter, there are innumerable instances in which the state also transfers wealth to the TCC by extracting income from workers to directly finance militarized accumulation.

The Precariat and Cognitive Labor

It had already become evident in the late twentieth century that the restructuring of world capitalism associated with globalization and CIT has involved a polarization of the working class between those whose work has been deskilled and routinized and those who moved into the ranks of so-called "knowledge workers" engaged in high-skilled (and allegedly high-paid) labor. These workers are what Robert Reich has called "symbolic analysts" and others have referred to as those performing immaterial labor.[56] While defenders of global capitalism have argued that the number of those engaged in well-paid cognitive labor will multiply, digitalization to the contrary appears to bring about the expanded commodification of this cognitive labor and the proletarianization and precariatization of those who perform such labor. This process involves the real subsumption of cognitive labor. Formal subsumption refers to the process by which people are separated from their means of survival or production, such as land or small businesses, so that they are forced to find ways to work for capital, whereas real subsumption refers to the subordination of workers into the capitalist production process as it is directly controlled by capital in the factory, the plantation, service sector, or in this case, through control over immaterial labor in the Internet. Real subsumption involves the total corporeal discipline, oppression, and domination of labor, so that one loses whatever is left of individual power and autonomy, incorporated, in Marx's words as a "living appendage" into the production process.

(More generally, beyond specifically cognitive labor that I focus on here, digitalization deepens the real subsumption of labor to capital worldwide. For example, if small farmers are formally subsumed to capital by their dependence on capitalist markets and credits, and increasingly on seeds and other inputs, they can be said to be formally subsumed to capital. But when they lose their land they face not formal but real subsumption. To the extent that the new technologies accelerate primitive accumulation and dramatically expand the ranks of the working class by displacing small independent producers—merchants, farmers, independent professionals—they expand the sphere of real subsumption. The real subsumption of cognitive labor is but the most dramatic indication of how digitalization accelerates this process.)

There is an important generational dimension to the new capital-labor relations insofar as the "millennial generation" is the first to be born into a digital world in which precarious work is becoming the norm and which could become *normalized* in the absence of a class-conscious movement against precariatization. The twentieth-century social contract that regulated work is a thing of the past for many, perhaps most of the millennial generation born between 1980 and the turn of century, and even more so the next generation that some have referred to as "Generation Y,"[57] this at a time when the global working class increasingly resembles a global army of youth. "While countries across Europe and East Asia are grappling with declining birthrates and aging populations, societies across the Middle East, Africa, and South Asia are experiencing youth booms of staggering proportions," noted one 2016 report. "More than half of Egypt's labor force is younger than age 30. Half of Nigeria's population of 167 million is between the ages of 15 and 34. In Afghanistan, Chad, East Timor, Niger, Somalia, and Uganda, more than two-thirds of the population is under the age of 25" and 300 million Indians were under the age of 15.[58] The global youth face a wave of labor-replacing technology and the real prospects of laborless production. At the same time, global marketing tantalizes youth with an endless stream of products and services. How will the youth of today respond politically to the contradiction of being swept up in this ubiquitous culture-ideology of consumerism and the reality of unemployment and poverty?

Young knowledge workers in particular are set to swell the ranks of the increasingly impoverished and alienated digital proletariat. A growing portion of this proletariat labors by supplying "on-demand" digital services online, what is sometimes dubbed the "human cloud." While neo-liberal economists and policy makers refer to them as "self-employed entrepreneurs," they are in effect outsourced contract workers laboring in the absence of any job stability or income security, entirely at the whim of those who contract them. The notion of a "sharing economy" gives the sense of control and autonomy even as the work involved becomes ever more precarious and disciplined. Firms such as Freelancer.com and UpWork contracted more than five million people to work remotely online in 2017. Such "micro-work" sites as Mechanical Turk, a service operated by Amazon, contracts some 500,000 "Turkers" who earn a few cents for each task performed.[59] In this world of cognitive proletarians whose labor is entirely unregulated, Amazon advertises its services by proclaiming, "you decide how much to pay workers for each assignment."[60] "All across the world," notes Starzmann, "uncountable solitary figures have committed themselves to lives in front of screens, fingers moving across keyboards ceaselessly—thinking, typing, producing."[61] And Bradley and Lee warn that the "revolutionary energy [of this young digital proletariat] is spent elsewhere—on computer games, porn, gambling, endless forms of intoxication to escape the reality of the working day."[62]

Here we need to explore the implications of such a shift for subject formation, for consciousness, and for what Pierre Bourdieu has termed "habitus," as "an acquired system of generative schemes" adjusted to a given set of social conditions.[63] The development of inter-subjectivities and class consciousness are impeded by the individuated and isolated nature of much cognitive labor. What type of a worldview may come out of this work absent some political mobilization outside of the work process? Cognitive workers may be more inclined to identify with middle and professional strata rather than with the global working class to which most belong. Fragmentation of the labor process and of work into scattered and irregular moments of labor power throws up new challenges to the organization of the working class and to the development of working-class consciousness. To this must be added the all-powerful role of the global corporate media, and the colonization by capital of social media, in shaping consciousness. Social media has become tremendously popular among young people, occupying enormous amounts of their time. Yet in the absence of a larger organized movement that brings people together around emancipatory projects, it tends to fragment and individualize what in essence is collective existence, generating an infinite amount of micro-spaces that undermine the development of collective consciousness and forms of social action (it also makes possible frightening new modalities of corporate and state surveillance, as I discuss in the next chapter).[64]

The transformations that CIT promises to bring are distinct from previous waves of technological change, in which labor shed from sectors replaced by automation became absorbed into new economic activities. For instance, the rise of the automobile industry destroyed industries dedicated to horse-based transportation but created vast new industrial and managerial employment in the auto industry. And earlier computerization created an abundance of high-skilled knowledge jobs. But now, as human knowledge is transferred to machines through machine learning, machines become valuable substitutes for humans at multiple levels.[65] CIT is like a utility (e.g., electricity) insofar as each new productive activity takes full advantage of the utility, and in doing so, brings big data into play. The "big data revolution" means that the data captured on work performed in knowledge-based occupations at the workplace and in the market may lead to direct automation of specific tasks and jobs. As algorithms generated by big data become predictable enough to make cognitive labor more and more redundant to a whole host of activities, from medical diagnosis to legal advice, it is clear that acquiring education and skills will no longer assure protection against job automation.

Many young people continue to place their hopes on higher education to escape the fate of the precariat, but training is becoming more and more disconnected from income. In the United States, higher education became a strategy for deferring unemployment, especially since the financial collapse of 2008. There was an unprecedented increase in university enrollment of over five million from 2001 to 2018, and enrollment numbers were expected to climb another 15 percent in subsequent years. The price for tuition and fees during this period jumped 157 percent in private institutions and 237 percent in public schools.[66] Student-loan debt, owed by more than 44 million borrowers, surpassed $1.5 trillion in 2019, over twice the total U.S. credit-card debt.[67] This debt is a claim on the future wages of these students, and in at least 20 states, debtors can be denied driver's licenses and professional licenses if they do not maintain debt payments. Their precarious situation creates the conditions for lives as precarious workers in the future. Nowhere is this more evident than in the shift to contract (adjunct) professors, who by 2019 taught some 70 percent of all university courses, constituting a growing army of "academic precariat." These professors generally hold doctorates, having achieved the highest level of formal education, yet often work for less-than-subsistence wages.

Laborless Production?

Yet much cognitive labor could itself become replaced by artificial intelligence. The expansion of surplus humanity and precariousness is not a result of digitalization as much as an expression of the problem of capitalism in its "normal" development. Marx argued in *The Grundrisse* that at a certain point in the development of production, science and technology become qualitative forces of production that can increasingly generate value independent of "living" human labor (e.g., through automation).

Crisis provides transnational capital with the opportunity to accelerate this process of forcing greater productivity out of fewer workers. The largest employers in the United States "have emerged from the economy's harrowing downturn loaded with cash thanks to deep cost-cutting that helped drive unemployment into double digits ... and [resulted in] huge gains in worker productivity," observed one report on the aftermath of the 2008 crisis.[68] The ongoing rise in the organic composition of capital through investment in constant capital intended to increase the rate of exploitation and/or to undercut worker resistance eventually results in a qualitatively new situation in which value-generating technology makes the labor power of large swaths of the working class not just cheapened and deskilled, but entirely unnecessary, swelling ever further the ranks of surplus humanity.

Already, each time we pick up the phone, we have become accustomed to computers replacing telephone operators, customer service representatives, and so on. Notwithstanding the argument put forth by apologists for the ruling order that the digital economy will bring high-skilled, high-paid jobs, we have seen that everything indicates quite the opposite: the digital economy will continue to aggravate the trend towards ever more mass un- and underemployment along with precarious forms of employment. The digital and platform economy makes it easier to coordinate and outsource workers as it simultaneously disaggregates the working class and aggregates capital. As noted in the previous chapter, we are poised to see the digital decimation of major sectors of the global economy. Anything can be digitalized, and this is increasingly almost everything. Automation is now spreading from industry to the financial, service, and agricultural sectors and is expected to even replace professional work such as lawyers, financial analysts, doctors, journalists, accountants, insurance underwriters, and librarians.[69] Anecdotes abound on the automation taking place in virtually every branch of the economy, including those considered labor dependent and previously not subject to automation. A 2017 story in the *Los Angeles Times*, for instance, reported the first pizza restaurant company in the Bay Area, Zume, to become fully robotized. According to the story, the whole pizza restaurant industry, and fast food more generally, could soon follow suit.[70]

Short of full automation, the ever rising organic composition of capital (that is, the increase in fixed capital as machinery and technology relative to living labor) leads to more and more being produced with fewer and fewer precarious workers. In the United States, the net increase in jobs since 2005 has been almost exclusively in unstable and usually low-paid work arrangements. Amazon, with a workforce of 230,000 and tens of thousands of seasonal workers, is notorious for the brutal sweatshop-like labor conditions in its warehouses and logistical networks, described as "the future of low-wage work."[71] (Meanwhile, Amazon CEO Jeff Bezos became the richest man in the world in 2017, with a net worth of over $100 billion, while thousands of Amazon employees require food stamps to make ends meet.) Indeed, digital-driven production seeks to lower wage, capital, and overhead costs—ultimately to achieve what the Nike Corporation refers to as "engineering the labor out of the product."[72]

Revealingly, the U.S. labor market added 9.4 million jobs between 2005 and 2015, including 9.1 million precarious jobs, so that the net increase in jobs since 2005 has been solely in these unstable work arrangements.[73] A billion-dollar data center built in 2011 by Apple in North Carolina created a mere 50 full-time positions.[74] At peak employment in 1979, General Motors alone had nearly 840,000 jobs and reported earnings of $11 billion, whereas in 2012 Google employed only 38,000 yet generated profits of $14 billion. Ford points out:

> YouTube was founded in 2005 by three people. Less than two years later, the company was purchased by Google for about $1.65 billion. At the time of its acquisition, YouTube employed a mere sixty-five people, the majority of them highly skilled engineers. That works out to a valuation of over $35 million per employee. In April 2012, Facebook acquired photo-sharing start-up Instagram for $1 billion. The company employed thirteen people. That's roughly $77 million per worker. Fast-forward another two years to February 2014 and Facebook once again stepped up to the plate, this time purchasing mobile messaging company WhatsApp for $19 billion. WhatsApp had a workforce of fifty-five – giving it a valuation of a staggering $345 million per employee.

Founder and chairman of the World Economic Forum Klaus Schwab, among others, has estimated that some one-half of all jobs in the United States are at risk of being automated and that the destruction of jobs will take place at a much faster pace than such shifts experienced during earlier industrial-technological revolutions under capitalism.[75] In the Philippines, 100,000 outsourced workers earn a few hundred dollars a month searching through the content on social media such as Google and Facebook and in cloud storage to remove offensive images.[76] Yet they too stand to be replaced by digital technology, as do millions of call-center, data-entry, and software workers around the world, along with their counterparts in manufacturing and in other service-sector jobs.[77] A 2017 United Nations report estimated that tens if not hundreds of millions of jobs will disappear in the coming years as a result of digitalization. As an example, the report estimated that more than 85 percent of retail workers in Indonesia and the Philippines were at risk. It also said that the spread of online labor plat-forms would accelerate a "race to the bottom of working conditions with an increasingly precarity."[78]

Even jobs once thought immune from automation, such as construction and agriculture, are becoming automated. Much labor for capitalist agricul-ture around the world is performed by internal and transnational migrants. Migrant workers around the world provide transnational agribusiness with a vulnerable pool of super-exploitable and super-controllable labor, subject to vicious campaigns of racism and xenophobia. Now, however, "the impact [of robotic agriculture] is already evident in some areas that used to employ large numbers of farmworkers," notes Ford. "In California, machines skirt around the daunting visual challenge of picking individual almonds by simply grasping the entire tree and violently shaking. Overall, agricultural employment in California fell by about 11 percent in the first decade of the twenty-first century, even as the total production of crops like almonds, which are compatible with automated farming techniques, has exploded."[79] Driscoll's now employs Agrobot, a robotic strawberry picker in its Califor-nia fields, and the California wine industry has re-engineered the bulk of its vineyards to allow machines to span vines like a monorail and strip them of grape clusters or leaves.[80]

Yet the displacement of millions as refugees from economic collapse, social strife, military conflict, and climate change, suggests that the tide of migrants and refugees is likely to become a tidal wave in the coming years. The "catastrophic convergence of poverty, violence, and climate change," writes Parenti, will result in a projected 700 million climate refugees over the next few decades. Pentagon planners, he notes, call climate change a "threat multiplier" as extreme weather and water scarcity inflame and escalate existing social conflicts, leading to "militarized management of civilization's violent disintegration."[81] One United Nations report warned of an emerging "climate apartheid," whereby "the wealthy pay to escape overheating, hunger, and conflict while the rest of the world is left to suffer." In "such a setting," warned the report, "civil and political rights will be highly vulnerable."[82] What will happen to these most vulnerable among the world's precarious population, migrants and refugees, already a major target for the social control and repression of the global police state, if their labor becomes unnecessary? This problematic is generalizable: once masses of people are no longer needed on a long-term and even permanent basis there arises the political problem for the system of how to control this expanded mass of surplus humanity.

Global Social Apartheid: The Green Zone and the Grey Zone

How will the system control a vast surplus population pushed out of the productive economy, thrown into the margins, and subject to a downward spiral of misery and destruction, into a *mortal cycle of dispossession-exploitation-exclusion*? Even in the richest country in the world, the United States, 78 percent of workers already live paycheck to paycheck.[83] In Europe, one-quarter of the population in the 27 EU member states in 2016 was at risk of poverty, severely materially deprived, or living in households with very low work intensity.[84] Worldwide, 50 percent of all people live on less than $2.50 a day and a full 80 percent live on less than $10 per day. One in three people on the planet suffer from some form of malnutrition, nearly a billion go to bed hungry each night, while the United Nations forecasts this figure to rise to two billion by 2050 if current trends persist. Another 2 billion suffer from food insecurity. Twenty-five thousand people die each day due to hunger as the TCC extends agribusiness into what were local farming preserves. From 2006 to 2018, TNCs financed by global banks invested several hundred billion dollars in 78 countries from all continents to buy some half a billion acres of farmland, as corporate farming for export replaces the use of this land as a local food source, causing rising levels of hunger.[85] In China, the transition into global capitalism "is leading to rising unemployment, economic insecurity, inequality, intensified exploitation, and declining health and education conditions," observes one study. "Pension and social welfare payments are almost nonexistent. People struggle to pay for medical treatment: clinics and hospitals require patients to pay cash in advance. A serious illness can spell financial ruin for an entire family."[86] Strikes, protests, petitions, demonstrations, building seizures, ethnic conflicts, and riots are escalating throughout China. Indeed, the Chinese government spent more in 2011 ($111 billion) on internal security than on defense ($106 billion).[87] The story repeats itself around the world: as the mass of humanity face a wretched and uncertain future, rebellion is breaking out everywhere—much of it spontaneous and unorganized, and some of it destructive and self-destructive.

Dominant groups face the challenge of how to contain both the real and potential rebellion of surplus humanity. It is the possibility of such a rebellion that so terrifies the likes of Johann Rupert (who I quoted at the start of this chapter) and the TCC and that gives impetus to a global police state. Greater discipline is required both for those expelled and made surplus and those incorporated under the new regimes of super-exploitation, which also means new methods of social control and subjugation. Savage global inequalities are politically explosive and to the extent that the system is simply unable to incorporate surplus humanity it turns to ever more violent forms of containment. The methods of control include sealing out the surplus population, through border and other containment walls, deportation regimes, systems of mass incarceration and spatial apartheid. They also include the deadly new modalities of policing and repression made possible by applications of digitalization and Fourth Industrial Revolution technologies.

The dual functions of the global police state—accumulation and social control—are played out in the militarization of civil society and the crossover between the military and the civilian application of weapons, tracking, security, surveillance, and other systems of control. The result is permanent low-intensity warfare, alongside "hot wars" and counterinsurgency, against communities in rebellion, especially racially oppressed, ethnically persecuted, and other vulnerable communities, as theaters of conflict spread from active war zones to urban and rural localities around the world that are not formally inside the war zones. A global police state brings all of global society into what in Pentagon jargon is called "battlespace." The type of permanent global warfare waged against the outcast and the downtrodden does not, in most cases, involve the "total wars" of the twentieth-century world conflagrations.[88] Any such total war today would likely spell the end of world civilization. Yet in many respects, global police state is more totalitarian, bringing together states with the TCC in ways that make this permanent warfare as much private as public, as we will see in the next chapter.

As digitalization concentrates capital, heightens polarization, and swells the ranks of surplus labor, dominant groups turn to applying the new technologies to mass social control and repression in the face of real and potential resistance. CIT has revolutionized warfare and the modalities of state-organized violence (see the next chapter). The new systems of warfare and repression made possible by more advanced digitalization include AI-powered autonomous weaponry such as unmanned attack and transportation vehicles, robot soldiers, a new generation of super-drones and flybots, hypersonic weapons, microwave guns that immobilize, cyber-attack and info-warfare, biometric identification, state data mining, and global electronic surveillance that allows for the tracking and control of every movement. These combine with a restructuring of space that allow for new forms of spatial containment and control of the marginalized.

The profound reconfiguration of space facilitated by digitalization is captured by the notion of global green zoning. "Green zone" refers to the nearly impenetrable area in central Baghdad that U.S. occupation forces established in the wake of the 2003 invasion of Iraq. The command center of the occupation and select Iraqi elite inside that green zone were protected from the violence and chaos that engulfed the country. Urban areas around the world are now green zoned through gentrification, gated communities, surveillance systems, and state and private violence. Inside the world's green zones, elites and privileged middle and professional strata avail themselves of privatized social services, consumption, and entertainment. They can work and communicate through the Internet and satellite, sealed off under the protection of armies of soldiers, police, and private security forces. At the high end of global green zones are the super-rich, who inhabit a world of their own and are connected to one another in networks that run through the global cities. As they snatch up luxury properties in such places as Monaco, Shanghai, Hong Kong, New York, London, and Paris, they raise property values to astronomical levels, resulting in further expulsions of the poor and hardening the dividing lines between the haves and the have-nots. "We are dealing here with a fundamental reorganization of metropolitan space, involving a drastic diminution of the intersections between the lives of the rich and of the poor, which transcends traditional social segregation and urban fragmentation," warns Davis.[89] This is a new *transnational* space. Middle classes and elites that are integrated into global markets have no need for "national" economies to supply them while globalizing technologies and medias allow them to integrate socially and culturally with their counterpart communities around the world. This new metropolitan landscape is "defined by Airbnb, Uber, helipads for the nouveau rich, artisanal grocers, novelty fitness clubs, private roads, and relentless condo tower construction," observes Johnson. The flip side, of course, is "pacification and removal of the poor, architectural innovation, and new forms of enclosure."[90]

Green zoning takes on distinct forms in each locality. While on sabbatical in 2015, I witnessed in Palestine such zoning in the form of Israeli military checkpoints, Jewish settler-only roads, and the apartheid wall. In Mexico City, the most exclusive residential areas in the upscale Santa Fe district are accessible only by helicopter and private gated roads. In Johannesburg, a surreal drive through the exclusive Sandton City area reveals rows of mansions that appear as military compounds, with private armed towers and electrical and barbed-wire fences. In Cairo, I toured satellite cities ringing the impoverished center and inner suburbs where the country's elite could live out their aspirations and fantasies. They sport gated residential complexes with spotless green lawns, private leisure and shopping centers, and English-language international schools under the protection of military checkpoints and private security police. Closer to home for me, in Silicon Valley, aspiring knowledge workers from around the world pursue their dreams of affluence at the thousands of high-tech companies, also from around the world. A full 60 percent of the Valley's high-tech workforce are affluent and upwardly mobile immigrants from dozens of countries, including India and China, as well as Vietnam, Zimbabwe, and Cuba, to name a few, serviced by an army of impoverished (and often migrant) workers. The Bay Area has seen, alongside the tech-fueled gentrification, an aggressive policing of displaced poor and low-income communities. Million-dollar homes—protected by million-dollar security systems—spring up alongside a proliferation of homeless shelters and recreational vehicles parked by the wayside that house whole families.[91]

In between green zones and those of outright warfare, policing and other forms of containment become normalized against the lumpenprecariat subject to repressive discipline. This is the so-called *grey zone*, where much of humanity is coming to reside. The global police state centers around the grey zone. Here is where we find the prison-industrial complexes, immigration and refugee repression and control systems, mass surveillance, the criminalization of outcast communities and ubiquitous, often paramilitarized policing. "'High intensity policing' and 'low intensity warfare' threaten to merge," according to Graham. "Western security and military doctrine is being rapidly re-imagined in ways that dramatically blur the juridical and operational separation between policing, intelligence and the military; distinctions between war and peace; and those between local, national, and global operations."[92] In the United States, the Pentagon began transferring early in the new century billions of dollars in military hardware to police departments around the country, giving rise to a class of so-called "warrior cops."[93] As police become militarized and as militaries take on more and more policing functions, the line between the two dissolves into what one British general called "war amongst the people."[94]

Megacities are the new battleground where the global police state is developed and deployed. Here is how Graham summarizes how the global police state is activated in the grey zone:

> Cities in both domains [in North and South] are starting to display startling similarities. In both, hard, military-style border fences and checkpoints around defended enclaves and 'security zones' superimposed on the wider and more open city, are proliferating. Jersey-barrier blast walls, identity check points, computerized CCTV, biometric surveillance and military styles of access control protect archipelagos of fortified social, economic, political or military centers from an outside deemed unruly, impoverished or dangerous. In the most extreme example, these encompass green zones, military prisons, ethnic and sectarian neighborhoods and military bases; they are growing around strategic financial districts, embassies, tourist and consumption spaces, airport and port complexes, sports arenas, gated communities and export processing zones.[95]

Sometimes the green and the grey zones are separated literally by walls. Israel's apartheid wall, an imposing 450-mile barrier that it has illegally constructed inside occupied Palestinian territory, is perhaps the most notorious case of walling. But the practice has been spreading around the world. In Lima, Peru, the affluent residents from the neighborhood of Casuarinas, one of the city's most exclusive gated communities, commissioned a 10-kilometer wall as a barrier against the impoverished inhabitants of the neighboring San Juan district, in what has come to be known as the *Muro de la Verguenza*, or Wall of Shame. "For decades, residents of Casuarinas had interacted with residents of San Juan only insofar as they employed them as maids, nannies, security guards, and gardeners, who were required to enter through the neighborhood's front gate at the base of the hill of Sucro," observes Campoamor. "In a city where even middle-class neighborhoods often have some sort of gate, Casuarinas is known for its particularly elaborate security apparatus. Three distinct checkpoints—one for residents, one for visitors, and one for pedestrians—ensure that only authorized individuals gain entry."[96]

There is an important element of perception management at play in green zoning and grey zoning. Green zones are visible—or made visible by corporate media and advertising; with their tourism, upscale shopping, conspicuous consumption, and real estate development, they give the impression of overall prosperity, whereas grey zones are made invisible, meant to be blotted out from public perception. These impressions are helped along by official data using standard measures that show a decrease in unemployment here, a rise in per-capita GDP there, leading to what Sassen sees as a de facto redefinition of the economy. Such a redefinition "makes 'the economy' presentable, so to speak," while "the reality at ground level is more akin to a kind of economic version of ethnic cleansing in which elements considered troublesome are dealt with by simply eliminating them." [97] This shrinking and redefinition of economic space that allows the ruling groups to represent economies as "back on track" holds for a growing number of countries" around the world. Masked by such redefinition is the hardships of un- and underemployment, poverty, social austerity, poor health, open and disguised homelessness, suicides, and substance addiction that become a part of everyday life for those expelled and thrust into the grey zone, subject to the state and private violence of the global police state.

Containing surplus humanity also involves a mobilization of the culture industries and state ideological apparatuses that dehumanize victims of global capitalism as dangerous, depraved, and undeserving at the same time as they inculcate petty consumerism and flight into fantasy. We should recall that it is only when hegemony breaks down that ruling groups rely on the direct coercion of the state's repressive apparatuses and private organs of violence. The Italian communist Antonio Gramsci developed the general concept of hegemony to refer to the attainment by ruling groups of stable forms of rule based on "consensual" domination of subordinate groups. Gramsci's notion of hegemony posits distinct forms, or relations of domination, in brief: *coercive domination* and *consensual domination*. Hegemony may be seen as a relationship between classes or groups in which one class or group exercises leadership over other classes and groups by gaining their active consent. Hegemony is thus rule by consent, or the cultural and intellectual leadership achieved by a particular class, class fraction, strata, or social group, as part of a larger project of class rule or domination. All social order is maintained through a combination of consensual and coercive dimensions; in Gramsci's words, hegemony is "consensus protected by the armor of coercion." [98]

The more mass capitalist culture infects the thinking and attitudes of the population the less the dominant groups must resort to use harsher forms of coercion to sustain their rule. As this mass culture becomes incorporated into the logic of a global police state, a neo-fascist culture emerges through militarism, misogyny, extreme masculinization, and racism. Such a culture generates a climate conducive to mass violence, often directed against the racially oppressed, ethnically persecuted, women, and poor, vulnerable communities. The omnipresent media and cultural apparatuses of the corporate economy, along with capitalist schooling, aim to colonize the mind—to impose a dull uniformity, to numb the senses, to pacify and undermine the ability to think critically or outside the dominant worldview. In this sense, it is thoroughly totalitarian. Warfare and police containment have become glorified, as well as normalized and sanitized for those not directly at the receiving end of armed aggression and global police state. "Militainment"—portraying and even glamorizing war and violence as entertaining spectacles through Hollywood films and television police shows, computer gaming, and corporate "news" channels—may be the epitome of a sadistic capitalism. It desensitizes, bringing about complacency and indifference and legitimating the authoritarianism of the dominant system.

But as the legitimacy crisis spreads and cultural hegemony breaks down all around the world, ruling groups have turned to social cleansing of surplus humanity through criminalization, as is the case with the bogus wars on drugs and terror. In the wake of the September 11, 2001 attacks, 140 countries passed draconian "anti-terrorist" security legislation that often made legal the repression of social movements and political dissent, according to a 2012 report by Human Rights Watch. "The counterterror laws enacted around the globe represent a dangerous expansion of powers to detain and prosecute people, including peaceful political opponents," it warned. "The elements that raise grave human rights concerns include overly broad and vague definitions of terrorism—such as 'disrupting the public order'—as well as sweeping powers for warrantless search and arrest, the use of secret evidence, and immunity for police who abuse the laws."[99] In 2011, the U.S. government authorized the indefinite military detention without charge or trial of anyone suspected of "terrorism."

A more sweeping criminalization, including criminalizing a wide range of acts of survival, is needed to expand the penal system as a method of social control of the dispossessed. Incarceration increasingly serves, as Bauman argues, as "an alternative to employment: a way to dispose of, or to neutralize a considerable chunk of the population who are not needed as producers."[100] In the United States, the imprisoned population is made up of the poorest and most excluded sector of the population. More than half of all prisoners did not hold full-time jobs at the time of their arrest. Two-thirds came from households whose annual income amounted to less than half the poverty line, and more than half were Latino or black, although these groups accounted for only 25 percent of the general population. "When considering the economic costs of mass incarceration," notes Jay, "it is essential to keep in mind the benefits to capital provided by punitive policies that reduce social protest and coerce workers into accepting lower wages."[101] The prison warden at Marion, the first "Supermax" prison in the United States, could not be more clear on the matter: "The purpose of the Marion control unit is to control revolutionary attitudes in the prison system and in society at large."[102]

In many cases, criminalization makes surplus humanity *both* a structural and a legal location, as in the legal criminalization of immigrant workers in the United States. In Denmark, the government announced in 2018 plans to legalize discrimination against poor and immigrant communities through a bill that would set apart as "ghettos" communities where more than 50 percent of residents are non-Western immigrants, where unemployment is above 40 percent, and where the average income is less than 55 percent of the average for the region.[103] The United Nations Special Rapporteur on Extreme Poverty and Human Rights, Philip Alston, warned in a 2017 report on poverty and inequality in the United States:

> In many cities, homeless persons are effectively criminalized for the situation in which they find themselves. Sleeping rough, sitting in public spaces, panhandling, public urination and a myriad of other offenses have been devised to attack the "blight" of homelessness. Even more demanding and intrusive regulations lead to infraction notices, which rapidly turn into misdemeanors, leading to the issuance of warrants, incarceration, the incurring of unpayable fines, and the stigma of a criminal conviction that in turn virtually prevents subsequent employment and access to most housing.[104]

In fact, in California, there are no less than 592 laws restricting standing, sitting, resting, sleeping, camping, panhandling, or food sharing for homeless people in public, and 781 separate laws restricting non-public spaces.[105]

In sum and to recap, there is a dangerous spiral here in the contradiction between a digitalization that throws ever more workers into the ranks of surplus humanity and the need for the system to unload ever greater amounts of accumulated surplus. In addition, surplus humanity cannot consume and so, as their ranks expand, the problem of overaccumulation becomes exacerbated. Once masses of people are no longer needed on a long-term and even permanent basis, there arises the political problem of how to control this expanded mass of surplus humanity. Greater discipline is required, both for those who manage to secure work under new regimes of precarious employment and super-exploitation, and for those expelled and made surplus. The entire social order becomes surveilled. Systems of state and private surveillance now have the ability to monitor any corner of the world and any transaction that cannot be carefully concealed. The global order as a unity becomes increasingly repressive and authoritarian. Projects of twenty-first-century fascism gain traction, as mechanisms of cultural hegemony that involve the manipulation of anxieties and desires and of structural (economic) control such as debt, combine with heightened coercive control. The militarization of cities, politics, and culture in such countries as the United States, Israel, and South Africa, the spread of neo-fascist movements in North America, Latin America, India, and Europe, the rise of authoritarian regimes in Turkey, the Philippines, Honduras, and elsewhere, are inseparable from these countries' entanglement in webs of global wars and militarized global accumulation, or a global war economy. We now turn to this global war economy.

3

Militarized Accumulation and Accumulation by Repression

Corruption, cozy business relationships between rulers and entrepreneurs, the free-for-all looting of national resources, hundreds of millions of profits to be made by all concerned, suppression and the impoverishment of the local population—all this requires Presidential Guards, elite special ops units, exaggerated militaries, ubiquitous security forces and the infusion of arms ... Profits are there to be made, power to be wielded by classes of people who have vested interests. "International warlordism" best describes this world-system. Its closed loop of transnational corporations, their commercial and military agents on the ground, corrupt politicians and ruling-class collaborators, security forces and local warlords enforce "order" and keep everything moving—while suppressing the groaning masses.

Jeff Halper, in *War Against the People*[1]

For a commercial company trying to make investments, you need a stable environment. Dictatorships can give you that.

Shell Oil executive[2]

In their classical 1966 study *Monopoly Capitalism*, Paul Baran and Paul Sweezy argued that the capitalist system needed rising levels of military spending as an outlet for ever greater amounts of accumulated surplus. "Here at last monopoly capitalism had seemingly found the answer to the 'on what' question," they wrote with regard to the rising Pentagon budget. "On what could the government spend enough to keep the system from sinking into the mire of stagnation? On arms, more arms, and ever more arms."[3] The concept of military Keynesianism in the post-World War II period thus referred to expanding military budgets to offset stagnation in the capitalist economy, in the same way that Keynesian policies more generally sought to create demand and stimulate the economy. U.S. President Dwight D. Eisenhower first coined the term "military-industrial complex," famously warning in his farewell address in 1961 that "an immense military establishment and a large arms industry" had emerged as a hidden force in U.S. politics.[4]

More than half a century later, it is time to update our understanding of the relationship between militarization and capitalism. If military Keynesianism referred to the purchase by the state of weapons systems and military equipment from industrial subcontractors as a subsidy to private capital, there has been in recent years, and especially since the events of September 11, 2001, a much more sweeping militarization of the global capitalist economy and society. War profiteering, far from new, is as old as war itself. All wars are for the appropriation of surplus in the broadest sense; beyond outright plunder, wars are for the creation, defense, and reproduction of the conditions under which surplus can be generated by some groups and appropriated by others. What requires analysis is the mode of this appropriation through warfare and violence and the role that it plays within the larger political economy, what I call here *militarized accumulation* and *accumulation by repression*.

While the old-style military Keynesianism is still in place, the concept of militarized accumulation points to the more expansive role that generating war, repression, and systems of transnational social control now play as they move to the very center of the global economy.* A global police state spans systems of mass incarceration, immigrant detention and deportation, refugee control systems, the construction of border and containment walls, mass surveillance, urban policing, the deployment of paramilitary and private mercenary armies and security forces, and so on. These have all become important sources of profit making that have helped offset the pressures of overaccumulation. As uninvested capital accumulates, enormous pressures build up to find outlets for unloading surplus. A convergence comes about around global capitalism's political need for social control and repression and its economic need to perpetuate accumulation in the face of stagnation. If it is evident that unprecedented global inequalities can only be sustained by ubiquitous systems of social control and repression, it becomes equally evident that quite apart from political considerations, the TCC has acquired a vested interest in war, conflict, and repression as a means of accumulation. As war and state-sponsored violence become

---

* Militarized accumulation and accumulation by repression are not identical. The latter refers more specifically to profit making through direct repression of, for instance, migrants or social movements. Militarized accumulation is the more encompassing category and they are coextensive enough that at most times I will collapse the two into the former.

increasingly privatized, the interests of a broad array of capitalist groups shift the political, social, and ideological climate towards generating and sustaining social conflict—such as in the Middle East—and in expanding systems of warfare, repression, surveillance, and social control.

The rise of a global police state involves a tighter integration of capital and the state; their articulation in new ways that fuse together key sectors of the economy around militarized accumulation. This mass of intertwined transnational capital is more and more dependent on a global war economy that in turn relies on perpetual state-organized war making, social control, and repression. A cursory glance at U.S. news headlines in the first years of the Trump government underscores these dynamics. The day after Donald Trump's electoral victory, the stock price of Corrections Corporation of America, the largest for-profit immigrant detention and prison company in the United States, soared 40 percent, given Trump's promise to deport millions of immigrants (see below).[5] Military contractors such as Raytheon and Lockheed Martin report spikes in their share value each time there is a new flare-up in the Middle East conflict. Within hours of an April 6, 2017 U.S. Tomahawk missile bombardment of Syria, the company that builds those missiles, Raytheon, reported an increase in its stock value by $1 billion. In 2018, Trump announced with much fanfare the creation of a sixth military service, the "space force." What went less reported is that a small group of former government officials with deep ties to the aerospace industry had pushed behind the scenes for its creation as a way to hype military spending on satellites and other space systems.[6]

The so-called wars on terrorism and drugs, the undeclared wars on immigrants, refugees, and gangs (and poor, dark-skinned, and working-class youth more generally), and the hot wars around the world, amount to vast programs for global accumulation through militarization and repression. The "war on terrorism" launched in the wake of the September 11, 2001 attacks legitimated an escalation of military ("defense") spending[†] and the imposition of the new transnational social control systems in the name of security. Most commentators focus on strategic and geo-political dimensions of these hot and low-intensity wars. While such considerations are

---

[†] As an aside, the language we use is part of the ideological and cultural dimension of struggles between oppressors and oppressed. It is now nearly universal to refer to the Pentagon and other military budgets as "defense spending." Yet there is nothing defensive about this spending. The U.S. military is an *offensive* war machine employed against the world's people. The Israeli "defense" industry, which together with high-tech is the mainstay of that country's economy, launches *offensives* against Palestinians struggling for freedom and supplies dozens of governments around the world with weapons to repress their populations. And so on.

critically important, we do not want to lose sight of the underlying structural process driving militarized accumulation: the TCC and its political
and state agents must commodify more and more spheres of global society,
including war, social conflict, and repression, in the face of overaccumulation and stagnation, and they must also develop systems of social control
that can contain the real and potential rebellion of the global working and
popular classes. The circuits of militarized accumulation coercively open
up opportunities for capital accumulation worldwide, either on the heels
of military force or through states' contracting out to transnational corporate capital the production and execution of social control and warfare.
Hence the generation of conflicts and the repression of social movements
and vulnerable populations around the world becomes an accumulation
strategy that conjoins with political objectives and may even trump those
objectives.

The attacks of September 11, 2001 were a turning point in the construction of a global police state. They mark the start of an era of permanent
global war. The Austrian economist Joseph Schumpeter coined the term
"creative destruction" in reference to how capitalism constantly "creates and
destroys" in its cycles of development.[7] Now "creative destruction" appears
to drive the logic of militarized accumulation. Permanent war involves
endless cycles of destruction and reconstruction, each phase in the cycle
fueling new rounds and accumulation. The Pentagon budget increased
91 percent in real terms between 1998 and 2011, and even apart from
special war appropriations, it increased by nearly 50 percent in real terms
during this period. *Worldwide*, total defense outlays grew by 50 percent
from 2006 to 2015, from $1.4 trillion to $2.03 trillion,[8] although this
figure does not take into account secret budgets, contingency operations,
and "homeland security" spending.[9] According to the Homeland Security
Research Corporation, an industry group, the global market in homeland
security reached $431 billion in 2018 and was expected to climb to $606
billion by 2024.[10] In the immediate aftermath of the attacks, the average
stock price of private military companies listed on stock exchanges jumped
some 50 percent in value.[11] In the decade from 2001 to 2011, military
industry profits nearly quadrupled.[12] In total, the United States spent a
mind-boggling nearly $6 trillion from 2001 to 2018 on its Middle Eastern
wars,[13] which by 2015 had killed some four million people.[14] As spin-off
effects of this military spending flow through the open veins of the global
economy—that is, the integrated network structures of the global production, services, and financial system—it becomes increasingly difficult

to distinguish between military and non-military dimensions of a global war economy.

The United States remains the world's most powerful military state, by far, and its intervention around the world has escalated in the past few decades. It maintains over 800 military bases in 70 countries and territories (the UK, France, and Russia trail distantly behind, with about 30 foreign bases each).[15] I have discussed at considerable length elsewhere how U.S. intervention and the preponderant role of the United States in the global police state must be understood less as a bid for a new U.S. "hegemony" conceived of domination over other states than as the most powerful instrument in the arsenal of global capitalism through which the mass of the world's poor and working peoples are contained and controlled and the world is further opened up to the TCC plunder.[16] The underlying class relation between the TCC and the U.S. national state needs to be understood in these terms. As the most powerful component of the transnational state (TNS), the U.S. state apparatus attempts to defend the interests of transnational investors and the overall system and to confront those political forces around the world that in one way or another threaten those interests or threaten to destabilize transnational processes. As one senior U.S. government official put it, U.S. military forces and intelligence agencies are deployed around the world to ensure "the viability and stability of major global systems: trade, financial markets, supplies of energy, and climate."[17] In theoretical terms, the U.S. state becomes the *point of condensation* for pressures from dominant groups around the world to resolve the intractable problems of global capitalism.

In 2015, the Chinese government announced that it was setting out to develop its own military-industrial complex modeled after the United States, in which private capital would assume the leading role.[18] This is crucial because China may compete geo-politically with other states, but Chinese transnational capitalists and the state-party elite are deeply integrated into global financial circuits and invested in global banking conglomerates that in turn are interlocked with the U.S.-led military-industrial-security complex. Moreover, most military contractor and private security firms are publicly traded and draw in investors from China and elsewhere around the world. The giant global financial institutions link Western military-industrial conglomerates with Chinese-based state banks and corporations involved in the Chinese military build-up. Blackrock, for instance, holds major investments in Lockheed Martin, Northrop Grumman, and Boeing and also in the Bank of China, China

Communications Construction Corp, China Construction Bank, China Rail Engineering, PetroChina, and so on.[19] As we saw in Chapter 1, global financial circuits are so thoroughly integrated and entangled that it becomes near impossible to separate out national circuits in an analysis of militarized accumulation, which is not to say that geo-political tensions are absent—indeed, *they are reaching explosive levels*—but rather, we need to come up with alternative ways of explaining these tensions, such as crises of state legitimacy and the drive to generate conflict in order to realize militarized accumulation.

Military expansion around the world has taken place through parallel, and often conflictive, processes, yet all show the same relationship between state militarization and global capital accumulation. Global military deployment led by the United States "serves to protect power-elite capital investments around the world," asserts Philipps. "Wars, regime changes, and occupations performed by military and intelligence agencies remain in service to investors' access to natural resources, free flow of capital, debt, collection, and speculative advantages in the world marketplace."[20] The board of directors and financial donors of the Atlantic Council, which was founded in 1961 by NATO members as a private organization to prepare policy recommendations on security matters, reads like a veritable who's who of the top global corporations, including the global financial institutions and tech giants. Its 2016 report on the ongoing wars in the Middle East was unambiguous in calling for U.S.-led NATO involvement to promote neo-liberal economic policies that open up the region to transnational corporate investment: "An associated task is to support and facilitate 'Big Bang' Regulatory Reforms to foster greater trade, investment, and economic integration, with a special focus on empowering entrepreneurs."[21]

We saw in Chapter 1 how the public finances of the capitalist state have been reconfigured to reduce or even eliminate the state's role in social reproduction and to expand its role in facilitating transnational capital accumulation through austerity, bail-outs, corporate subsidies, and state debt as governments transfer wealth directly and indirectly from working people to the TCC. It is crucial to see how militarized accumulation has played the central role in this reconfiguration as states are reduced to pimping for the global military-industrial-security complex. In the United States, a cumulative $5.6 trillion budget surplus had been projected prior to September 2001. But subsequently massive military budgets turned this surplus almost overnight into a deficit that had surpassed $21 trillion by

2018. Escalating military spending is covered by borrowing from transnational finance capitalists. The money is then spent to finance the circuits of militarized accumulation and paid back to the original lenders with interest. This process that fuses financial and militarized accumulation becomes abundantly clear when we consider that the *interest payments alone* on the debt incurred to prosecute the Iraq and Afghanistan wars is estimated to exceed $7.5 trillion by 2050.[22]

This pattern is replicated in Europe and elsewhere around the world. Spain's military spending increased by 29 percent from 2000 to 2008, buying weapons systems from transnational arms suppliers that were for the most part simply put in storage.[23] Subsequent state debts and deficits then set the country up for an economic freefall when the 2008 crisis hit. Greece steadily ramped up its military budget in the 2000s, registering the highest military spending relative to GDP in all of Europe and purchasing billions of dollars in arms from weapons producers in the EU, the United States, and Russia, even as debt spiraled and the economy went into sharp decline starting in 2009. "No one is saying 'buy our warships or we won't bail you out.' But the clear implication is that they will be more supportive if we do," said one aide to then Greek prime minister George Papandreou in 2012.[24] The Syriza government that came to power in 2015 on the heels of a mass uprising against austerity then found the sovereign debt so overwhelming that it was forced to submit to austerity and privatization imposed by the EU on behalf of private creditors.

It is difficult to track the scale of militarized accumulation relative to capital's multiple circuits—that is, to measure a magnitude for the significance of global police state to the global economy as a whole. Worldwide, official state military outlays in 2015 represented about 3 percent of the gross world product of $75 trillion (this does not include state military spending not made public). But militarized accumulation involves much more than activities generated by state military budgets. As we shall see below, there are vast sums involved in state spending and private corporate accumulation through militarization and social control, and other forms of generating profit through repressive social control that do not involve militarization per se, such as structural controls over the poor through debt-collection enforcement mechanisms or accumulation opportunities opened up by criminalization (see below and Chapter 2). Given how thoroughly entangled they are with one another in the global economy, it is difficult to separate out distinct sectoral circuits of accumulation in our analysis. For instance, it becomes near impossible to separate such sectors in the global economy as fossil-fuel production, mining, and agribusiness, from the militarized and repressive dimensions of these activities. Oil and gas, to take one example, represent some 3 percent of the gross world product,[25] a percentage similar to state military spending. But it is simply impossible to disentangle this sector from the Middle East wars and other conflicts around the world, so much so that it is stitched into the global police state, as are other extractive industries (see below).[26]

From the perspective of the TCC, we may ask just how functional and strategic in the long run is rising dependence of the global economy on militarized accumulation; to what extent it is in the best long-term interests of global capital to become so dependent on a global police state? I will return in the next chapter to the prospects that other policies and accumulation strategies *may* come into play in the future that take precedence over those related to a global police state.

The Privatization of War and Repression

The German sociologist Max Weber famously defined the state as that institution that exercises a legitimate monopoly of violence over a given territory. If this held true for much of the modern era (since the Treaty of Westphalia in 1648), it is no longer so. The state attempts to sustain accumulation by contracting out the exercise of this violence to transnational capital. This is a two-way street, insofar as capital pressures the state to open up opportunities for unloading surplus and generating profit through militarization and state-sanctioned repression. The more state policy is oriented towards war and repression, the more opportunities are opened up for transnational capital accumulation; the more the political and corporate agents of transnational capital seek to influence state policy in this direction, the more political systems and capitalist culture becomes fascistic.

The various wars, conflicts, and campaigns of social control and repression around the world involve the increasing fusion of private accumulation with state militarization. In this relationship, the state facilitates the expansion of opportunities for private capital to accumulate through militarization. The most obvious way that the state opens up these opportunities is to facilitate global weapons sales by military-industrial-security firms. This mechanism dates back to the onset of military Keynesianism, but the amounts they now involve were simply unimaginable in the earlier era. In 2017, for instance, the U.S. government signed a deal for private firms to supply $350 billion in arms to the Saudi regime.[27] Between 2003 and 2010 alone, the developing world bought nearly half a trillion dollars in weapons from arms dealers. Global weapons sales by the top 100 weapons manufacturers and military service companies increased by 38 percent between 2002 and 2016. These top 100 companies across the globe, excluding China, sold $375 billion in weapons in 2016, generating $60 billion in profits, and employing over three million workers.[28]

Yet the relationship between the state and private capital in militarized accumulation is more than state spending to pay contractors for military hardware. The state increasingly turns over the very design and execution of war, repression, and security to the TCC. The U.S.-led wars in Iraq and Afghanistan opened enormous opportunities for private military and security firms, precipitating the explosion in private military and police contractors around the world deployed to protect the TCC and global capitalism. The onslaught of privatized warfare was led in the Middle East by the notorious Blackwater mercenary company, exposed in 2007 by reporter Jeremy Scahill in his bestseller, *Blackwater: The Rise of the World's Most Powerful Mercenary Army*.[29] Private military contractors in Iraq and Afghanistan during the height of those wars exceeded the number of U.S. combat troops in both countries, and outnumbered U.S. troops in Afghanistan by a 3-to-1 margin.[30] In 2017, the founder of Blackwater, Erick Prince, along with Stephen Feinberg, a billionaire financier who owns the military contractor and private security firm Dyncorp, submitted a proposal to the Trump administration, at the request of Trump advisors, to literally privatize the entire U.S.-NATO war in Afghanistan, although the plan had not at the time of writing (mid-2019) been approved.[31]

Beyond the United States, private military and security firms have proliferated worldwide and their deployment is not limited to the major conflict zones in the Middle East, South Asia, and Africa. In his study, *Corporate Warriors*, Singer documents how private military forces have come to play an ever more central role in military conflicts and wars. Although written in 2003, a wealth of subsequent evidence confirms that the turn towards privatization exploded in the wake of the Middle East wars.[32] "A new global industry has emerged," noted Singer. "It is outsourcing and privatization of a twenty-first century variety, and it changes many of the old rules of international politics and warfare. It has become global in both its scope and activity." The operations of private military firms (PMFs) "are not restricted to any one geographic area or type of state. PMFs have been active on every continent but Antarctica."[33] He goes on:

"The changes that this phenomenon portends are tectonic. The emergence of a privatized military industry may well represent the new business face of warfare."[34] And beyond the many based in the United States, PMFs come from numerous countries around the world, including Russia, South Africa, Colombia, Mexico, India, the EU countries, and Israel, among others. If it is a mistake to see PMFs as national companies, it is also a mistake to see them as somehow disentangled from the integrated mass of transnational capital. Many PMFs are subsidiaries of other transnational corporations. For instance, Vinnell is but a branch of BDM (Braddock, Dunn and McDonald), a military contractor that is in turn owned by the Carlyle Group, one of the largest private equity (holding) companies in the world, with investors from 75 countries and cross-investment with hundreds of companies from around the world.

Beyond wars, private military forces open up access to economic resources and corporate investment opportunities—deployed, for instance, to mining areas and oil fields—leading Singer to term PMFs "investment enablers." In effect, one branch of the TCC, the PMFs, accumulates its capital by opening up opportunities for other branches of the TCC—for instance, energy, mining and agribusiness conglomerates—to accumulate capital. Or to put it another way, the PMFs make profit by carrying out direct violence so that other transnational corporations may profit through the structural violence of dispossession and exploitation. At other times, PMF interventions are to put down popular rebellions, such as the Mexican government's contract with the South Africa firm Executive Outcomes to quell the indigenous Zapatista uprising in Chiapas. PMFs work for whoever will pay them. Their clients include states, corporations, landowners, non-governmental organizations, even the Colombian and Mexican drug cartels. The single largest client is the Pentagon, which from 1994 to 2002 alone entered into over 3,000 contracts with U.S.-based firms at a cost of more than $300 billion: "Every major military operation in the post-Cold War era has involved considerable levels of support and activity by private firms offering services that the U.S. military used to perform on its own."[35]

U.S.-based Halliburton and Carlyle were the most notorious of the military-civilian companies that benefitted from the Middle Eastern wars, since numerous top-level officials of the government of President George Bush held major shares of these companies, including the families of President Bush and Vice President Dick Cheney. But companies receiving contracts for the Middle Eastern wars came from all over the world.

From 2005 to 2010, the Pentagon spend $146 billion on private military contractors for the Iraq-Afghanistan war theater,[36] contracting some 150 firms from around the world for support and security operations in Iraq alone.[37] In the wake of the September 2001 attacks, private contractors were getting roughly half of the entire U.S. defense budget each year.[38] By 2018, private military companies employed some 15 million people around the world, deploying forces to guard corporate property, provide personal security for TCC executives and their families, collect data, conduct police, paramilitary, counterinsurgency and surveillance operations, carry out mass crowd control and repression of protesters, manage prisons, run private detention and interrogation facilities, and participate in outright warfare.[39]

These firms were increasingly integrated into the transnational corporate and financial networks of the TCC, and their boards of directors and advisors, notes Phillips, "represent some of the most powerfully connected people in the world, with multiple socio-political links to governments, military, finance, and policy groups."[40] The leading global financial corporations are so thoroughly invested in the well-known military-industrial-security corporations of the twentieth century, such as Lockheed-Martin, Northrop Grumman, Boeing, and Raytheon, that what appears is a fusion of the traditional military-industrial complex with transnational finance capital and the tech sector. To take but one example, the following transnational financial investment firms hold multi-million and billion dollar holdings in Lockheed-Martin: State Street ($15.2 billion), Capital Group ($12.17 billion), Vanguard ($6.5 billion), Blackrock ($6.1 billion), Bank of America ($3.1 billion), Morgan Stanley ($703 billion), Goldman Sachs ($474 million), Credit Suisse ($149 million), and so on.[41] These same financial conglomerates, as we saw in the previous two chapters, are heavily invested in the tech giants. As the fate of Silicon Valley and Wall Street become tied to that of warfare and repression, this Silicon Valley-Wall Street nexus becomes in turn interlocked with the military-industrial-security complex. As we enter the third decade of the new century, we have reached a point where the war and repression machine is driven by its obligation to shareholders rather than to any public interest (however so mis-defined). "It just hits you as a ton of bricks," said one senior U.S. military official. "The Department of Defense is no longer a war-fighting organization, it's a business enterprise."[42]

In the 1990s, the U.S. government began to outsource the analytical and operational work of its 16 spy agencies to private contractors. By 2006, these 16 agencies were allocating 70 percent of their combined budget to for-profit contractors. What one former U.S. military official called the "intelligence-industrial complex" had become by 2008 a $50 billion market serviced by hundreds of transnational corporations. Tasks outsourced to private companies included running global spy networks, intelligence analysis, signals intelligence collection, surveillance, drafting policy reports and intelligence briefings, covert operations, and the torture of prisoners. Following the September 2001 events, the number of such contract employees of the CIA came to exceed the agency's own full-time workforce, and even made up more than half of its covert operations branch. Among the largest private companies contracted by spy agencies, Booz Allen Hamilton, itself partly owned by the Carlyle Group, commanded a private intelligence army at least ten thousand strong, while about half of the 42,000 employees of the Science Applications International Corporation (SAIC) held U.S. government security clearances.[43] Shorrock estimated that 80 percent of the approximately 45,000 private-sector employees working for the intelligence-industrial complex worked for just five mega-corporations following a wave of mergers in the 2010s. These were: Leidos, in part held by Lockheed Martin; Booz Allen Hamilton; CSRA Inc., which among other things manages drone platforms around the world; SAIC, which runs the CIA drone assassination fleet and operates military satellites, and CACI International, which among other things provides "counterinsurgency targeting" to NATO.[44]

Meanwhile, the private security (policing) business, a subset of the privatization of war and security, now dwarfs public security around the world. Singer notes:

> The private security business is one of the fastest growing economic sectors in many countries ... There has been a dramatic growth in the U.S. security industry since 1990. The amount spent on private security is 73 percent higher than that spent in the public sphere, and three times as many persons are employed in private forces as in official law enforcement agencies. Linked with this trend, "gated communities" are now the norm in residential construction, with more than 20,000 such communities in the United States; in fact, four of every five new communities in the United States are guarded by private forces. Aside from formal policing work, private security firms are taking on a wider variety of other homeland security functions once performed by governments. For example, industry leader Wackenhut runs prisons in thirteen states in the United States and in four foreign countries. It

also provides SWAT teams that protect nuclear weapons facilities in South Carolina and Nevada from terrorist threats. The same trends are taking place around the globe. In South Africa, the ratio of private security personnel to uniformed police officers is approximately four to one. In the UK and Australia, it is two to one. Private security personnel within Britain (roughly 250,000) actually outnumber the British army. In parts of Asia, the private security industry has grown at 20 percent to 30 percent per year. Even in communist China, some 250,000 guards are employed by the private security industry. Perhaps the biggest explosion of private security is the near complete breakdown of public agencies in postcommunist Russia, with over 10,000 new security firms opening since 1989.[45]

Since Singer wrote these lines in 2003, in fact, the private security business has continued to grow exponentially. G4S, the world's largest private security firm, has become the third larger private employer in the world (after Walmart and Foxconn), with 660,000 employees and annual revenue of over $10 billion.[46] There were an outstanding 20 million private security workers worldwide in 2017, and the industry was expected to be worth over $220 billion by 2020. In half of the world's countries, private security agents outnumber police officers. Even *Forbes* had to acknowledge that escalating global inequality has driven the sector's meteoric rise. "With more and more individuals joining the billionaire club, demand for services such as alarm monitoring and armored transport are skyrocketing, resulting in private security companies becoming a symbol of the global wealth divide."[47] Private armed forces offer systems of privatized security to corporate clients and affluent residents from green zones. In Detroit, for instance, the private security firm Securitas reported a 25 percent annual rate of growth of its services to private clients from 2013 to 2019. Another company, Threat Management Center, boasts a client roster in the city of over 5,000 private citizens and 100 businesses.[48]

It is important to state the obvious here: corporations accrue police powers and usurp the authority of states as they hire private military and security forces to do their bidding free from any restraint. Several centuries ago, in the heyday of European colonial exploits in Asia, British and Dutch chartered companies were authorized by their imperial governments to amass and deploy their own private armies for colonial expeditions in India, Indonesia, and elsewhere. This bygone era has now been resurrected under the contemporary conditions of global capitalism as the TCC conquers and re-colonizes the world.

Silicon Valley and Surveillance Capitalism

CIT has revolutionized warfare, the modalities of state and private violence, and the instruments of social control. The so-called "Revolution in Military Affairs" (RMA) started in the late twentieth century but with the application of more advanced digital and Fourth Industrial Revolution technologies, this RMA appears to be entering a new stage. Virtually every new technology becomes employed in various combinations with traditional armed, police, and intelligence forces and involves an inter-operability of all ways to conduct warfare, social control, surveillance, and repression. To reiterate what we observed in the previous chapter, chilling new systems of warfare and repression made possible by more advanced digitalization include AI-powered autonomous weaponry such as unmanned attack and transportation vehicles, robotic soldiers, a new generation of superdrones and flybots and other micro-drones, hypersonic weapons, microwave guns that immobilize, nano-weaponry, cyber-attack and info-warfare, biometric identification, bio-weapons state and private data mining, and global electronic and sighting surveillance that allows for the tracking and control of every movement. State data mining and global electronic surveillance expand the theater of conflict from active war zones to militarized cities and rural localities around the world.[49] These combine with a restructuring of space that allow for new forms of spatial containment, surveillance, and control of the marginalized.

This RMA has opened up new possibilities for ruling groups to exercise what in the military jargon has been referred to as "full spectrum dominance," or "total battlespace awareness." This battlespace becomes all encompassing: traditional physical space (land, sea, air), cyberspace, political systems, "the information environment," the electromagnetic spectrum, social media, and so on.[50] All of global society becomes a highly surveilled and controlled, and wildly profitable battlespace. We must not forget that these technologies of the global police state are driven as much, or more, by the drive to open up new outlets for accumulation as they are by strategic or political considerations. The rise of the digital economy and the blurring of the boundaries between the military and the civilian sectors appear to fuse several factions of capital around a combined process of financial speculation and militarized accumulation. The market for new systems made possible by digital technology runs into the hundreds of billions. The global biometrics market, for instance, was expected to jump from its $15 billion value in 2015 to $35 billion by 2020.[51] Financial capital supplies the credit for investment in the tech sector and in the technologies of the global police state. Tech firms develop and provide the new digital technologies that are now of central importance to the global economy. Ever since NSA whistleblower Edward Snowden came forward in 2013, there has been a torrent of revelations on the collusion of the giant tech firms with the U.S. and other governments in the construction of a global police state. And the military-industrial-security complex applies this technology, as it becomes an outlet for unloading surplus and making profit through the control and repression of rebellious populations and through privatized warfare.

In his eye-opening study *Surveillance Valley: The Secret Military History of the Internet,*[52] investigative journalist Yashar Levine chronicles the little-known history of how CIT and the Internet were developed in the 1960s by the U.S. state and military-industrial corporations as instruments of war, counterinsurgency, surveillance, and political repression, with an eye towards dual use in military and commercial application. The U.S. government then turned the Internet over to corporate consortiums starting in the late 1980s, just as Silicon Valley was emerging as a global hub of the new information technology. As the first wave of digitalization took off in the 1990s, the emerging tech industry was thus conjoined at birth to the military-industrial-security complex and the global police state. But the nascent industry set out to deliberately rebrand itself as a progressive rebel advancing an enlightened countercultural movement. The propaganda campaign has been somewhat successful in turning the tycoons at the high-tech summit of global capitalism such as Bill Gates, Steve Jobs, and Elon Musk into techno-folk heroes among some youth dazzled and drawn into a cult of information technology.[53] Yet behind this public relations veneer, over the years Google supplied mapping technology used by the U.S. Army in Iraq, hosted data for the Central Intelligence Agency, indexed the National Security Agency's vast intelligence databases, built military robots, co-launched a spy satellite with the Pentagon, and leased its cloud computing platform to help police departments predict crime. "And Google is not alone," notes Levine. "From Amazon to eBay to Facebook ... Some parts of these companies are so thoroughly intertwined with America's security services that it is hard to tell where they end and the U.S. government begins."[54]

Data mining is not only highly profitable in commercial marketing campaigns; it is key to the systems of surveillance and control of the global police state. As digitalization has expanded, we move to a point where virtually all communication beyond face-to-face, every transaction and every activity in the institutions of society becomes digital data. These unfathomable stores of data are at the disposal of the corporation and the states that collect them. Google appears to have taken the lead in Silicon Valley's turns to more expansive mining and commodification of the data trail. "Uber, Amazon, Facebook, eBay, Tinder, Apple, Lyft, Four-Square, Airbnb, Spotify, Instagram, Twitter, Angry Bird. If you zoom out and look at the bigger picture, you can see that, taken together, these companies have turned our computers and phones into bugs that are plugged in to a vast corporate-owned surveillance network," observes Levine. "Where we go, what we do, what we talk about, who we talk to, and who we see— everything is recorded and, at some point, leveraged for value," so much so that it earned Google $90 billion in revenue and $20 billion in profits in 2017.[55]

In her study *The Age of Surveillance Capitalism*, Shoshona Zuboff of the Harvard Business School shows how data extraction and analysis has reached a height of ubiquity unimaginable only a few years ago. Virtually all of the information in the world is now digitalized, giving incredible power to those who can collect, sift through, and analyze this data.[56] Zuboff is correct in seeing Google and the other tech corporations as driven by the vast new opportunities for profit making that big data now opens up, observing that "this new market form is a unique logic of accumulation in which surveillance is a foundational mechanism in the transformation of investment into profit."[57] But here we want to stress how "this new market form" is in turn hitched to the global police state. Then-CIA director Michael Hayden was quite candid in 2013 when he explained that in the years following September 11, 2001, the agency "could be fairly charged with the militarization of the world wide web."[58] Insofar as here we are concerned with militarized accumulation, it has become clear that the difference between commercial and military profiling and data mining is illusory. The same platforms and services that Google deploys to monitor people's lives and collect their data is put to use running huge swaths of the U.S. military and spy agencies and police departments, as well as the corporations of the military-industrial-security complex. The fusion of Silicon Valley with this complex got a boost at the turn of the century, when the CIA launched a venture capital fund, In-Q-Tel, to invest in start-ups and align the agency more closely with Silicon Valley. One of these start-ups, Keyhole, financed by the CIA in partnership with the National Geospatial-Intelligence Agency (NGA, which delivers satellite intelligence to the CIA and the Pentagon), was then bought outright by Google in 2004.

A more advanced integration began from that year among Google and the rest of Silicon Valley with the apparatus of the U.S. military and national security state and the more traditional companies of the military-industrial complex such as Raytheon, Northrop Grumman, and Lockheed Martin. The behemoth of the Internet companies, Google, led the way, partnering with these traditional military contractor companies and with "just about every major military and intelligence agency," with the State Department, the FBI, and other federal agencies: "Google didn't just work with intelligence and military agencies but also sought to penetrate every level of society, including civilian federal agencies, cities, states, local police departments, emergency responders, hospitals, public schools, and all sorts of companies and nonprofits." And it does not stop at Google. Amazon, Paypal, Facebook, eBay among the Internet giants, along with numerous smaller companies, also signed contracts worth billions of dollars with the CIA, the NSA, the Pentagon, local police stations, and so on.[59] Amazon CEO Jeff Bezos, the richest man in the world, sits on the Defense Innovation Advisory Board, a Pentagon initiative launched in 2016 to bring to the U.S. military high-level officers from leading Silicon Valley companies.[60] Two years earlier, Amazon had signed a $600 million deal with the CIA.[61] As social media became weaponized, another CIA-backed company, Geofeedia, which allows its clients to display social media posts from specific geographic locations, had in 2016 500 police departments as clients and touted its ability to monitor unions, protests, rioting, and activist groups. Geofeedia and other CIA-backed companies "paid Facebook, Google, and Twitter for special access to social media data—adding another lucrative revenue stream to Silicon Valley."[62]

We saw in the previous chapter the role that mass media and the entertainment industry (telling the two apart is often impossible) play in shaping social consciousness. Indeed, the culture of global capitalism is a powerful and omniscient force, if not omnipotent, for there are multiple cultures of resistance that push back, as well as contradictions between the dominant cultural narratives and people's lived reality and material conditions. Corporate media is global in its reach and influence, a highly concentrated "media monopoly" cross-invested with the entertainment industry, transnational financial institutions, and technology corporations, and with revenue topping $2 trillion in 2017. Transnational media practices "reflect and reproduce the transnational transformation of capitalism," notes Artz in his study *Global Entertainment Media*. The transnational media conglomerates "are instruments of and for the transnational capitalist class."[63] In turn, the same global financial giants that we have identified at the core of the global economy spread their investment tentacles throughout Silicon Valley as well as in corporate media and entertainment. For instance, Blackrock, Vanguard, State Street, JP Morgan Chase, Capital Group, and Goldman Sachs have combined holdings of some $40 billion in Comcast Corporation, which provides media and television broadcasting, Internet, cable and other communication services. These same leading financial conglomerates also hold tens of billions of dollars in the Walt Disney Company, a vast corporate conglomerate that employs some 200,000 people worldwide, had revenue in 2016 of $55.6 billion, and in turn has holdings in broadcasting, entertainment, parks, and hotels among its vast empire, including, for example, the American Broadcasting Corporation (meanwhile, workers at Disney's Anaheim, California resort are paid so little that two-thirds say they don't have enough food to eat three meals a day[64]). The same patterns hold for the other media monopolies, such as Bertelsmann, Viacom and CBS, Time Warner, and so on.[65]

The media-financial-CIT nexus is enormously influential in shaping the culture and ideology of global capitalism and reproducing the system's hegemony. Corporate media "manipulates feelings and cognition of human beings worldwide," notes Phillips, and promotes "entertainment viewing as a distraction to global inequality."[66] Corporate media receives some 70–80 percent of its broadcast and print content from what Phillips calls public relations and propaganda (PRP) firms, with nearly all content inside the global corporate media system made up of pre-packaged managed news, opinion, and entertainment:

The preparations for and the reporting on ongoing wars and terrorism fits well into the ideological kaleidoscope of pre-planned news. Government and private public relations specialists provide ongoing news feeds to the transnational media distribution systems. The result is an emerging macro-symbiotic relationship between news dispensers and news suppliers. Perfect examples of this relationship are the press pools organized by the Pentagon both in the Middle East and in Washington D.C., which give pre-scheduled reports on wars and terrorism to selected groups of news collectors (journalists) for distribution through their specific media organizations.[67]

The point here is that Hollywood, the entertainment industry, and the corporate media have become weaponized, swept up into the circuits of militarized accumulation. They play a central role in the cultural and ideological campaign to legitimate and normalize a global police state as they help to construct the hegemonic order, and as they themselves profit from war and social control. The global police state weaves itself into the fabric of everyday life through mass media and entertainment. U.S. military and intelligence agencies, for instance, influenced over 800 major movies and 1,000 television shows from 2005 to 2016, turning Hollywood into a potent propaganda machine for war and repression.[68] The list of films and television shows in which the military and intelligence agencies has exerted influence is simply staggering, ranging from dozens of Hollywood blockbusters such as *Top Gun, Windtalkers, An Officer and A Gentleman, Stripes, Independence Day, Jurassic Park, Blackhawk Down, The Hunt for Red October, Patriot Games*, the James Bond series, *Hulk, Transformers*, and *Meet the Parents*, and TV programs ranging from *America's Got Talent, Oprah, NCIS, The Jay Leno Show*, to numerous documentaries aired by PBS, the BBC, and the History Channel.

At every level, digitalization and big data pave the way for "surveillance capitalism" and take the Taylorist disciplining of labor to heights that could not be imagined in the twentieth century. Big data is a powerful instrument of capital in its ceaseless class struggle with labor. As Ford observes:

> Big data and smart algorithms that accompany it are having an immediate impact on workplaces and careers as employers, particularly large corporations, increasingly track a myriad of metrics and statistics regarding the work and social interactions of their employees. Companies are relying ever more on so-called people analytics as a way to hire, fire, evaluate, and promote workers. The amount of data being collected on individuals and the work they engage in is staggering. Some companies capture every keystroke typed by every employee. Emails, phone records, web searches, database queries and accesses to files, entry and exit from facilities, and untold numbers of other types of data may also be collected—with or without the knowledge of workers.[69]

Beyond this control over labor in the workplace, the entire social order becomes surveilled. Systems of state and private surveillance now monitor any corner of the world and nearly every transaction that cannot be carefully concealed. The French philosopher Michel Foucault feared the panopticism at work in specific institutions. He could surely not have imagined how in this dictatorship of transnational capital the dominant groups have come to achieve a vast panoptical surveillance of the entire planet, a surveillance that is at once in function of control and accumulation.

Criminalization and Militarized Accumulation

In the previous chapter, we saw that criminalization is a mechanism to facilitate the repression of dissent and the social control of surplus humanity. But criminalization is also a method that the state uses to create special dedicated markets for private profit.[70] It is the most clear-cut method of accumulation by repression. This type of criminalization activates "legitimate" state repression to enforce the accumulation of capital, including by institutionalizing through the coercive apparatuses of the state diverse mechanisms of secondary exploitation (see the previous chapter). In turn, the state turns to private capital to carry out repression against those criminalized.

There has been a rapid increase in imprisonment in countries around the world, led by the United States, which has been exporting its own system of mass incarceration. In 2019, it was involved in the prison systems of at least 33 different countries. U.S. programs in these countries included the construction of new prisons, prison guard training, accreditation, data management, and overall design. In Mexico, as part of the so-called "war on drugs" (see below), the United States funded a boom in federal prison construction, which increased from five to 14.[71] Around the world there were 10.7 million people held in penal institutions. The United States led the way, with 2.3 million prisoners, followed by China, with 1.65, and then Brazil, Russia, India, Thailand, Indonesia, Turkey, Mexico, and the Philippines. While the global prison population grew by 24 percent from 2000 to 2018, the population in Oceania behind bars increased by 86 percent, in the Americas by 41 percent, in Asia by 38 percent, and in Africa by 29 percent (by contrast, it decreased by 22 percent in Europe).[72]

There is a vast literature now on mass incarceration in the United States, a country that provides a case study on the carceral state. Among the many studies of the rise of this prison-industrial complex, Ruth Wilson

Gilmore, in *Golden Gulag*, shows how California, perhaps the epicenter of the strategy of mass incarceration, led the way in "the biggest prison building project in the history of the world." She shows how the defeat of radical struggles alongside the accumulation of surplus capital led to a strategy of caging surplus labor, made up of young people from racially and ethnically oppressed groups in vast disproportion to the population at large.[73] Nationwide, the imprisoned population increased 900 percent in the past four decades, reaching 2.3 million people in 2018.[74] But this figure does not include another five million people who are out of prison but under one or another form of carceral surveillance, such as in halfway houses, on probation or parole; nor does it include the tens of millions with an arrest or conviction record, pretrial detainees and juveniles held in detention centers. The *Prison Policy Initiative* reports that people *go to jail* 10.6 million times each year in the United States.[75]

This carceral state opens up enormous opportunities at multiple levels for militarized accumulation. Worldwide, there were in 2001 nearly 200 privately operated prisons on all continents and many more "public-private partnerships" that involved privatized prison services and other forms of for-profit custodial services such as privatized electronic monitoring programs. The countries that were developing private prisons ranged from most member states of the EU, to Israel, Russia, Thailand, Hong Kong, South Africa, New Zealand, Ecuador, Australia, Costa Rica, Chile, Peru, Brazil, and Canada. The companies running these private prisons were themselves giant transnational corporations, including the U.S.-based but globally traded Corrections Corporation of America (CCA), Geo Group, and Management and Training Corporation and the UK-based G4S and Serco, linked in turn to the financial industry.[76] Private prisons in the United States date back to the 1970s, when private corporations first started to take over the operation of halfway houses. In the 1980s, the CCA became the first for-profit prison company to win a contract to run a private facility. Since 2000, the number of people in private prisons in the United States increased by 47 percent compared to an overall rise in the prison population of 9 percent. In 2018, the U.S. Bureau of Prisons announced that it was expanding the use of private prisons for those held in federal facilities.[77] Since government agencies paid private companies per prisoner, it is in the interests of these companies and their investors to expand the prison population as much as possible, to hold prisoners as long as possible, and by extension, to expand the methods of criminalization.

These U.S. private prisons held just under 10 percent of the total federal and state prison population, leading some to dismiss their importance. But this figure is highly misleading because, even when prisons remain public, there is widespread privatization of prison services, such as health care, education, food, telephone, and transportation, as well as "public-private partnerships," private juvenile detention centers, and halfway houses (to which must be added the immigrant detention centers discussed below).[78] Moreover, since the total number of those imprisoned peaked in the early 2010s, there has been a steady if very slow decline in the total number of prisoners, in part, as a result of the growing movement for criminal justice reform.[79] This decline, however, has been countered by new forms of privatized carceral control, what some have called "community cages": day reporting centers, intermediate sanctions facilities, halfway houses, and electronic monitoring. Electronic monitoring programs more than doubled in the United States in the 2010s and are estimated to become a $6 billion industry.[80] As one executive from the Geo Group, which undertook in the 2010s a wave of acquisitions of firms supplying these "community cages" program, explained: "We believe that the emphasis on offender rehabilitation and community reentry programs as part of criminal justice reform will create growth opportunities for our company."[81]

The carceral state also provides capital with a ready supply of captive and super-exploitable labor. In 2017, some 15 percent of inmates in federal and state prisons performed work for such companies as Boeing, Starbucks, and Victoria's Secret, while migrants detained for violating immigration laws are one of the fastest growing segments of prison labor. In Colorado, for instance, some 1,600 prisoners in 2014 were employed by private companies manufacturing furniture, in the dairy industry, car repair, landscaping, and the military industry, making less than one dollar an hour.[82] "For Private business, prison labor is like a pot of gold," note Goldberg and Evans in their 2012 essay, "The Prison-Industrial Complex and the Global Economy": "No strikes. No union organizing. No unemployment insurance or workers' compensation to pay. New leviathan prisons are being built with thousands of eerie acres of factories inside the walls. All at a fraction of the cost of 'free labor'."[83] And on top of this, more and more prisons are charging prisoners for basic necessities, from medical care to toilet paper and even "room and board" charges. Cash-strapped state and local governments have increasingly attempted to generate revenue by charging fees to people convicted of crimes—and even just those who have unpaid fines for traffic violations and other petty offenses—including fees for public defenders, prosecutors, court administration, jail operation, and probation supervision. And those who are unable to pay these fees are locked up, often for years.[84]

There are many methods of criminalization. The commodification of debt, as we saw in Chapter 2, has generated new modalities of exploiting surplus humanity while at the same time it has become a powerful tool for disciplining the global working class. In addition to the extraction of value through secondary exploitation, debt bondage is increasingly bound up with militarized accumulation and the global police state. In the United States, an estimated 77 million people—one in three of the adult population—have a debt that has been turned over to private collection agencies. These collection agencies that skim off a portion of the profit that original creditors make on the debt have been given draconian power by the courts, prosecutor offices, and the police and prison systems of the debtfare state to punish debtors and enforce repayment, even when the debtor may be unemployed or otherwise unable to pay. In recent years, thousands of these debtors have been arrested and jailed and millions more are threatened with debt because they owe money, from car payments to utility bills, student loans, and medical fees, or because a check bounced. This criminalization of private debt, according to one American Civil Liberties Union report, "happens when judges, at the request of collection agencies, issue arrest warrants for people who fail to appear in court to deal with unpaid civil debt judgements." In many cases, these debtors are unaware they were sued for repayment or did not receive notice to show up in court.[85] In turn, these severe sanctions compel workers to accept work under even the most exploitative of conditions, as the state reinforces this compulsion by tying public assistance to such work ("workfarism").

Criminalization has made the private bail-bond industry immensely profitable. The inability to pay bail is a critical factor in pre-trial mass incarceration; on any one day some 400,000 people in the United States are held in jail awaiting trial.[86] When poor people cannot afford to pay bail, they must turn to private bail-bond companies.

While the bail-bond industry portrays itself as small "mom and pop" operations, transnational insurance companies dominate the industry, make billions of dollars a year in profit from poverty, and promote ongoing criminalization of the poor.[87] Just nine large companies underwrite a majority of the approximately $14 billion in bail bonds issued each year. These companies, in turn, are often subsidiaries of large transnational corporations traded in global stock markets. These corporations, often operating through the American Legislative Exchange Council (see below), have pushed for changes in laws, regulations, and practices to dramatically expand the for-profit bail system and block reform. From 1990 to 2009, the number of people forced to turn to bail doubled while bail amounts have risen. The result of bail corporations' control, says one report, "is that millions of people are no longer free: people stuck in jail and families stuck in debt to create profit for these corporations." It goes on:

> With little accountability, the for-profit bail industry has thus created a way to profit from usurping the role and function of the courts, trapped families in debt while escaping from scrutiny for consumer practices, made armed arrests and surveilled people without meaningful oversight by police, and evaded insurance regulators … Like payday lenders who profit from families' needs for immediate funds, bail corporations take advantage of the urgent crisis of detention to lock people and their families in bad contracts, surveillance and control, and debt. No matter the eventual outcome of the case, even in cases in which the arrest itself is determined to be wrongful, the money that families scrape together to pay bail corporations is lost to them forever.[88]

The War on Migrants and Refugees[89]

The massive displacement unleashed by capitalist globalization, state and private violence, and military conflict has resulted in an unprecedented wave of worldwide migration in recent years. In 1960, there were some 75 million immigrant workers (workers who have left their country of origin) worldwide and 100 million in 1980. According to the low-end estimate of the United Nations, this figure shot up to some 200 million immigrant workers worldwide in 2005, double the figure from 1980. The International Labor Organization then put the figure for 2014 at 232 million.[90] In addition, there are nearly 70 million people worldwide who have been forcibly displaced due to wars and political repression and are counted as refugees, but who, if they have been displaced outside their country, would likely also need to be considered part of the global migrant workforce.[91] Moreover, these figures do not take into account several hundred million Chinese who have migrated from the interior of that country to the coastal cities to work in the industrial coastal areas and who constitute in the practice an immigrant workforce deprived of labor rights and access to social services as a result of Chinese internal pass and residency laws, known as the *hukou system*.[92] As this worldwide migrant population increases, borders around the world are militarized, states are stepping up repressive anti-immigrant controls, and native publics are turning immigrants into scapegoats for the spiraling crisis of global capitalism. Yet "there is a point at which borders cease to be geographical lines and filters between states," notes Graham, "and emerge instead as increasingly interoperable assemblages of control technologies strung out across the world's infrastructures, circulations, cities, and bodies."[93] Globally, according to the International Organization for Migration, an estimated 40,000 people died between 2005 and 2014 navigating these control technologies as they attempted to cross borders.[94]

This migrant population serves global capitalism well. It provides an almost inexhaustible labor reserve for the global economy. Transnational labor mobility has made it possible for the TCC to reorganize labor markets around the world and to recruit a transient workforce that is disenfranchised and easy to control. Repressive state controls over the migrant population and criminalization of non-citizen workers makes this sector of the global working class vulnerable to super-exploitation and hyper-surveillance. In turn, this self-same repression in and of itself becomes an ever more important source of accumulation for transnational capital. It is a source of accumulation in a double sense. First, every phase in the war on immigrants has become a wellspring of profit making, from private, for-profit detention centers and the provision of services inside public detention centers such as health care, food, phone systems, to other ancillary activities of the deportation regime, such as government contracting of private charter flights to ferry deportees back home, and the equipping of armies of border agents. In the United States, the Department of Homeland Security issued more than 344,000 contracts for border and immigration control services worth $80.5 billion between 2006 and 2018.[95] Second, if this war opens vast new outlets for unloading surplus, it also provides capital with the opportunity to intensify exploitation, to drive down black and informal market wages, and to place downward pressure more generally on wages.

The war on immigrants in the United States provides a textbook case study on militarized accumulation and accumulation by repression. By one estimate, the border security industry was set to double in value from approximately $305 billion in 2011 to some $740 billion in 2023.[96] The day after Donald Trump's November 2016 electoral victory, the stock price of Corrections Corporation of America (CCA, which later changed its name to CoreCivic), the largest for-profit immigrant detention and prison company in the United States, soared 40 percent, given Trump's promise to deport millions of immigrants. Earlier in 2016, CCA's CEO Damon Hiniger reported a 5 percent increase in first-quarter earners as a result of "stronger than anticipated demand from our federal partners, most notably Immigration and Customs Enforcement," as a result of the escalating detention of immigrant women and children fleeing violence in Central America.[97] The stock price of another leading private prison and immigrant detention company, Geo Group, saw its stock prices triple in the first few months of the Trump regime (the company had contributed $250,000 to Trump's inauguration and was then awarded with a $110 million contract to build a new immigrant detention center in California).[98] Hundreds of private firms from around the world put in bids to construct Trump's infamous U.S.-Mexico border wall.[99] Given that such companies as CoreCivic and Geo Group are traded on the Wall Street stock exchange, investors from anywhere around the world may buy and sell their stock, and in this way develop a stake in immigrant repression quite removed from, if not entirely independent, of the more pointed political and ideological objectives of this repression.

The U.S.-Mexico border was already by the end of the twentieth century one of the most militarized stretches of land in the world, with ten guards for every mile for the length of the 2,000-mile border. Many stretches along the frontier are akin to a war zone.[100] U.S. President Donald Trump's fanatical campaign to "build the wall" was distinct in rhetoric only from the border militarization pursued by his predecessors, Democratic and Republican alike. The government claims a 100-mile-wide "constitutional suspension zone" inside the entire U.S. border in the name of immigration control, including the coasts, encompassing some 200 million people. In this zone, the state claims the power to set up check points, to determine anyone's status, to conduct stop and search at will, and to seize and copy laptops and cell phones.[101] In the 1990s, the U.S. Congress and the Department of Defense set aside the U.S.-Mexico border for the development of high-tech military and security industrial development. Researcher Juan Manuel Sandoval traces how the border region has been reconfigured into a "global space for the expansion of transnational capital" centered around high-tech military and aerospace-related industries, military bases, and the deploying of other civilian and military forces for combating "immigration, drug trafficking, and terrorism through a strategy of low-intensity warfare" on the U.S. side, along with the expansion of *maquiladoras* (sweatshops), mining, and industry on the Mexican side in the framework of capitalist globalization and North American integration. He shows how the border region has become a single integrated site of intensive militarized accumulation that is in turn integrated into the larger worldwide circuits of global capitalism.[102]

The activities of the American Legislative Exchange Council, or ALEC, expose the inner connections between corporate interests, the state, militarization and policing, and anti-immigrant and other neo-fascist tendencies in civil society.[103] ALEC brings together state and federal elected officials and law enforcement and criminal justice system representatives with some 200 of the most powerful transnational corporations, among them, ATT, Coca Cola, Exxon Mobile, Pfizer, Kraft Foods, Walmart, Bank of America, Microsoft, Nestlé, AstraZeneca, Dow Chemical, Sony, and Koch Industries, this latter one of the biggest ALEC funders. ALEC develops legislative initiatives that advance the transnational corporate agenda, hammering out in its gatherings draft criminal justice, anti-union, tax reform, financial and environmental deregulation and related bills that are then tabled by state and local elected officials associated with ALEC. These bills have included the notorious "three strikes law," that mandates 25 years to life sentences for those committing a third offense (even for minor drug possession), and "truth in sentencing," that requires people to serve all of their time with no chance of parole.

In 2009, ALEC members and representatives from the CCA drafted a model anti-immigrant law that was then introduced into the Arizona state assembly by Assemblyman Russell Pearce, an ALEC board member. The bill, known as law SB1070, passed with the support of 36 co-sponsors, 30 of who received campaign contributions from CCA lobbyists as well as from lobbyists for Geo Group and another private prison company, Management and Training Corporation. The bill was then signed by Arizona Governor Jan Brewer, who herself has close ties to CCA and to ALEC.[104] SB1070 legalized racial profiling by instructing state law enforcement agents to detain and question anyone who appeared to be undocumented and authorizing anyone to sue police who failed to do so, requiring in effect everyone to carry proof of citizenship or legal residence at all times. Although some of the most draconian provisions were struck down later by federal courts, the Arizona law became a model for "copycat" legislation passed in five other states and introduced in several dozen more. In 2010 and 2011 alone, 164 such laws were passed by state legislatures. A study of the virulently racist anti-immigrant bloc behind these laws and other campaigns of private and state persecution of immigrants reveals the extensive interlocking of far-right and neo-fascist organizations in civil society, government agencies and elected officials (local and federal), politicians, and corporate and foundation funders, lobbies, and activists.[105]

The private immigrant detention complex is a boom industry. Undocumented immigrants constitute the fastest growing sector of the U.S. prison population and are detained in private detention centers and deported by private companies contracted out by the U.S. state. As of 2010, there were 270 immigration detention centers that caged on any given day over 30,000 immigrants and annually locked up some 400,000 individuals, compared to just a few dozen people in immigrant detention each day prior to the 1980s[106]—that is, prior to the launching of capitalist globalization and the new transnational systems of labor recruitment and control associated with it. Under the Obama presidency, more immigrants were detained and deported than at any time in the previous half century. Detentions and deportations then escalated further under Trump, thus continuing the pattern in place since the 1980s. Some detention centers housed entire families, so that children were behind bars with their parents. Since detainment facilities and deportation logistics are subcontracted to private companies, capital has a vested interest in the criminalization of immigrants and in the militarization of control over immigrants—and more broadly, therefore, a vested interest in contributing to the neo-fascist anti-immigrant movement.

A month after SB1070 became law, Wayne Callabres, the president of Geo Group, held a conference call with investors and explained his company's aspirations. "Opportunities at the federal level are going to continue apace as a result of what's happening," he said, referring to the Arizona law. "Those people coming across the border being caught are going to have to be detained and that to me at least suggests there's going to be enhanced opportunities for what we do." The 2005 annual report of the CCA stated with regard to the profit-making opportunities opened up by the prison-industrial complex:

> Our growth is generally dependent upon our ability to obtain new contracts to develop and manage new correctional and detention facilities … The demand for our facilities and services could be adversely affected by the relaxation of enforcement efforts, leniency in conviction and sentencing practices or through the decriminalization of certain activities that are currently proscribed by our criminal laws.[107]

By the second decade of the twenty-first century, over 350,000 immigrants were going through privately run prisons for the undocumented each year and record numbers were being deported, even though the absolute number of immigrants had declined.

As the war on immigrants escalated, so too did profit-making opportunities opened up by the war. It was revealed in 2017 that some 60,000 immigrants held in Geo Group detention centers were being coerced into performing all sorts of labor to upkeep the company's facilities in exchange for $1 a day in pay. By relying on the free work of the detainees, charged a lawsuit filed against the company, Geo Group maintained an entire facility in Colorado with just one janitor on the payroll.[108] The government's Immigration and Customs Enforcement (ICE) agency also turned to privatizing flights deporting immigrants. One of several companies contracted by ICE, CSI Aviation, received more than $300 million in contracts to provide ICE with air passenger service in the three years from 2014 to 2016. A government report found that ICE was often paying for charter flights that were mostly empty. Not just detention and deportation, but everything in between, from food, phone systems, and other services provided to the detention facilities, are contracted out to private companies. This includes government contracts to private companies for GPS ankle monitors placed on detainees released on bond, even though the detainees must themselves pay hundreds of dollars a month to wear the monitors.[109]

As we have seen, digitalization opens up new technological possibilities for developing and deploying the global police state. The tech sector in the United States has become heavily involved in the war on immigrants as Silicon Valley plays an increasingly central role in the expansion and acceleration of arrests, detentions, and deportations. As their profits rise from participation in this war, leading tech companies have in turn pushed for an expansion of incarceration and deportation of immigrants and lobbied the state to expedite the use of its social control and surveillance technologies in anti-immigrant campaigns. According to one report:

> Immigrant communities and overpoliced communities now face unprecedented levels of surveillance, detention, and deportation. Tech innovation and infrastructure makes this possible, allowing immigration enforcement to rely on policing through huge databases, computer programs, tech employees analyzing big data, and shareable cloud-based storage. These systems accumulate unprecedented amounts

of personal and private information and enable the rapid expansion of information-sharing capabilities among city, state, and regional law enforcement agencies, as well as some foreign governments, for the purpose of finding, deporting, and detaining immigrants. Immigration enforcement and detention is now big business for Silicon Valley. ICE [Immigration and Customs Enforcement], DHS [Department of Homeland Security], and many other law enforcement agencies spend billions of taxpayer dollars on procuring and maintaining these new systems. Currently, about 10 percent of the DHS $44 billion budget is dedicated to data management. A handful of huge corporations, like Amazon Web Services and Palantir, have built a "revolving door" to develop and entrench Silicon Valley's role in fueling the incarceration and deportation regime.[110]

Two tech giants, Amazon and Palantir, have developed advanced biometric identification, data collection, and tracking systems for ICE and other government agencies through its cloud computing, what the report calls the "cloud industrial complex." Amazon and other tech and military-industrial companies, among them Adobe, IBM, Oracle, Salesforce, Lockheed Martin, Symantec, Raytheon (which by way of example is involved in supplying "border security" in more than 24 countries across Europe, the Middle East, Asia, and the Americas[111]), and Zoom, lobbied the government and spent thousands of dollars in contribution to congressional election campaigns for approval of the federal government's $20 billion "Cloud First" program, which has involved, among other aspects, the migration to Amazon's cloud computing of the entire DHS and ICE data portfolio. Following the lead of the giant tech companies, hundreds of small to mid-sized corporations compete to build information-sharing platform and software programs for advanced data collection and biometric tracking systems for DHS and ICE, while transnational tech companies based abroad have also been contracted, among them the French-based IDEMIA and Tokyo-based NEC Corporation. And lest we forgot, all these companies are publicly traded on global stock markets, so that any investors in these companies from around the world develop a stake in the war on immigrants in the United States.

In Europe, meanwhile, the refugee crisis and European Union's program to "secure borders" has provided a bonanza to military and security companies providing equipment to border military forces, surveillance systems, and IT infrastructure. As in the United States, these companies, far from passive beneficiaries of the crisis, have been behind the push to expand so-called "securitization." In 2007, the leading companies from Europe's military-industrial-security complex established the European Organization for Security to lobby governments to militarize borders and implement sweeping securitization programs. At the same time as these companies were benefitting from the multibillion-dollar border security contracts in Europe, they were granted licenses by EU member states to sell from 2005 to 2014 nearly $100 billion in arms to Middle East and North Africa (MENA) countries. The MENA regimes used the spike in arms sales to crack down on popular uprisings during the 2011 Arab Spring and to fuel armed conflicts.

War, state repression, and economic collapse drove millions of people from MENA to flee as refugees to safer locations in Europe in the wake of the Arab Spring. In turn, the refugee crisis—sensationalized by the corporate media and the European Right—proved a blessing for the corporate war complex. The budget for the EU border security agency, Frontex, increased a whopping 3,688 percent between 2005 and 2016, while the European border security market was expected to nearly double, from some $18 billion in 2015 to approximately $34 billion in 2022. Major transnational corporations that have both pushed for and profited from the securitization campaign include, among others, military supply, aerospace and technology conglomerates Airbus, Finmeccanica, Thales, and Safran, as well as the technology giant Indra Systems—all companies publicly traded on global stock markets. By the end of the second decade of the century, Europe's borders increasingly resembled those of the U.S.-Mexico border, with concrete walls, virtual walls, military patrols, monitoring and sniper towers, cameras, land radars and wireless telecommunication infrared surveillance, drones, carbon-dioxide probes, biometric identification systems, and immigration databases. "Collectively the evidence shows a growing convergence of interests between Europe's political leaders seeking to militarize the borders and its major defense and security contractors who provide the services," warned a 2016 report issued by the Amsterdam-based Transnational Institute. "Today we have an even more powerful military-industrial-security complex, using technologies that point outwards and inwards, that right now are targeted at some of the most vulnerable desperate people on our planet."[112]

Social Cleansing and Militarized Accumulation Around the World[‡]

Few developments in recent decades have been so functional to the global capitalist assault on the working and oppressed peoples of the Americas—and so illustrative of accumulation by repression—than the so-called "war on drugs." Journalists and academics exposed in the 1990s how the CIA shuttled arms to the Nicaraguan contras and other right-wing paramilitary groups in Central America and the Andes and brought back drugs to distribute in inner-city, largely African American, neighborhoods in the United States.[113] Michelle Alexander's 2012 bestseller, *The New Jim Crow*, exposed how the farcical war on drugs in the United States has been a mechanism for the mass incarceration of surplus African Americans, Latino and poor white labor.[114] Beyond the United States, dominant accounts portray the drug wars as a heroic struggle by the U.S., Mexican, and other governments in the Americas against depraved mafia cartels and criminal gangs, typically mystifying and sensationalizing the havoc as "senseless violence." Yet these same military and police are often deeply entrenched in drug trafficking.

Indeed, the war on drugs forms a bridge between the formal and informal, including criminal, economies of global capitalism. Capitalism has always been Janus faced—the flip side to its above-board "legal" and "legitimate" activities is the black or underground economy that is "illicit" and "illegitimate." These two faces are functionally integrated, from the key illegal activities that the U.S. mafia has performed for corporations throughout the twentieth century, to the international drug trafficking in Indochina that helped finance U.S. counterinsurgency and build a base for that region's integration into emergent globalized capitalism.[115] Gilber, among others, has shown how the U.S.-organized war on drugs in the Americas is not about ending the drug trade but about slicing up the spoils of this trade among underground cartels and military, economic and political elites. He shows, moreover, how the illicit trade is central to the predatory global banking system, into whose coffers tens of billions of drug profits are deposited and re-circulated to the financial networks of the global economy.[116] It is estimated that worldwide global drug trade was worth $435 billion in 2013,[117] and that much of this is re-circulated

---

‡ This section is not intended as a comprehensive account of social cleansing and militarized accumulation. That would take up multiple volumes. It is intended to highlight a few examples of how the global police state is deployed around the world in the intersection of its two dimensions: social control and militarized accumulation.

in the global financial system, constituting a critical intravenous for the anemic global economy. In this sense, the violent drug trade is itself a method of global capital accumulation that is militarized.[118] But it is much more. The drug wars constitute the axis around which the vast program of militarized accumulation and capitalist globalization revolves in Mexico, Colombia, and elsewhere in the Western Hemisphere, a multi-pronged instrument of the TCC for primitive accumulation that links the transnational military-industrial-security complex with neo-liberal reform, social cleansing of the poor, and repression of social movements.[119] "The war on drugs is a long-term fix to capitalism's woes," observes journalist Dawn Paley, "combining terror with policymaking in a seasoned neoliberal mix, cracking open social worlds and territories once unavailable to globalized capitalism."[120]

The United States invested from the late 1990s and on several tens of billions of dollars in the "war on drugs" in Latin America. These investments open up opportunities for accumulation at multiple levels. Military and police operations in the name of combating drug trafficking have resulted in Colombia, Central America, and Mexico in the mass displacement of local peasant, indigenous, Afro-descendant, and other communities in the countryside whose lands are then appropriated by local landowners and transnational capitalists. "Forcing out populations as a war strategy aims at impeding collective action, damaging social networks, intimidating and controlling the civilian population," notes Paley. "By moving people off the lands, new territories are opened up for these so-called frontier investments."[121] The operations in turn generate a steady supply of labor for agro-industrial, mining, and other extractive operations that have expanded in the region through capitalist globalization.[122] They provide a smokescreen for the repression of social movements and, especially in the case of Colombia, for counterinsurgency. And much of the monies end up in the coffers of transnational corporations. For instance, the U.S. government allocated $2.5 billion from 2008 to 2015 to the Merida Initiative, a program for assistance to the Mexican military allegedly to combat drug trafficking. Yet as one researcher pointed out, most of this money "does not even cross the border." Instead, it went directly from U.S. state coffers into the accounts of Texas-based Fairchild Aircraft that makes the radar planes flown by the Mexican Air Force, of Connecticut company Sikorsky, which makes the Blackhawk helicopters used by the Mexican Army, and to the California headquarters of General Atomics that makes the drones used to surveil the U.S.-Mexico border.[123]

Latin American is becoming a cauldron of state and private violence fused together for the purpose of repressing political revolt and opening up the continent to further corporate plunder. The region holds up a mirror to where the rest of the world is headed; it is emblematic of the global police state. Reflecting the resurgence around the world of far-right and neo-fascist forces (see next chapter), Latin America in recent years has seen a return to power of far-right repressive and authoritarian regimes, starting with the 2009 *coup d'état* in Honduras, followed by the 2016 "parliamentary coup" in Brazil against the governing Workers Party, as well as an escalation of repression throughout the region and a mobilization of far-right parties and business groups. "The current dictatorships present a civil image of respect for constitutional precepts, holding regular elections with the participation of political parties and other features of democratic regimes," notes Beinstein. "Political prisoners are almost always brought before judges who issue arbitrary verdicts but with an appearance of legality, the assassination of opposition figures go unreported by the corporate media, and state repression of political dissent is often blended with police violence against the poor, against popular protests, and against common delinquency."[124]

Central to this far-right turn in the region has been a racist, authoritarian, and militaristic retrenchment to consolidate and expand transnational corporate power.[125] In Mexico and Argentina, for instance, constitutions have been amended to allow the armed forces to carry out police functions, while U.S. special operations forces training missions tripled between 2007 and 2014.[126] According to "Security for Sale," a 2018 report by the Washington, D.C.-based Inter-American Dialogue, in 2017 over 16,000 private military and security companies in Latin America employed some 2.4 million people and often collaborated with state forces in repressing social movements. The lines between current and retired military and police personnel and these private companies are blurred, involving "an interwoven network of current military, former military, private security, business elites and government officials." In Mexico alone, the private security industry grew 180 percent from 2012 to 2018 and was worth $1.5 billion that year. In Brazil, the industry earns an astounding $14 billion annually.[127]

Latin American militaries have rapidly expanded in recent years in lockstep with a vast new round of transnational corporate penetration and appropriation of the region's abundant natural resources and labor supply. The Central American militaries grew by 20 percent since the 1990s. The Brazilian, Bolivian, Mexican, and Venezuelan militaries doubled in size during this time, and Colombia's military quadrupled. The rest of the region's militaries have grown in size by an average of 35 percent.[128] Militaries have been deployed to the region's megacities and often work alongside shadowy death squads in social cleansing and the repression of organized dissent.[129] There is a close overlap between transnational corporate plunder of the region's resources, states' deployment of military and police forces, paramilitarization, and the expansion of private security firms. These public and private forces are deployed both to open up the region's resources to the TCC and to provide security directly for transnational corporations. In Ecuador, for instance, the government deployed the military to evict the Indigenous Shuar and turn over their ancestral lands to a Chinese mining company. "Rather than calling in the military when situations get out of control, [states] have tasked the military with regularly monitoring and protecting important infrastructure and assets," note Kyle and Reiter. "Bolivia uses its military to protect natural gas pipelines, and in neighboring Peru, the government declared the country's only oil pipeline a 'strategic asset' and now tasks the military with protecting it from vandals."[130]

At the same time, some of the biggest customers for private security are these same extractive industries, natural resource projects, and agribusinesses. "From Mexico to Chile, companies and corporations in search of gold, water, oil, coal, gas, iron, timber and other lucrative exports hire armed guards to protect their investments," noted the Inter-American Dialogue report. Often there are

> ... local populations protesting these activities, and at times they have been met with violence. Lack of political will to hold companies and their contracted security providers to account has led to multiple cases in which private security personnel have clashed with local populations and activists, resulting in killings that remain in impunity. There is often a close-knit network between business, private security, the military and the government. This network often offers protection to the elite when tensions rise between environmental activists and local populations and landholders and business owners ... All over the region, in Brazil, Mexico, Peru, Guatemala, Colombia and elsewhere, traffickers, gangs, security forces, militias and private security firms—the lines between which often blur—have been found to kill, assault and threaten indigenous rights defenders and environmental activists. After Brazil, Colombia is the second-deadliest place for environmental defenders,

registering 95 deaths between 2015 and 2017. Along with criminal groups, the private security sector and the military have been implicated in these killings.[131]

It seems little has changed since the fifteenth- and sixteenth-century Conquest. The TCC is the new Conquistador.

Israel, meanwhile, perhaps more than any other country in the world exhibits an entire economy and political-colonial system predicated on militarized accumulation. It tops the list of countries most involved in intense international conflicts of the last two hundred years.[132] The country is at the very heart of the global police state, listed by the Global Militarization Index as "the most militarized nation in the world."[133] In the 1980s and 1990s, Israel moved from a traditional economy based largely on agriculture and national industry to a war and high-tech economy, as Tel Aviv and Haifa became Middle Eastern outposts of Silicon Valley. Israel has more technology stocks listed on the NASDAQ Exchange—many of them security related—than any other foreign country. The attacks of September 11, 2001 then allowed Israel to accelerate the development of, and export around the world, a so-called "homeland security industry." Israel has been exporting arms around the world almost since its inception in 1948.[134] The Israeli economy feeds off local, regional and global violence, conflict, and inequalities. But in the wake of 9/11, it carved out a unique niche as a provider worldwide of weapons sub-systems, technologies, and training for the global homeland security industry that have "dual use" applicability to both military and civilian markets, doing arms and security business with some 130 countries. The 400 public and private military firms, many of them publicly traded, sold some $30 billion worldwide in arms from 2000 to 2007. To this must be added the homeland security, intelligence, and policing exports of these military firms and several hundred other firms selling domestic security goods, technologies, and services. The country has 200 cybersecurity companies and is now the number two worldwide exporter of cyber products and services.[135]

The secret to securing this niche, notes Israeli researcher Jeff Halper, is the use of Occupied Palestinian Territory as a laboratory for testing these weapons, security, and intelligence systems and technologies so that they can be marketed globally as "combat tested." Its largest corporations sponsor war and conflict: "The Occupation represents a resource for Israel in two senses: economically it provided a testing ground for the development of weapons, security systems, models of population control and tactics without which Israel would be unable to compete in the international arms and security markets."[136] Halper goes on to provide in chilling detail how the full panoply of weapons systems, and surveillance and intelligence technologies it has developed have been broadly deployed against Palestinians in the Occupied Territories:

> The Occupied Palestinian Territory has been transformed into probably the most monitored, controlled and militarized place on earth. It epitomizes the dream of every general, security expert and police officer to be able to exercise total biopolitical control. In a situation where the local population enjoys no effective legal protections or privacy, they and their lands become a laboratory where the latest technologies of surveillance, control and suppression are perfected and showcased, giving Israel an edge in the highly competitive global market. Labels such as "Combat Proven," "Tested in Gaza," and "Approved by the IDF [Israeli Defenses Force]" on Israeli or foreign products greatly improves their marketability.[137]

These methods of control and repression fine tuned against the Palestinians have been exported by Israel to racist police in U.S. inner cities, Brazilian security forces that patrol the impoverished residents of the Rio *favelas*, Colombian and Guatemalan military and paramilitary forces in their battles against social movements, Central Asian intelligence officers monitoring human rights activists and journalists, Chinese Army agents developing domestic systems of social control, and corporate clients and repressive states and police agencies the world over.[138]

In China, there has been a rapid build-up of special operations forces aimed at internal social control in the face of a massive upsurge of workers' struggles and social protests (indeed, many see China as the emerging epicenter of global labor struggles).[139] The Chinese government spent more in 2011 ($111 billion) on internal security than on defense ($106 billion).[140] Alongside the growth of its military-industrial complex, high-tech systems of internal security and control are expanding rapidly in the country in the face of unrest generated by rising unemployment, sharp social polarization and escalating inequalities, economic insecurity, intensified exploitation, and declining health and education conditions. As the Chinese state attempts to head off political instability, Chinese citizens may be on the way to becoming the most surveilled population in the world. In 2016,

China had 176 million surveillance cameras in operation and this figure was expected to more than triple to reach 626 million by 2020.[141]

Contrary to the assumption that the state exercises exclusive authority over these developing systems of internal social control and mass surveillance, the internal security program involves the participation of private surveillance and other companies, such as, for instance, the collaboration of these companies with police departments to implement facial and gait recognition technologies to detect alleged criminals along with labor leaders and political dissenters in real time as they move through public spaces. The facial recognition project was launched in 2015 with the participation of various private technology and security companies, with the goal of having a database in place that can identify any of the country's 1.4 billion citizens within seconds.[142] This program for facial recognition surveillance is the fastest growing in the world, with a market worth $6.4 billion in 2017, compared to the U.S. market worth $2.9 billion that year, and was expected to grow by over 12 percent through to 2021.[143] The leading private Chinese-based company involved, Hangzhou Hikvision Digital Technology, already controls some 20 percent of the world market in CCTV cameras and video surveillance equipment and has been contracted by the U.S. Army and by the Memphis Police Department, among other clients.[144] Hikvision and another leading Chinese surveillance firm, Dahua, are both listed on the Shenzhen stock exchange. The global financial conglomerates UBS and J.P. Morgan are among the Hikvision's top ten shareholders (the Chinese government is a minority shareholder).[145]

Chinese surveillance technology is also being applied to a "social credit system" that the government plans to develop nationwide, a vast behavioral control system that ranks citizens based on their behavior and doles out rewards and punishments depending on scores. The all-intrusive systems being developed include holding people criminally liable for content posted in any group chat they initiate on messaging apps. Citizens are required by law to download apps that allow the government to monitor their cell-phone photos and videos. If someone makes political posts online without a permit or questions the government's official narrative on current events, your score decreases. Companies participating in the surveillance program include the global publicly traded tech conglomerates Alibaba and Tencent as well as a host of smaller companies, including SenseTime, Megvii, LLVision Technology, and Intellifusion, among others. The state's central system, known as the "Integrated Joint Operations Platform," draws on artificial intelligence, data mining and storage, and algorithm surveillance to aggregate data, analyze people's profiles, and predict who may pose a threat to the state.[146] Other Chinese-based and transnational corporations are rapidly expanding into the Chinese internal security market. In 2019, for instance, a spinoff from Blackwater, Frontier Services Group (FSG), struck a deal with the Chinese government to build a training facility for the program against the Uygur ethnic minority in the western province of Xinjiang. The Chinese state-owned conglomerate, Citic Group, owns a quarter of the stock of FSG, which is listed in the Hong Kong stock exchange.[147]

As I discussed above and in earlier chapters, several factions of capital have become heavily invested in the global police state and are linked together through the circuits of transnational finance capital and the application of new digital technologies. The financial sector, the military-industrial-security complex and the extractive industries are particularly dependent on a global police state and are in turn interwoven with high-tech or digital capital. The extractive and energy complexes must dislodge communities and appropriate their resources, which make them most prone to supporting or even promoting repressive and neo-fascist political arrangements through the global police state. Capital accumulation in the military-industrial-security complex depends on never-ending wars and on systems of repression. Financial accumulation requires ever greater austerity that is difficult, if not impossible, to impose through consensual mechanisms.

How these three sectors of capital came together in the United States with state and paramilitary forces was abundantly demonstrated in 2016 in a military-style counterinsurgency against indigenous activists and their allies who were peacefully protesting the construction of the Dakota Access Pipeline in lands near their Standing Rock Sioux reservation in North Dakota. Bankrolled by a consortium of banks that included Wells Fargo and Bank of America, the private Fortune 500 oil and gas company building the pipeline, Energy Transfer Partners, hired a mercenary and security firm known as TigerSwan, that originated as a Pentagon and State Department contractor for the Middle East wars. TigerSwan was charged with organizing a counterinsurgency campaign against the protesters in coordination with the company and with local, state, and federal law enforcement agencies, including National Guard troops. "Aggressive intelligence preparation of the battlefield and active coordination between intelligence and security elements are now a proven method of defeating pipeline insurgents," stated TigerSwan, in calling the anti-pipeline protesters "jihadist fighters" and the protest area a "battlefield." The "less than lethal" arsenal unleashed by the public-private counterinsurgency apparatus included rubber bullets, bean bag pellets, LRAD sound devices, water cannons, attack dogs, predator drones, metadata imaging, counter-intelligence, and psyops.[148] In the wake of Standing Rock, 56 bills were introduced in 30 states to restrict such protests.[149]

While the Standing Rock ordeal is a chilling case study in paramilitarization of the global police state, such operations carried out against social justice movements are now routine around the world.[150] A report by Lloyd's of London, a global insurance and financial conglomerate, warns that "instances of political violence contagion are becoming more frequent" and headed towards what it terms "PV [political violence] pandemics." It identifies so-called "super-strains" of PV as "anti-imperialist," "independence movements," social movements calling for the removal of an "occupying force," "mass pro-reform protests against national government[s]," and "armed insurrection" inspired by "Marxism" and "Islamism."[151] This "PV" is big business. According to the 2016 report, *Global Riot Control System Market, 2016–2020*, prepared by a global business intelligence firm whose clients include Fortune 500 companies, in the next few years there will be a multi-billion-dollar boom in the worldwide market for "riot control systems." The report forecast a dramatic rise in civil unrest around the world, driven by an increase in Standing Rock and Ferguson-style incidents. "Protests, riots, and demonstrations are major issues faced by the law enforcement agencies across the world," stated the report. "In addition the increase in incidents of civil wars in countries such as Syria, Iraq, Lebanon, and Egypt along with an increase in the global defense budget will generate demand for riot control systems." It predicted that countries in the Asia-Pacific region would experience the highest growth in the demand for "riot contagion" services and equipment. The escalating demand for "specialized equipment" is being driven by "the rise of urban warfare," stated the report, citing the 2014 Umbrella Revolution in Hong Kong, "which witnessed 100,000 protesters blocking the roads [and] led law enforcement agencies to adopt militarization" (it should be noted that the Hong Kong protesters were entirely peaceful).[152]

In sum, absent a change of course forced on the system by mass mobilization and popular struggle from below, mounting crisis will push militarized accumulation and accumulation by repression into more and more spaces in the global economy and society. The more the global economy comes to depend on this militarization and conflict, the greater the drive to war and the higher the stakes for humanity. There is a built-in war drive to the current course of capitalist globalization. Historically, wars have pulled the capitalist system out of crisis while they have also served to deflect attention from political tensions and problems of legitimacy. The breakdown of hegemony points to the political dimensions of global capitalist crisis. We now turn to responses from above and from below to this crisis of hegemony and to possible alternative futures.

4

The Battle for the Future

The future cannot be a continuation of the past and there are signs, both externally, and, as it were, internally, that we have reached a point of historic crisis. The structures of human societies themselves, including even some of the social foundations of the capitalist economy, are on the point of being destroyed by the erosion of what we have inherited from the human past. Our world risks both explosion and implosion. It must change ... If humanity is to have a recognizable future, it cannot be by prolonging the past or the present. If we try to build the third millennium on that basis, we shall fail. And the price of failure, that is to say, the alternative to a changed society, is darkness.

Eric Hobsbawm[1]

It's a Class Struggle Goddammit!
Fred Hampton, Chicago leader of the Black Panther Party

If I had an hour to solve a problem I'd spend 55 minutes thinking about the problem and five minutes thinking about solutions.

Albert Einstein

We have explored in the previous chapters two of the three interrelated developments to which the global police state refers: the omnipresent systems of mass control and repression to contain the real and potential rebellion of the global working class and surplus humanity, and militarized accumulation as a strategy for unloading surplus accumulated capital. We now turn to the third development, the increasing move towards political systems that can be characterized as twenty-first-century fascism, or even in a broader sense, as totalitarian.[2] It is the increasing breakdown of capitalist hegemony that has prompted the TCC to impose ever more coercive and repressive forms of rule. Escalating inequalities and the inability of global capitalism to assure the survival of billions of people throw states into crises of legitimacy. The system may be approaching a general crisis of capitalist rule.

"The modern crisis ... is related to what is called the 'crisis of authority.' If the ruling class has lost its consensus, i.e., is no longer 'leading' but only 'dominant,' exercising coercive force alone, this means precisely that the great masses have become detached from their traditional ideologies, and no longer believe what they used to believe previously, etc.," wrote great Italian political thinker and socialist revolutionary, Antonio Gramsci, in what is perhaps the single most cited passage of his writings. "The crisis consists precisely in the fact that the old way is dying and the new cannot be born; in this interregnum a great variety of morbid symptoms appear."[3] He wrote this passage to describe the crisis of early twentieth-century capitalism in Europe, at a time when fascism had taken power in his own country. There can be little doubt that we are again in such a interregnum as the battle for the future shapes up. We have entered a fluid period of great uncertainly that opens up the dangers of neo-fascism, war, and ecological collapse, but also new possibilities for emancipatory projects.

The increasing influence around the world of neo-fascist, authoritarian, and rightwing populist parties and movements, symbolized above all by Trumpism in the United States, has sparked a flurry of debate on whether fascism is again on the rise.[4] There are no countries in the world that at the time of writing in mid-2019 have plunged into fascism. Nonetheless, the crisis has resulted in a sharp polarization between insurgent left and popular forces, on the one hand, and an insurgent far Right, on the other, at whose fringe are openly fascist tendencies. A project of twenty-first-century fascism is on the ascent in the civil societies of many countries around the world. The project has made significant advances in recent years in its competition to win state power, and in some cases, it has gained a foothold in the capitalist state. But a fascist outcome to the crisis of global capitalism is not inevitable. Whether or not a fascist project manages to congeal is entirely contingent on how the struggle among social and political forces unfolds in the coming years. If historically grounded and theoretically informed analysis helps to call out the danger that far-right insurgencies may develop into outright fascism, then this analysis becomes part of the political and ideological struggle to prevent such an outcome. We start with a theoretical excursion that draws on Gramsci's theory of hegemony.

Global Police State and Twenty-First-Century Fascism[5]

Fascism, whether in its classical twentieth-century form or possible variants of twenty-first-century neo-fascism, is *a particular response to capitalist crisis.* Trumpism in the United States, Brexit in the United Kingdom, the increasing influence of neo-fascist and authoritarian parties and movements throughout Europe (including Poland, Germany, Hungary, Austria, Italy, Holland, Spain, the UK, Denmark, France, Belgium, and Greece)[6] and around the world, such as in Israel, Turkey, Colombia, the Philippines, Brazil, and India, as distinct as they may be from one another, have in common that they represent far-right responses to the crisis of global capitalist hegemony.

For Gramsci, hegemony refers to a particular relation of social domination in which subordinate groups lend their "active consent" to the system of domination. Projects of hegemony involve not merely rule but political and ideological leadership of the dominant groups based on a set of class alliances and political blocs they have constructed. Hegemony must be constantly reconstructed because the possibility of hegemonic or consensual domination rests not just on the dominant groups achieving their political and ideological leadership but also on material foundations. This is to say that the ruling groups must also provide some sort of material (economic) "payoff" to significant sectors among the subordinate groups to allow for these sectors' social reproduction and stability—that is, for their well-being. No would-be ruling class can exercise hegemony without developing diverse mechanisms of legitimation and securing a social base—a combination of the consensual integration through material reward for some and the coercive exclusion of others that the system is unwilling or unable to co-opt. The point to underscore here is that the exclusion of billions even as globalization draws all into the new order, and the socioeconomic destabilization of many of those that had achieved some level of stability in the earlier eras, especially in the rich core countries of world capitalism, is now making it increasingly difficult for the ruling groups to reproduce the hegemony of the system.

Let us deepen this line of analysis, as it is crucial to understanding the rise of twenty-first-century fascism and a global police state. Gramsci argues that a class or class fraction achieves hegemony to the extent that it is able to present its own interests as the general interest of society, and insofar as "the interests of the dominant group prevail, *but only up to a certain point, i.e., stopping short of narrowly corporate economic interests.*"[7] What Gramsci means by this is that if the capitalist classes and their political agents in the state want to establish hegemony, they must at some point make concessions and reach compromises with subordinate groups that in some way prioritizes securing the overall stability of capitalist rule over the immediate aim of maximizing profits. Emergent transnational elites set about in the 1980s and 1990s to establish hegemony in global society by constructing a global capitalist historic bloc. What Gramsci means by an historic bloc is a "social ensemble" or a coalition that draws in the dominant strata and also establishes a social base beyond the ruling group. To be successful in constructing this historic bloc, the ruling group must be able to present its class project as in the general interest and gain the *consent* of those brought into the bloc through a combination of material reward (that is, some "payoff" to the subordinate social base) and ideological leadership. If all this seems excessively abstract, we will see momentarily how it helps us understand the turn to a global police state and the threat of twenty-first-century fascism.

It appeared for a time in the 1990s that transnational elites would be able to establish this historic bloc. The political and cultural agents of the TCC operating through transnational state institutions, the mass media, and the culture industries held up the globalization boom of the late twentieth century, coming as it did in the wake of the collapse of a socialist alternative and Third World revolutionary projects, as proof that global capitalism was the only alternative for the world, and one that would usher in a new age of prosperity and opportunity. But efforts to cement the bloc proved elusive. As the TCC went global, it turned to naked pursuit of its own corporate interests, unrestrained from national regulatory control and seemingly impervious to mass pressure from below. It could no longer even pretend to represent a "general interest," much less assure the social reproduction of enough among the global working and popular classes to secure its hegemony as global capitalism became ever more predatory, a veritable gangster capitalism. Under these conditions, coercive domination and violent exclusion came to prevail over consensual incorporation. By the turn of the century, counter-hegemonic forces spread and developed into a transnational movement against the depredations of neo-liberalism and for global justice, followed in the wake of the 2008 financial collapse by a global revolt that continues to this day.

When a crisis of political authority or hegemony does not find an organic solution, "it means that a static equilibrium exists (whose factors may be disparate, but in which the decisive one is the immaturity of the progressive forces)," wrote Gramsci. "It means that no group, neither the conservatives nor the progressives, has the strength for victory, and that even the conservative group needs a master."[8] In these moments, notes Gramsci, "the crisis creates situations which are dangerous in the short

run since the various strata of the population are not all capable of orient-
ing themselves equally swiftly, or of reorganizing with the same rhythm."[9]
Gramsci was writing in reference to the rise of fascism in Europe in the
1920s and 1930s. But his analysis goes far in identifying the current conjuncture, that of a sharp political polarization between left/progressive and
far-right responses to the crisis (and indeed the "immaturity of the progressive forces"). Neither left nor far-right forces have been able to gain the
upper hand as global capitalist hegemony breaks down.

The class character of fascism remains the same in the twenty-first
century as it was in the twentieth—a project to rescue capital from this
organic crisis—but the particular historical character of world capitalism
and of its crisis is substantially different at this time than in the previous
century. As I discussed in Chapter 1, the transnationalization of the leading
capitalist sectors around the world takes place within the political framework of a nation-state-based system of political authority. This disjuncture
generates a set of political and ideological contradictions that the system
has been unable to manage and that helps us to understand the specter
of twenty-first-century fascism. What, then, does twenty-first-century
fascism share with its twentieth-century predecessor and what is distinct?
Above all, fascism in the twentieth century involved the fusion of reactionary political power with *national* capital. It was, in part, the inability of
German and Italian national capital to out-compete the national capitals
of other European powers in the imperialist conquests of the turn of the
nineteenth century and following the German defeat in World War I that
led to a fascist response in the 1930s once the crisis hit full force. In distinction, twenty-first-century fascism involves the fusion of *transnational
capital* with reactionary and repressive political power—an expression of
the dictatorship of the TCC.

In addition, the fascist projects that came to power in the 1930s in
Germany, Italy, and Spain, as well as those that vied unsuccessfully to
win power in many European countries,[10] in the United States, and in
some South American countries, had as a fundamental objective crushing
powerful working-class and socialist movements. But in the United
States, Europe, and elsewhere, the revolutionary Left and the organized working class are now at a historically weak point. In these cases,
twenty-first-century fascism appears to be a *preemptive* strike at working
classes and at the spread of mass resistance through the expansion of a
global police state. The Fourth Industrial Revolution promises to increase
the ranks of surplus humanity and also impose greater competitive pres-

THE BATTLE FOR THE FUTURE

sures on the TCC, as we have seen, thus heightening its need to impose more oppressive and authoritarian forms of labor discipline on the global working class. Equally as important, dominant groups face the challenge of how to contain both the real and potential rebellion of surplus humanity. In the face of this challenge, capitalist states have appeared to abandon efforts to secure legitimacy among this surplus population and instead have turned to criminalizing the poor and the dispossessed, with tendencies towards genocide in some cases.

The Social Bases of Twenty-First-Century Fascism

Twentieth-century fascism took root in an earlier stage of capitalist development, when the middle classes and the petty-bourgeoisie that represented a significant portion of the population were experiencing a destabilization of their status and the threat of downward mobility into the ranks of the proletariat. Fascist movements offered the ruling groups the ability to successfully compete with mass working-class parties for the allegiance of the middle classes and the petty-bourgeoisie, although these movements did recruit among the working class as well. These strata came to be seen as the core social base of the fascist movements—instruments in the hands of national capitalist classes attempting to resolve the crisis of capitalism.[11] The middle classes and the petty-bourgeoisie are strata that own their own means of livelihood and therefore do not have to sell their labor to capital, among them, small shopkeepers and businesspeople, independent artisans and professionals, family farmers, and other small commodity producers. These strata were reduced to small pockets in the cores of world capitalism as proletarianization accelerated in the latter half of the twentieth century and especially in the age of globalization. While analysis of the petty bourgeoisie remains important in assessing current political processes, this class is not numerous enough to form a critical mass that could provide a viable social base for twenty-first-century fascism to triumph.

Today that role is played in the cores of world capitalism by certain sectors of the working class. Twenty-first-century fascist projects seek to organize a mass base among historically privileged sectors of the global working class, such as white workers in the Global North and urban middle layers in the Global South, that are experiencing heightened insecurity and the specter of downward mobility and socioeconomic destabilization. As with its twentieth-century predecessor, the project hinges on the psychosocial mechanism of displacing mass fear and anxiety at a time of acute capitalist crisis towards scapegoated communities, such as immigrants, Muslims and refugees in the United States and Europe, southern African immigrants in South Africa, Muslims and lower castes in India, Palestinians in Palestine/Israel, or the darker-skinned and disproportionately impoverished population in Brazil. Far-right forces do so through a discursive repertoire of xenophobia, mystifying ideologies that involve race/culture supremacy, an idealized and mythical past, millennialism, a militaristic and masculinist culture that normalizes, even glamorizes war, social violence, and domination, and a contempt rather than empathy for those most vulnerable. The key to this neo-fascist appeal is the promise to avert or reverse downward mobility and social destabilization; to restore some sense of stability and security.

This discursive repertoire of twenty-first-century fascism, of course, shares many features with classical twentieth-century fascism, including what Umberto Eco characterized as a "cult of tradition," "fear of diversity," a besiege mentality, a sense of deprivation of a clear social identity, "selective populism," and Orwellian "Newspeak."[12] However, these discursive and emotive elements take place under very different circumstances and historical moment in world capitalism. With regard to extreme masculinization, although here is not the place for discussion, the denigration of women in general and the sexual predation of Trump (and of Philippine President Rodrigo Duterte or Brazilian President Jair Bolsonaro, among others) that were on public display for all to see, almost seemed to be a point in his favor among his diehard base. This phenomenon may be a sexual sublimation of what are fears of social and economic emasculation. On the matter of contempt rather than empathy, witness Trump's notorious 2018 comments on poor countries being "shithole countries," his public mocking of a disabled reporter during his 2016 campaign for the presidency, and so on. It is not too much of an analytical stretch to associate such public displays of contempt with the process whereby policies of aggression and repression of these vulnerable groups achieve discursive or psycho-social legitimation in the common-sense consciousness of those who would provide the mass social base for a neo-fascist project.

There is a heavy overlap with ideologies of national regeneration, national/race purity, and a mystique of heroism that characterized twentieth-century fascism (although in the particular case of Trump, the latter resembled an extreme narcissistic mystique of his self). Twenty-first-century fascism, like its twentieth-century predecessor, is a violently toxic mix of reactionary nationalism and racism. The nation, argued Benedict Anderson, is an "imagined political community," in which "the nation is always conceived as a deep horizontal comradeship," regardless of the actual inequality and exploitation that exists.[13] In conjunction, argues Callinicos, racism offers workers from the dominant racial or ethnic group an imaginary solution to real contradictions; recognition of the existence of suffering and oppression, even though its solution is a false one.[14] Neo-fascist projects on the rise at this time offer precisely this mix of nationalism and racism in attempting to organize better-off sectors of the working class experiencing social and economic destabilization in the face of capitalist globalization.

The parties and movements associated with such projects have put forth a racist discourse, less coded and less mediated than mainstream politicians, targeting the racially oppressed, ethnic or religious minorities, immigrants and refugees in particular as scapegoats. It is crucial to note that deteriorating socioeconomic conditions do not automatically lead to a racist backlash. Political agents and state agencies must mediate a racist/fascist interpretation of these conditions.[15] While there is nothing inevitable about a fascist outcome to the current lurch to the far right, the more the current racist mobilization becomes entrenched the greater the danger of such an outcome. In the United States, the far Right and neo-fascists have been attempting to reconstruct the white racist historic bloc that to one extent or another reigned supreme from the end of post-Civil War reconstruction to the late twentieth century, but has become destabilized through capitalist globalization. In Europe, the far Right and the neo-fascist movements were following a very similar path to Trump's in terms of recruiting formerly privileged sectors among the working classes who are suffering under the crisis by scapegoating Muslims, immigrants, and other vulnerable sectors, promising to stabilize the situation for these precariatized sectors. In India, the ruling Bharatiya Janata Party, itself an outgrowth of the fascist Rashtriya Swayamsevak Sangh (known simply as RSS) movement,[16] combined a far-right Hindu nationalism with the scapegoating of the country's Muslim minority and aggression against the lower castes. In all these cases, "national" identity becomes a stand-in (that is, a code) for racist mobilization against scapegoats.

Yet the discourse of national regeneration is in sharp contradiction with the transnational integration of capital and a globally integrated production and financial system upon which hinge the class and status interests of the major capitalist groups and state elites. Here there is a critical distinction to be made between the conjuncture of fascist projects in the last century and those of the twenty-first century. Fascism in Germany and Italy arose at the height of nation-state capitalism and it did offer some material benefits—employment and social wages—to a portion of the working class through corporatist arrangements, even as it unleashed genocide on those outside the chosen group. In this age of globalized capitalism, there is little possibility in the United States or elsewhere of providing such benefits, so that the "wages of fascism" now appear to be entirely psychological. In this regard, the ideology of twenty-first-century fascism rests on irrationality—a promise to deliver security and restore stability that is emotive, not rational. It is a project that does not and need not distinguish between the truth and the lie.

In the United States, for example, the Trump regime's public discourse of populism and nationalism bore no relation to its actual policies. In its first year, Trumponomics involved deregulation—the virtual smashing of the regulating state—slashing social spending, dismantling what remained of the welfare state, privatizations, tax breaks to corporations and the rich, and an expansion of state subsidies to capital, in short, neo-liberalism on steroids. This is a distinction lost on many commentators. German monopoly capitalists turned to the Nazis to crush the powerful trade unions, and socialist and communist movements. But they also turned to the Nazi state to open up vast new opportunities for accumulation and to compete, including through territorial expansion, with capitalist groups from other countries. In sharp distinction to this fusion of German *national* capital with the fascist state, Trumpism has sought to open up vast new opportunities for profit making inside the United States (and around the world) for *transnational* capital. The Trump White House called for transnational investors from around the world to invest in the United States, enticed by a regressive tax reform, unprecedented deregulation, and some limited tariff walls that would benefit groups from anywhere in the world that establish operations behind them. "America is open for business," Trump declared at the 2018 meeting of the global elite gathered for the 2018 annual conclave of the World Economic Forum in Davis, Switzerland: "Now is the perfect time to bring your business, your jobs and your investments to the United States."[17]

The mechanisms of twenty-first-century fascism also involve ideological campaigns aimed at seduction and passivity among those locked out. The digital and communications revolution allows neo-fascism to draw on cultural and ideological apparatuses that were simply unavailable to the twentieth-century fascists. The newfound ability of transnational capital to achieve political domination through control over the means of intellectual production, the mass media, the educational system, and the culture industries allows it to achieve a much more profound and complete penetration into the spheres of culture and community, indeed, into the life world itself. Corporate marketing strategies depoliticize through the manipulation of desire and of libido so that the grievances and frustrated aspirations of the excluded become channeled into petty consumption and flight into fantasy rather than into placing political demands on the system through collective mobilization. The corporate media conglomerates worldwide barrage the global public with ideological justifications for global capitalism, control the flow of information in such a way as to censor information critical of the system, bombard the public with trivial information, and frame events in such a way that the system of global capitalism is normalized.

In this regard, I observed in my earlier work that the heightened role of political and ideological domination in this digital age through control over media and the flow of images and symbols would make any project of twenty-first-century fascism more sophisticated and, together with new panoptical surveillance and social control technologies, probably allow it to rely more on selective than generalized repression—unless a revolt from below comes to actually threaten the rule of the TCC. These new modalities of social control and ideological domination blur boundaries, so that there may be a constitutional and normalized neo-fascism (with formal representative institutions, a constitution, political parties, and elections), even as transnational capital and its representatives tightly control the political system and any dissent that actually threatens the system is neutralized if not liquidated.[18] We may see a "withering away" of constitutional order rather than a rupture, if the global police state and the impulse towards twenty-first-century fascism are not contained.

An essential condition for twentieth- and now for any twenty-first-century fascism is the spread of fascist movements in civil society and their fusion at some point with reactionary political power in the state. Gramsci reminds us that civil and political society are a unity; there can be no stable or hegemonic project without a correspondence between the two. "Today, there are two repressive and punitive apparatuses in Italy," observed Gramsci on the eve of the fascist takeover, "fascism and the bourgeois state. A simple calculus of utility induces us to expect the dominant class to combine these two apparatuses at some point."[19] Gramsci referred to the locus of social processes as the extended state, comprised of political society, or the state (government) proper, plus civil society. In fact, no state exhibits clear-cut boundaries between its institutions and others in a social formation; the boundary between state and civil society is an artificial conceptual line.

This distinction and the unity of political and civil society allow us to distinguish between right-wing authoritarianism and neo-fascism, since both are associated with the global police state. It is precisely because they are not the same that we must distinguish between the two. For our purposes, authoritarianism refers to rule by an expanding repressive apparatus of the state that strives to close off space through legal and extra-legal repression of popular mobilization from below in civil society. In Latin America, perhaps most emblematic of this authoritarianism, far-right repressive and authoritarian regimes have in recent years returned with a vengeance, as we saw in the previous chapter. Yet here is the critical distinction between repressive authoritarianism and neo-fascism: in Latin America, with the possible exception of Brazil and Colombia, we do *not* see in the same way as we do in the United States, in Europe, in India, or in Israel, the spread throughout civil society of neo-fascist movements and ideologies. In short, the region is being swept up into a global police state but in a way that is more appropriate to view as right-wing authoritarianism than as neo-fascism.

By conflating authoritarianism and fascism, we lose the ability to distinguish between the two. Twenty-first-century fascism and a global police state involve *a triangulation of far-right, authoritarian, and neo-fascist forces in civil society with reactionary political power in the state and transnational corporate capital*. Classical and current discussion on fascism also stress *national* military expansionism. We are indeed seeing an escalating militarization that involves the increasingly autonomy and power of the military, in the United States and in many countries around the world. But I believe *global police state* has more analytical purchase and is more robust as a concept in discussing the nature of the current global militarization. The global order as a unity is increasingly repressive and authoritarian and particular *forms* of exceptional national states or national polities, including twenty-first-century fascism, develop on the basis of particular national and regional histories, social and class forces, political conditions and conjunctures. Yet the militarization of cities, politics, and culture in such countries as the United States and Israel, the spread of neo-fascist movements in North America, Europe, Israel, and India, the rise of authoritarian regimes in Turkey, the Philippines, Honduras, and so on, are inseparable from these countries' entanglement in webs of global wars and militarized global accumulation, or global war economy.

An International of Twenty-First-Century Fascism?

It was above all the presidency of Donald Trump in the United States that sparked renewed fear of fascism. But the project of twenty-first-century fascism as a response to capitalist crisis is not tied to any one individual or government. To make sense of this, let us reiterate that civil and political society form a unity; there can be no stable or hegemonic project without a correspondence between the two. In the United States, a neo-fascist insurgency can be traced back to the far-right mobilization that began in the wake of the crisis of hegemony brought about by the mass struggles of the 1960s and the 1970s, especially the Black and Chicano liberation struggles and other militant movements by Third World peoples, the feminist, gay liberation, anti-war, counter-cultural, and militant working-class struggles.[20] Fascist movements expanded rapidly since the turn of the century in civil society and in the political system through the right wing of the Republican Party.

Trump proved to be a charismatic figure,[21] able to galvanize and embolden disparate neo-fascist forces, from white supremacists, white nationalists, militia, and neo-Nazis and Klans, to the Oath Keepers, the Patriot Movement, Christian fundamentalists, and anti-immigrant vigilante groups. Encouraged by Trump's imperial bravado, his populist and nationalist rhetoric, and his openly racist discourse, predicated in part on whipping up anti-immigrant, anti-Muslim, and xenophobic sentiment, they began to cross-pollinate to a degree not seen in decades as they gained a toehold in the Trump White House and in state and local governments around the country. Paramilitarism spread within many of these organizations and overlapped with state repressive agencies. In Oregon, for instance, the state Republican Party tapped armed right-wing militia to provide security for its events.[22] In New Mexico, an armed fascist militia organization, the self-proclaimed United Constitutional Patriots, linked up with border patrol agents in armed patrols along the border with Mexico in 2019. In April that year, they took it upon themselves to arrest some 300 border crossers.[23] The Southern Poverty Law Center reported a total of 954 hate groups in 2017, up from 917 the year before, and 689 "extreme antigovernment groups." According to the Center, "a spate of protests in liberal cities following the election allowed the militia movement, part of the larger antigovernment sector, to thrust itself into the spotlight of urban America in a significant way for the first time since the Oath Keepers deployed militants to protect mostly white-owned businesses in Ferguson, Missouri, in 2015."[24]

Yet Trumpism was but a *dramatic* (in the literal sense, as in drama, theatrics) intensification of—rather than a departure from—the far-right agenda of repressive capitalist globalization that dates back to the rise of Reagan and Thatcher governments in the United States and the United Kingdom. Trumpism and other far-right responses to the crisis of global capitalism sought to create a new balance of political forces in the face of the breakdown of the short-lived global capitalist historic bloc. We may be seeing the rise of Caesarism as discussed by Gramsci, in which a charismatic figure steps in to resolve an unstable stalemate in the balance of social and political forces or in a conjuncture of hegemonic breakdown. Gramsci noted that a Caesarist solution could arise without a Caesar, without any great "heroic" and representative personality, and in the absence of immediate mass repression. Instead, it may involve more authoritarian forms of parliamentary government that may or may not involve a rupture with constitutional order further on.

Trumpism and other such movements are a contradictory attempt to re-found state legitimacy under the destabilizing conditions of capitalist globalization. Nation-states face a contradiction between the need to promote transnational capital accumulation in their territories and their need to achieve political legitimacy. As a result, states around the world have been experiencing spiraling crises of legitimacy that generate a bewildering and seemingly contradictory politics of crisis management that appears as schizophrenic in the literal sense of conflicting or inconsistent elements. This schizophrenic crisis management also helps explain the resurgence of far-right and neo-fascist forces that espouse rhetoric of nationalism and protectionism even as they promote neo-liberalism. Trumpism and similar movements in Europe and elsewhere were not departures from but incarnations of an emerging dictatorship of the TCC. In the United States, the TCC was delighted with Trump's neo-liberal policies but divided over his brash, buffoon-like conduct and his neo-fascist political inclinations.[25] To paraphrase the great Prussian military strategist, Carl von Clausewitz, who famously said that "war is the extension of politics by other means," Trumpism, and to varying degrees other far-right movements around the world, were the extension of capitalist globalization by other means, namely by an expanding global police state and a neo-fascist mobilization.

Its nationalist discourse notwithstanding, the Trump regime was not opposed to capitalist globalization (he was himself a member of the TCC) but in fact pursued a program of neo-liberalism on steroids and "globalization by other means,"[26] involving an intensification of neo-liberalism in the United States together with a heightened role for the state in subsidizing transnational capital accumulation in the face of stagnation and overaccumulation. Trump's populism and protectionism had little policy substance; it was almost entirely symbolic—hence the significance of his fanatical "build the wall" rhetoric, symbolically essential to sustain a social base for which the state can provide little or no material bribe. Such "symbolic capital," as French sociologist Pierre Bourdieu would call it, is necessary under these conditions to reproduce material rule of the TCC and its agents.[27] There is indeed a mounting backlash against capitalist globalization among the popular and working classes and more nationally oriented sectors of the elite, as well as from right-wing populists, as evidenced in the rise of right-wing populist movements throughout Europe that call for a withdrawal from globalization processes. These developments underscore the highly conflictive nature of global capitalism and uncertainty as to further globalization in the face of the explosive contradictions and the widespread opposition that it generates.

When Trump did impose tariffs on imported steel and aluminum in 2018, and then further tariffs the following year, for instance, he was opposed by much of the TCC and the political elite in the United States, including much of his own Republican Party and even sectors of the steel industry that relied on cheaper imported steel for the production of intermediate and finished steel products.[28] Indeed, support for the tariffs came principally from trade union bureaucrats; Trump's move was really about appeasing his restless working-class social base. Recall, as well, that his predecessors, from Clinton, to Bush, and then to Obama, all closely identified with neo-liberal globalization, also imposed tariffs at one point or another in their administrations. More generally, the tendency under way towards an expansive global police state, neo-fascist mobilization, and schizophrenic crisis management, were quite evident well before Trumpism and were not tied to it.

Twenty-first-century fascism cannot be understood as a nation-state project in this age of global capitalism—in the sense not that it could not take hold in a single nation-state but that its impulse springs from the crisis brought about by a capitalist globalization that has integrated all nation-states into the circuits of global capital and involves a transnational mobilization of far-right and neo-fascist forces. This is important because much recent discussion on neo-fascism frames it in just such terms and emphasizes nationalism as an immanent feature of fascism. Yet as I have emphasized above, and in distinction to the twentieth century, the current nationalist discourse among far-right groups is entirely political-ideological insofar as the programmatic content of far-right forces such as Trumpism and others seeking to win the state is decidedly not national but global, albeit under the changing conditions of crisis and the breakdown of hegemony.

Neo-fascist groups in civil society such as the white nationalists in the United States may promote an inward national program, but these civil society groups by themselves do not amount to fascism as a system. For fascism to emerge, as I have already discussed, these groups must fuse with (transnational) capital and the state, yet the TCC has no interest in economic nationalism. Capitalist globalization has generated mass discontent and insecurity. The anti-globalism and economic nationalism espoused by far-right groups—and used by those groups in their recruitment strategies in a toxic mix of racism and nationalism—reflects real social discontent. The contradictions of capitalist globalization, as I have emphasized, take on distinct political expressions, including the rise of a far Right bidding for state power and new political alliances and coalitions that threaten to tear asunder ruling-class consensus around globalization. The pretense of economic nationalism disrupts global supply chains and undermines TCC interests. It opens up severe splits in ruling blocs, erodes the ruling groups' capacity to rule, and heightens the political crisis.

Beyond the United States, an International of twenty-first-century fascism seemed to be emerging. Far-right and neo-fascist groups around the world, for instance, celebrated the October 2018 electoral victory of Brazilian fascist Jair Bolsonaro. Former Trump advisor and neo-fascist organizer Steven Bannon served as an advisor to the Bolsonaro campaign,[29] while Italy's extreme-right interior minister Matteo Salvini declared in an exuberant tweet that was shared by U.S. neo-Nazi leader Richard Spencer that "even in Brazil, the citizens have sent the Left packing." *The Guardian* of London warned in its headline coverage that "Trump joy over Bolsonaro suggests new rightwing axis in Americas and beyond."[30] Beyond such political agents of twenty-first-century fascism as Bannon or Salvini, the TCC had banked on Bolsonaro and was delighted with his victory. As in the United States under Trump, Bolsonaro proposed the wholesale privatization and deregulation of the economy, opening up the Amazon to lumber, mining and transnational agribusiness interests, regressive taxation and general austerity, alongside mass repression and criminalization of social movements and vulnerable communities opposed to this program. The day after Bolsonaro's victory, noted one observer, the "world's capitalists are salivating over the new investment opportunities" that Bolsonaro promises.[31] Capital markets and Brazilian funds spiked on the world's stock exchanges the day after his electoral victory. Here we see the "wages of fascism" for a global capitalism in crisis.

Global Reformism: Saving Capitalism from Itself

There is growing alarm among reformist elements of the transnational elite that worsening inequalities threatens the stability of global capitalism and that there must be some sort of redistribution. These elites have been scrambling to find ways to reform the system in order to save capitalism from itself and from more radical challenges from below. In 2017, Mark Bertolini, the CEO of Aetna, a $250 billion healthcare company, warned, "Doing nothing, in the current model around capitalism, will destroy capitalism. When 65 percent of people under the age of 35 believe that socialism is a better model, we have a problem. So unless we change it, it will change—and maybe not in a good way."[32] These concerns may become more widespread as the system spirals into deeper crisis. "A crisis exists, sometimes lasting for decades," observed Gramsci. "This means that incurable contradictions have come to light within the structure and that the political force positively working to preserve the structure itself are nevertheless striving to heal these contradictions, within certain limits."[33] Marx and Engels similarly noted in *The Communist Manifesto* that elements among the capitalist class are "desirous of redressing social grievances in order to secure the continued existence" of their rule.[34]

Unlike the neo-fascist response to the crisis, the reformist strategy calls for imposing some restraint on the immediate goal of profit making in the interests of securing the overall stability of capitalist rule. In the view of the reformers, it is not the capitalist system itself but its particular institutional organization that is to blame for inequalities. They believe the system can be reformed by policies such as those proposed by Thomas Piketty in *Capital in the Twenty-First Century*,[35] a book received upon its release in 2013 by wild enthusiasm on the part of the academic, media, and political establishment precisely because it converged with the reformist agenda of a rising number of transnational elites and intelligentsia. The would-be reformers call for a limited re-regulation of global market forces, mildly redistributive measures such as increased taxes on corporations and the rich, a more progressive income tax, the reintroduction of social welfare programs, and a "green capitalism."[36] They were also concerned that extreme levels of inequality would undermine the prospects for growth and profit making. The Organization of Economic Cooperation and Development (OECD), the club of the 34 richest countries, for instance, warned in a 2015 report that the "global inequality gap" has "reached a turning point." The report did not have much to say about the social injustice that such inequality represents, nor about the mass suffering it brings about. It did, however, highlight that "high inequality drags down growth," and recommended raising taxes on the rich.[37]

Tellingly, some of the very economists and policy makers who designed the neo-liberal program and pushed it on the world through such transnational state institutions as the World Bank, and the International Monetary Fund, and the U.S. and other powerful national states, are now leading critics of "market fundamentalism," a phrase first coined by George Soros. A Hungarian-born billionaire financier and speculator, Soros achieved notoriety in 1992 when he threw the British economy into a tailspin by unloading some $10 billion worth of pounds onto international currency markets, making him a profit of $1 billion overnight. The Wall Street tycoon first coined the phrase "market fundamentalism" in his best-selling 1998 book, *The Crisis of Global Capitalism*, which argued that blind faith in market forces was leading to widening inequalities and ongoing crises that threatened the stability of the system.[38] Another leading voice among the reformers is Joseph Stiglitz, who as senior vice president and chief economist of the World Bank from 1997 and 2000, helped impose neo-liberalism around the world, but then came out against neo-liberalism in the wake of the 1997–98 Asian financial crisis. More recently, Lawrence Summers joined the ranks of the reformers. Previously, he displayed impeccable neo-liberal logic in 1991 by claiming, as chief economist at the World Bank, that dumping toxic waste in Third World countries would bring economic benefits. "I have always thought that the under-populated countries in Africa are vastly UNDER-polluted [*sic*]," wrote Summers, "their air quality is probably vastly inefficiently low compared to Los Angeles or Mexico City." From the World Bank, Summers went on to design free trade and other neo-liberal policies for the Clinton and then later the Obama administrations.[39] Fast forward to 2012; Summers argued that escalating inequality should be tempered because it is fueling a growing disillusionment with capitalism.[40]

Perhaps most emblematic of the neo-liberals-cum-reformers is Jeffrey Sachs. As a consultant for international financial institutions and governments Sachs designed and imposed the very first neo-liberal structural adjustment program, on Bolivia, in 1985. The program decimated Bolivia's poor: purchasing power dropped by 70 percent nearly overnight, unemployment shot up to 25 percent as thousands were fired and strikes made illegal, and throwing millions into untold hardship as nearly all social welfare benefits were swept away.[41] The succession of mass popular uprisings against Sachs's program eventually culminated in the indigenous revolution that brought Evo Morales to the presidency in 2006. From Bolivia, Sachs went on to pioneer the "shock program" of structural adjustment in Russia following the collapse of the Soviet Union, resulting in an overnight drop of 50 percent in the GDP, a tenfold increase in poverty and a spike of 75 percent in the mortality rate for workers. He drafted programs for the transition to capitalism in Poland and elsewhere in Eastern Europe, including overnight austerity and the wholesale transfer to private banks and corporations of large blocs of formerly state assets.

As global capitalism entered into crisis, these and other one-time apostles of neo-liberalism have framed the public agenda on global poverty and inequality. Their books have become best-sellers and standard texts in university courses.[42] They have helped to establish the hegemony of a mildly reformist discourse within this agenda that actually embraces the continuation of a campaign to open up the world to transnational capital within a new framework of transnational regulation and mild redistribution through taxation and limited social safety nets. As case in point, the reformers promoted the United Nation's Millennium Development Goals (Sachs served as chief UN strategist for the Goals), which were promulgated with much fanfare in 2000 at the United Nations Millennium Summit. The Goals put forth a set of eight development goals to be achieved by 2015, among them: a reduction by half the proportion of people living in extreme poverty and who suffer from hunger; universal primary education; a reduction by two-thirds the mortality rate among children under five and by three-quarters the maternal mortality rate; halt and reverse the incidence of major diseases; promote gender equality and the empowerment of women, and so on. However, the prescription put forth to achieve these lofty goals was based on a more thoroughgoing privatization of health and educational systems, further freeing-up of the market from state regulations, greater trade liberalization and more structural adjustment, and the conversion of agricultural lands into private commercial property—in other words, an intensification of the very capitalist development that has generated the social conditions to be eradicated.

The transnational elite reformers appear now to pin their hopes on the possibility that the global economy can be regenerated and further crisis averted through large-scale investment in worldwide infrastructure and in a "green capitalism" that involves environmental technologies. "Unlike accumulation by repression, green capitalism has the capacity to restore a degree of democratic legitimacy and incorporate important sectors of the environmental and social movements into a new hegemonic bloc," argues Jerry Harris in a reply to my analysis of militarized accumulation:

> Talk of a Green New Deal is rapidly spreading in U.S. media and polit-ical circles [while] the Chinese state and the country's green energy private sector have begun to exert leadership. Combined with the One Belt One Road project to build massive new infrastructure throughout the Global South, a new strategic direction for transnational capital-ism begins to appear, one which is in harmony with the imperatives of growth and markets.[43]

It is certainly plausible that digitalization or a "green capitalism" will unleash a new round of capitalist expansion that could temporarily offset the crisis of overaccumulation. However, even assuming that "green capitalism" is not an oxymoron and may actually forestall ecological holocaust,[44] such expan-sion would not necessarily push back the threat of a global police state. For that to happen it would have to involve a worldwide redistribution of wealth downward that could diminish global inequalities, exclusion, and immiseration, and therefore attenuate the system's imperative of expand-ing social control and repression. Absent such a redistribution, there is no reason to expect that TCC investment in a private, for-profit alterna-tive energy industry or infrastructure would resolve the plight of surplus humanity and the precariat.[45] Similarly, it is certainly *feasible* that digitali-zation may have a different impact on the global economy and global labor than that discussed in Chapter 2, or that reform policies may counter the current tendency towards the expansion of surplus and precarious labor. This is to say that whether or not a global police state becomes entrenched is contingent on the outcome of the struggle among social forces and their distinct political projects.

The hope placed in a "green capitalism" embraced by enlightened elites, in this regard, reflects liberal approaches that tend to assume that the crisis of humanity can be resolved without a confrontation with the powers that be in global society, and that groups and classes whose interests are fundamentally antagonistic can be brought together in some unified project on the basis of moral persuasion or an appeal to reason. The underlying assumption seems to be that those who rule over us need only be enlightened by this appeal to ethics and reason—or that they need only be told that a course other than global police state is in their own long-term strategic interests—rather than a struggle to build counter-power from below and dethrone these rulers. Yet it must be reiterated time and again that it is capital's implacable drive to accumulate that leads it to plunder the environment, to expropriate land and resources, to waste and pillage communities everywhere, and to impose a global police state to contain the explosive contradictions of an out-of-control system.

This all comes down not to technical considerations such as green technology or politics from above, as reformist elites become aware of the threat of ecological collapse, but to *the outcome of social and class struggle*. Redistribution and ecology must be forced on the system through mass struggle from below. Let us recall that the original New Deal in the United States, from which the Green New Deal movement in that country takes inspiration, was *forced* on the ruling groups by mass working-class struggles. Alliances with reformers among the transnational elite may be important, but so too is pushing beyond the reformist approach to the global crisis. This approach is entirely inadequate because it bypasses the questions of *power* and of corporate control over the planet's productive resources that are at the very heart of global capitalism and its crisis. Any resolution to this crisis requires a radical redistribution of wealth *and power* downward to the poor majority of humanity. Social justice requires a measure of transnational social governance over the global production and financial system as a necessary first step in this radical redistribution, which in turn must be linked to the transformation of class and property relations and a struggle for what ultimately must be an eco-socialism.

Widening splits among the ruling classes and the unraveling of the post-WWII international order open up new possibilities for those from below struggling for more far-reaching change to seek strategic political alliances. What position should the Left and progressive forces put forward with regard to the reformist elite? The threat of neo-fascism and ecological collapse poses the need for broad class alliances, or united front politics. Historically, such fronts have subordinated the Left to the reform-oriented and "democratic" bourgeoisie. We need urgently to build a united front

THE GLOBAL POLICE STATE

against fascism to push back the global police state. But any strategy of broad anti-fascist alliances is also *necessarily a fight against the TCC*. Efforts to forge such a united front must foreground a clear and sharp analysis of global capitalism and its crisis. It must strive for popular and working-class forces to exercise their hegemony over any such alliances.

History has shown us that the major changes have come at times of acute crisis, when the ruling groups are divided, and when there are powerful mass social movements from below. The major reform movements of the 1930s and the 1960s, for instance, came out of militant mass struggles placing demands on the state and elites for radical change. If particular corporate groups (e.g., the alternative energy industry) and reformist elements among the transnational elite can be brought on board a project of radical transformation this is both welcome and necessary, but not at the expense of substituting an anti-capitalist and socialist agenda with a liberal agenda of mild reform. This is *not* an argument against reform. We must fight for any and every reform that helps people survive the depredations of global capitalism and that pushes forward environmental policies and democratic liberties. But given the depth and nature of the crisis, I am not convinced that this time around anything short of the overthrow of capitalism can prevent our destruction.

Revitalizing the Left

As capitalist crisis throws more people into uncertain futures, socialism appears to be increasingly viewed in a favorable light, especially among youth. In the United States, where anti-communism and the celebration of capitalist individualism has long dominated popular consciousness, one 2019 survey found that 61 percent of U.S. citizens between the ages of 18 and 24 viewed socialism in a positive light, as well as over 50 percent of millennials.[46] Dominant groups have taken notice of the increasingly popularity of socialism. In his 2019 State of the Union speech, U.S. President Donald Trump declared that the United States would "never be a socialist country," while Speaker of the House Nancy Pelosi repeatedly declared that "We [the Democrats] are capitalists."[47] The TCC has also taken notice. In a 2019 letter to the bank's shareholders, the head of JP Morgan, billionaire Jamie Dimon, attacked socialism as "a disaster" that produces "stagnation, corruption, and authoritarianism"[48] (seemingly oblivious to the fact that global capitalism is producing chronic stagnation, widespread corruption, and a free fall into authoritarianism). These spokespeople from the ruling groups would certainly have no reason to speak about socialism were it not back on the popular agenda.

How to get to eco-socialism? As socialism regains its popularity, there has recently been an explosion of works in the English language on what a post-capitalism future may look like and how we would get there.[49] But we are far indeed from moving from the ideas put forth in these works to mass socialist movements around the world. We are "now in the phase of the 'autumn of capitalism' without this being strengthened by the emergence of 'the people's spring' and a socialist perspective," contended Samir Amin in 2018.[50] It is true that the failure of elite reformism and the unwillingness of the transnational elite to challenge the predation and rapaciousness of global capital have helped to open the way for the far-right response to the crisis. The political and economic elite, if they are unable to stabilize capitalism through moderate reform, will be all too willing to turn to authoritarianism and neo-fascism to secure capitalist control. And if a program of mild reform alongside capitalist globalization fails to resolve the plight of masses of people, some of these masses will embrace the neo-fascist alternative in a desperate bid for stability, as is now happening. If the Right has been deft to draw on the well-known nationalist, populist, xenophobic, and racist repertoire to channel rising anxieties and transform mass anti-systemic sentiment into support for neo-fascist and authoritarian programs, we cannot lay all the blame on the failure of elite reform. The Right has in part been empowered to do so by the failure of the Left to develop and defend a viable alternative.

A global revolt has spread since the 2008 collapse, ranging from Occupy Wall Street, Black Lives Matter, the immigrant rights movement, the Dakota Access Pipeline protests, and fast food workers' struggles in the United States, to the leftist parties Podemos and Syriza in Europe, Extinction Rebellion in the United Kingdom, the Yellow Vest movement in France, the Arab Spring in the Middle East and North Africa, the Shack Dwellers' Movement and other poor people's campaigns in South Africa, the radical Chilean student movement, mass worker struggles in India and China, and the uprising against the military regime in the Sudan, among many others. This global revolt has certainly been uneven. It has come in waves that are often followed by repression, cooptation, and dissipation. Some of these, such as the Arab Spring movements, have taken tragic turns, while far-right forces have been able to mobilize mass discontent as well. In many of these revolts, social movements seem to have been clear on what they are struggling against—the Mubarak dictatorship in Egypt, austerity in Europe, the privatization of education in Chile, the 99%, and so on. But in many cases, the absence of a concrete, viable socialist-oriented program and of political organizations that could push such a program has helped the dominant groups and their representatives to undercut the revolt.

These lessons are brought home in Latin America, where the "Pink Tide" (left turn) that took place early in the new century raised great hopes and expectations. The Pink Tide governments were swept to power in elections that took place on the heels of mass rebellions against neo-liberalism. These governments challenged and even reversed the most glaring components of the neo-liberal program. Yet the structural power of transnational capital, and especially of global financial markets, over the effort by states and social movements to undertake transformations is enormous and pushed the Pink Tide states to accommodate these markets. These structural constraints along with U.S. and local right-wing hostility cannot be underestimated. Nonetheless, and leftist rhetoric aside, the Pink Tide governments based their strategy on a vast expansion of raw material production in partnership with foreign and local contingents of the TCC.

The model of "assistencialism" which was developed involved social assistance programs based on capturing and redistributing surplus generated by an expansion of mining, carbon-based energy resources, large-scale agribusiness, and mega-infrastructural projects to extract these resources and export them to the world market, rather than by a more fundamental transformation of property relations or a more direct challenge to the prerogatives of transnational capital. With the exception of Venezuela during the height of the Bolivarian Revolution, what stood out was the absence of any shift in basic property and class relations despite changes in political blocs, a discourse in favor of the popular classes, and an expansion of social welfare programs. The spread of transnational corporate mining and agro-industry brought about a greater concentration of land and capital and heightened the structural power of the TCC over leftist states. As a result, the Pink Tide countries became ever more integrated into the transnational circuits of global capitalism and dependent on global commodity and capital markets.

The popular masses were clamoring for more substantial transformations. The turn to the Left did open up space for these masses to push forward their struggles. Yet states often suppressed demands from below for deeper transformation in their drive to attract transnational corporate investment and expand extractivist accumulation. These states demobilized social movements, absorbing their leaders into the government and the capitalist state, and subordinated their mass bases to the Left parties' electoralism. Because there were no more substantial structural transformations that could address the root causes of poverty and inequality, these social programs were subject to the vagaries of global markets over which the Pink Tide states exercised no control. Once the 2008 world financial crisis hit, they came up against the limits of redistributive reform within the logic of global capitalism. The extreme dependence on raw materials exports threw these countries into economic turmoil when global commodities markets collapsed, undermining governments' abilities to sustain social programs and generating political tensions that helped fuel popular protest and open up space for a right-wing resurgence.[51] There emerged an evident disjuncture throughout Latin America—*symptomatic of the worldwide phenomenon on the Left*—between mass social movements that are at this time resurgent, and the institutional and party Left that has lost the ability to mediate between the masses and the state with a viable project of its own.

These observations point to a broader discussion on why the Left's response to crisis has been so weak relative to that of the far Right that I cannot explore here. In the West, a part of the story is the embrace by significant portions of the Left of the limitations set by postmodern identitarian politics that celebrated a world of "differences" and endless fragmentation, in which capitalism, at most, became "just another" among the multiplicity of oppressive systems. Although the heyday of postmodernism may have passed, the political behavior patterns that came with it is still very much present in popular social justice struggles in the West. What Reed regards as "infrapolitics," that flows from celebrating this fragmentation and romanticizing "everyday resistance," makes it impossible to build any type of unity around a common program.[52] Similarly, Srnicek and Williams critique "folk politics" in their study *Inventing the Future*. "Under the sway of folk-political thinking, the most recent cycle of struggles—from anti-globalization to anti-war to Occupy Wall Street—has involved the fetishization of local spaces, immediate actions, transient gestures, and particularisms of all kinds," they observe. "Rather than undertake the difficult labor of expanding and consolidating gains, this form of politics has focused on building bunkers to resist the encroachments of global neoliberalism. In doing so, it has become a politics of defense, incapable of articulating or building a new world." The utopian potentials "inherent in twenty-first-century technology," they conclude, "cannot remain bound to a parochial capitalist imagination: they must be liberated by an ambitious left alternative." Yet leftist movements often eschew programs and organizations that involve representation: "Leftist movements under the sway of folk politics are not only unlikely to be successful—they are in fact incapable of transforming capitalism."[53]

Such identitarian politics should *not be confused* with struggles against particular forms of exploitation and oppression that different groups face. Ethnic, racial, gender, and sexual oppression are not tangential but constitutive of capitalism. There can be no general emancipation without liberation from these forms of oppression. But the inverse is just as critical: all the particular forms of oppression are grounded in the larger social order of global capitalism that perpetually regenerates these oppressions. Postmodern narratives and identitarian politics alienated a whole generation of young people in the late twentieth and early twenty-first centuries from embracing a desperately needed Marxist critique of capitalism at the moment of its globalization. The best identitarian politics can aspire to are symbolic vindication, diversity (often meaning diversity in the ruling bloc), non-discrimination in the dominant social institutions, and equitable inclusion and representation *within* global capitalism.

The transnational elite was all too willing to embrace such a politics of "diversity" and "multiculturalism" in the wake of the mass struggles of the 1960s and 1970s as a strategy to channel the struggle for social justice and anti-capitalist transformation into non-threatening demands for inclusion, if not outright cooptation. The strategy served to eclipse the language of the working and popular classes and of anti-capitalism. It helped to derail ongoing revolts from below. To beat back the descent into global police state and twenty-first-century fascism, we need to bring together the multiplicity of fragmented struggles, which requires moving beyond identitarian and "folk" politics. As vital rebellion now breaks out everywhere, it is urgent to revitalize a Marxist critique of global capitalism and its crisis as a guide to an emancipatory working-class politics that can win over the would-be social bases of twenty-first-century fascism.

This challenge is ironically facilitated by globalization, which has also helped generate deeper organic linkages between the oppressed and exploited across national and regional borders, giving rise to a truly global working class. This working class in all its diversity, and whose 3.2 billion members in countless ways pursue everyday survival strategies and mount resistance to exploitation and oppression, must become the major agent in the struggle against the global police state and for a socialist future. Already globalization has helped generate an emerging transnational unionism. "Globalization may have opened as many doors as it closed," notes Munck. "At the most basic level, the globalization of communication has countered one of the most formidable barriers to global action. With email, social media, and other online platforms, workers enjoy better tools to organize across countries." Indeed, he concludes, "globalized capitalism may have created the basis for a new global working class, not only in material conditions but also in consciousness."[54] In recent years, workers from many different countries have joined transnational unions, sometimes through mergers of what were national-based unions and at other times by forming entirely new worker organizations. The International Trade Union Confederation brought together 207 million workers from 163 countries in 2019. The IndustriALL global union, a merged industrial global union, had in that year 50 million members and 800 affiliated national unions around the world.[55]

Beyond those formally organized, as digitalization continues to fragment and individuate the labor process, a key challenge for the reconstruction of emancipatory projects is solidarity among workers who experience individuated isolation with those who face extreme vulnerability in precarious employment and those who are excluded and therefore not in a position to withdraw their labor. The conditions that the lumpenprecariat face, combined with the isolation and individuated nature of cognitive workers, suggest that the axis of class consciousness and collective agency surely must involve a shift from isolated points of production to everyday life, communities, and the political system. How do we link a politics of everyday life to projects of collective emancipation beyond the local, keeping in mind the fragmentation of struggles, whether at the local or world level, that are always specific and conducted in particular places and subject-matters, such as ecology, women's rights, social services, and community demands? Any fight-back will have to challenge exclusion and struggle against precarious work arrangements alongside the more traditional struggles of those who may be formally employed. The repertoire of global working-class and popular struggles must involve strategies, in addition to strike activity, for the widespread disruption of the system, insofar as those excluded cannot fight by withdrawing their labor.

A hopeful sign of what may be to come in this fight-back took place on May 8, 2019. On that day, Uber drivers in cities around the world went on strike to protest low wages that the company pays its drivers and against their status as "independent contractors," which allows the multi-billion-dollar company to avoid providing health care, pension, or any other benefits, and to shift to the drivers themselves the burden of maintaining the means of production (their cars). Billed as the opening salvo in an emerging labor movement of "gig workers", the worker action was notable on four accounts. First, it involved precisely those precarious workers whose labor places them at the very cutting edge of global economy, the so-called "platform" or "gig economy." Second, it was truly global, with reports of work stoppages from the United States, Brazil, Australia, Nigeria, Costa Rica, Kenya, the United Kingdom, and elsewhere, suggesting a hitherto unseen transnational coordination and solidarity. Third, the workers clearly understood how to confront capital: their stoppage was timed to take place on the same day as Uber's Initial Public Offering (IPO) and may have been responsible for the IPO's disappointing results.[56] Finally, the action showed that even the most atomized workers as those in the ride-hailing industry are—or may become—conscious of their collective interests and able to collectively confront capital.

A New International?

In my view, if we are to face the onslaught of the neo-fascist Right, the Left worldwide must urgently renovate a revolutionary project and a plan for re-founding the state. It must do so across borders under an umbrella forum that puts forth a minimum program around which popular and working-class forces can unite, and that establishes mechanisms to articulate struggles across nations and regions to coordinate a fight-back against the ravages of a predatory global capitalism. Such a forum or organization must be for and by these global working and popular classes, one that is not open to the TCC and its agents, that is explicitly opposed to global capitalism, that is predicated on system change, and that puts forth a minimum program and a renewed socialist vision that incorporates the idea of an ecological socialism. Eco-socialism is predicated on a fundamental proposition: achieving ecological equilibrium and an environment favorable to life is incompatible with capitalism's expansive and destructive logic. A non-ecological socialism is a dead end, and a non-socialist ecology cannot confront the present ecological crisis.[57]

In fact, a number of calls have gone out in recent years for the formation of a new world party or International.[58] Just a month before his untimely death, the political economist Samir Amin published a call for the establishment of a global Fifth International in a "Letter of Intent for an Inaugural Meeting of the International of Workers and Peoples."[59] The World Social Forum (WSF) was founded in 2001 as a "movement of movements" in the wake of the late twentieth-century upsurge of struggles against globalization. It brought together hundreds, perhaps thousands of social movements from around the world in annual meetings to network and share the experience of their varied struggles. However, the WSF explicitly rejected a political program and thus contributed to the separation of left political parties and organizations from mass social movements. For a fight-back to be successful, we need to build a program around which a united front against fascism can be organized.

Whereas the First, Second, Third, and Fourth Internationals were all umbrella international organizations for socialist political parties, the WSF prohibited political parties from participating. I concur with Amin that we need to "establish a new Organization and not just a 'movement'" or a "discussion forum." Any new forum, in my view, must incorporate both social movements and left political organizations and parties. This is to say that a new International would be distinct from the first four and also from the WSF, which was an international of social movements only. Commitment to a minimum program and to joining forces around such a program with political parties may be tough for social movements to swallow. It is true, as those who shy away from building or even working with left political organizations observe, that the "vanguardist" model of revolution in the twentieth century (as an aside—this was less due to Lenin's approach than to a fetishization of that approach) involved control of social movements from below by political parties that sought to snuff out their autonomy, and moreover, that some left political organizations in and out of the government in the new century continue to seek such control over social movements from below.

Any new International will have to deal with the matter of elections and of the capitalist state. We have learned that subordinating the popular agenda to winning elections will only set us up for defeat, even if we must participate in electoral processes when possible and expedient, and even as the electoral arena may be a strategic space of struggle. But we have also learned from recent experience of the leftist party Syriza in Greece and the Pink Tide governments in Latin America, as well as social democratic governments that came to office around the world in the late twentieth century, that once a left force wins government office (which is *not the same as state power … state power is imposed structurally by transnational capital*), it is tasked with administering the capitalist state and its crisis and is pushed into defending that state and its dependence on transnational capital for its reproduction, which places it at odds with the same popular classes and social movements that brought it to power.

Clearly, a new International must put forth a model of revolutionary struggle in which social movements from below exercise complete autonomy from political parties and from states that may be captured by such parties. If the Left attempts to control or place brakes on mass mobilization and on autonomous social movements from below, if it suppresses the demands of the popular masses in the name of "governance," pragmatism, or electoral strategies, it will be betraying what it means to be the Left. It is only such mass mobilization from below that can impose a counterweight to the control that transnational capital and the global market exercise from above over capitalist states around the world. The matter is one of the ability of autonomous mass social movements from below to *force* states to undertake transformations that challenge the prerogatives of transnational capital. This in turn involves rethinking the triangular relations among states, left parties, and mass social movements as part of any revitalized left program. We need a global organizational framework that can help close the disjuncture between the resurgence of mass social movements and the institutional or party Left.

I have strived in this study to provide a theoretical understanding of the system of global capitalism and the processes of transformation that this system is currently experiencing. A renewed socialist Left cannot be at the political forefront of the global revolt if, as Elbaum reminds us, it is not at the same time at the intellectual forefront of the study of global capitalism.[60] To reiterate, as the popular revolt breaks out everywhere, we must put forward a revitalized Marxist critique of global capitalism and its crisis *as a guide to an emancipatory working-class politics that can win over the would-be social bases of twenty-first-century fascism and establish a working-class hegemony in the revolt.* What are the fissures in the system? What is the structure of power and how are the ruling groups organized worldwide? What viable forms of struggle from below for system change does this new epoch offer? And critically, how can a revolutionary ecological socialist movement play a critical role in the global revolt?

We must remember that the dictatorship of transnational capital is *reactive.* It is the breakdown of global capitalist hegemony that has prompted the TCC to impose a global police state. When the next big economic collapse hits, the Left and resistance forces from below must be in a position to seize the initiative and to push back at the global police state. Capital may be on a tactical offensive, but it is at this time on the strategic defensive, insofar as it is responding to a crisis that it cannot resolve. Can we turn its strategic defensive into *our* strategic offensive?

Notes

Introduction: "George Orwell Got It Wrong"

1. Liza Elliott, *Everything is Known* (Birmingham, AL: Red Camel Press, 2018), pp. 9–10, 20–21.
2. Nick Srnicek and Alex Williams, *Inventing the Future: Postcapitalism and a World Without Work* (London: Verso, 2016, revised edition), pp. 1–2.

Chapter 1   Global Capitalism and its Crisis

1. What appears here is a very brief summary of my extensive writings on capitalist globalization as a new epoch with its particular, novel features. See, among other works: William I. Robinson, *A Theory of Global Capitalism: Production, Class, and State in a Transnational World* (Baltimore, MD: Johns Hopkins University Press, 2004); Robinson, *Global Capitalism and the Crisis of Humanity* (New York: Cambridge University Press, 2014); *Robinson, Into the Tempest: Essays on the New Global Capitalism* (Chicago, IL: Haymarket, 2018).
2. Eric Hobsbawm, *The Age of Extremes* (New York: Vintage Books, 1994), p. 277; original emphasis.
3. The best single work on the anatomy of the global economy, and especially the global production system, remains Peter Dicken, *Global Shift: Mapping the Changing Contours of the World Economy* (New York: Gilford, 2015, seventh edition).
4. On the TCC, see discussion in Robinson's works cited in endnote 1. For a concise summary of the development of this concept and a review of the scholarship, see William I. Robinson and Jeb Sprague, "The Transnational Capitalist Class," in Mark Juergensmeyer, Saskia Sassen, and Manfred Steger (eds.), *Oxford Handbook of Global Studies* (New York: Oxford University Press, 2018).
5. For detailed discussion and data on this point, see various chapters in Robinson, *Into the Tempest*. Here is one interesting, though hardly the most significant, indicator: of the world's 2,158 billionaires in 2017, 631 came from North America (which includes Mexico), 475 from Greater China, 414 from Western Europe, 295 from South-East Asia, 163 from Eastern Europe, 84 from Central and South America, 52 from the Middle East and Africa, 43 from Oceana. See Rupert Neate, "World's Billionaires Became 20% Richer in 2017, Report Reveals," *The Guardian*, 26 October 2018, accessed on 9 April 2019 at www.theguardian.com/news/2018/oct/26/worlds-billionaires-became-20-richer-in-2017-report-reveals.

6. Stefania Vitali, James B. Glattfelder, and Stefano Battiston, 2011. "The Network of Global Corporate Control," *PLOS ONE*: 1–36, accessed on 12 March 2019 at www.scribd.com/doc/70706980/The-Network-of-Global-Corporate-Control-by-Stefania-Vitali-James-B-Glattfelder-and-Stefano-Battiston-2011.

7. Peter Phillips, *Giants: The Global Power Elite* (New York: Seven Stories Press, 2018), p. 35.

8. There is simply no precedent in the history of capitalism of such an extreme concentration and centralization of capital on a global scale, nor for the speed with which it has proceeded. From 1998 to 2018, TNCs spent $44 trillion in takeovers. In the United States, corporate profits rose from 1.9 percent of the GDP in 1978 to 4.5 percent in 2018. See Patrick Foulis, "An Age of Giants," *The Economist*, 17 November 2018, special report insert, pp. 4–5.

9. Phillips, *Giants*, p. 153.

10. Phillips, *Giants*, p. 162.

11. This is not the place to review that literature. But see, inter alia: summary discussion and references in Robinson, *Global Capitalism and the Crisis of Humanity*, Chapter 4; Andrew Kliman, *The Failure of Capitalist Production: Underlying Causes of the Great Recession* (London: Pluto, 2011); and "Radical Perspectives on the Crisis," a website of dozens of articles on Marxist crisis theory and the contemporary crisis. Available at: https://sites.google.com/site/radicalperspectivesonthecrisis/finance-crisis. Michael Roberts, *Marx 200* (London: Lulu, 2009).

12. There is a vast and very rapidly growing literature on the global ecological crisis. See, inter alia: John Bellamy Foster, Richard York, and Brett Clark, *The Ecological Rift: Capitalism's War on the Earth* (New York: Monthly Review Press, 2011); Jason W. Moore, *Capitalism in the Web of Life: Ecology and the Accumulation of Capital* (London: Verso, 2015); Naomi Klein, *This Changes Everything: Capitalism Versus the Climate* (New York: Simon & Schuster, 2015); Elizabeth Kolbert, *The Sixth Extinction: An Unnatural History* (New York: Picador, 2015).

13. On this threat, see Marek Hrubec, "Threat of Limited Nuclear War," *Critical Sociology*, 19 September 2018, online edition, accessed on 15 March 2019 at https://journals.sagepub.com/eprint/R48PdvKxqIVIQTvnbveb/full.

14. Joah Bierman, "A Sales Pitch for Davos Globalists," *Los Angeles Times*, 26 January 2018, p. A3.

15. "We have a strong U.S. exposure," explained one ArcelorMittal executive. "We are a net beneficiary of the trade actions": Jeff Stein, "Trump Cozies Up to Steel," *Los Angeles Times*, 8 October 2018, p. A12. While the Trump rhetoric railed against "foreign" car imports and in favor of "U.S. cars," in fact, the auto industry in the United States is intricately tied to a global web of factories, supply chains, and international markets, and the enmeshing of capitals across auto TNCs so thorough, that lays waste to the view that there are national car companies that compete with one another internationally. Honda produces and sells more cars in the United States than General

Motors, which produces and sells the majority of its cars outside the United States. For these details, see Thomas Suh Lauder, "Can Trump's Plans Rev Up the U.S. Auto Industry?," *Los Angeles Times*, 20 February 2017, p. A8.

16. Most observers, fixed as they are in a state-centrism and a nation-state/interstate framework of analysis that attributes global political dynamics to capitalist competition among nation-states, fail to see how the political contradictions generated by the legitimacy crisis feed back into economics. As *The Economist* reported in its 26 January 2019 report, "Snowbalization," U.S.-based TNCs were hesitant to swap board seats with Chinese-based firms, not because of inter-corporate competition but because they feared that President Donald Trump's political rhetoric over China would bring them political flak. In this way, politics becomes overdetermined. The state-centric approaches violate the fundamental methodological tenet of Marxism, for which the story starts with the mode of production and class relations, from which state forms derive.

17. While I cannot elaborate here, the arguments put forward by critics—usually dogmatic Marxists—of my theory of global capitalism and my take on these matters of geo-politics, Trumpism, etc., commit three fallacies (that is, they violate three rules of critical social science inquiry): 1) they fail to see the need to distinguish surface appearance from underlying essence—that is, they take surface appearance at face value; 2) they see contradictions such as those I have discussed here as anomalies that belie my arguments rather than seeing contradictions as an intrinsic aspect of reality; 3) they critique my arguments without addressing the data I put forward to support them and often without presenting any counter-data. To take but one example of this third fallacy, it may *appear* that U.S.–Chinese competition has to do with competition between U.S. and Chinese capitalist groups, but there is vast, ever-growing, and at this point overwhelming evidence of the transnational integration of what appear in popular parlance as "U.S." and "Chinese" companies. Suffice it to point out here that even Chinese state-owned enterprises (SOEs) are themselves cross-invested with TCC groups from all over the world. A full 86 percent of SOEs that list A shares on stock markets have less than 20 percent state ownership and corporate investors from around the world are heavily invested in these SOEs (see, e.g., the report by Daniel H. Rosen, Wendy Leutert, and Shan Guo, "Missing Link: Corporate Governance in China's State Sector," Asia Society/Rhodium Group, November 2018, accessed on 7 May 2019 at https://asiasociety.org/sites/default/files/inline-files/ASNC_Rhodium_SOEReport.pdf). And as Jerry Harris shows, the giant global financial institutions, including Blackrock, J.P. Morgan, Barclays, and UBS, as well as public and private investment banks around the world, such as the European Investment Bank and the World Bank's International Finance Corporation, are all heavily invested in Chinese state-private banks. See "Who Leads Global Capitalism?: The Unlikely Rises of China," *Class, Race and Corporate Power*, 6(1), 2018, accessed on 7 May 2019 at https://digitalcommons.fiu.edu/cgi/viewcontent.cgi?referer=https://www.google.com/&httpsredir=1&article=1119&context=classracecorporatepower).

18. Klaus Schwab, "Global Corporate Citizenship: Working with Governments and Civil Society," *Foreign Affairs*, January–February 2008, pp. 108–109.
19. Karl Marx, "Wage Labor and Capital," in Robert C. Tucker (ed.), *The Marx-Engels Reader* (New York: W.W. Norton, 1978), p. 214.
20. There is a great deal of good literature on Fordism and Keynesianism. David Harvey's *The Condition of Post-Modernity* (Cambridge, MA: Blackwell, 1990), although somewhat outdated, remains an important statement on the subject. See also: Ash Amin (ed.), *Post-Fordism: A Reader* (Cambridge, MA: Blackwell, 1994), Robert W. Cox, *Production, Power, and World Order: Social Forces in the Making of History* (New York: Columbia University Press, 1987); William I. Robinson, *Global Capitalism and the Crisis of Humanity* (New York: Cambridge University Press, 2014).
21. Thomas Piketty demonstrates these swings in the profit rate in *Capital in the Twenty-First Century* (Cambridge, MA: Harvard University Press, 2014), figure 6.8, p. 227. The absolute volume of corporate profit worldwide amounted to $2 trillion in just the first quarter of 2019, nearly double the amount ten years earlier. See "Corporate Earnings: Earnings Reprieve," *The Economist*, 20 July 2019, p. 52.
22. Greg Sargent, "'There's Been Class Warfare for the Last 20 Years, and My Class has Won," *Washington Post*, 30 September 2011, accessed on 15 March 2019 at www.washingtonpost.com/blogs/plum-line/post/theres-been-class-warfare-for-the-last-20-years-and-my-class-has-won/2011/03/03/gIQApa FbAL_blog.html?utm_term=.486c085504e7.
23. For one account of this rising immiseration, see Gary Leech, *Capitalism: A Structural Genocide* (London: Zed, 2012).
24. Martin Ford, *The Rise of the Robots* (New York: Basic Books, 2015), p. 198.
25. Robert Cox and Eliza Rosenbaum, "The Beneficiaries of the Downturn," *New York Times*, 28 December 2008, accessed on 9 April 2019 at www.nytimes.com/2008/12/29/business/29views.html.
26. See Greg Jensen, Atul Narayan, Daniel Crowley, and Sam Green, "Peak Profit Margins? A Global Perspective," Bridgewater Associates, 27 March 2019, accessed on 24 April 2019 at www.bridgewater.com/research-library/daily-observations/peak-profit-margins-a-global-perspective/?fbclid=IwA RofnkRcMxDcG3oUaDCgRUz5UlE44vhHrfqy3011zNXYQvMJMDFl NKyTRXo.
27. Oxfam (London), *Wealth: Having It All and Wanting More*, online report accessed on 4 March 2018 at the Oxfam website: http://policy-practice.oxfam.org.uk/publications/wealth-having-it-all-and-wanting-more-338125.
28. *The Economist*, "The Problem with Profits," 26 March 2016, accessed on 2 February 2018 at www.economist.com/news/leaders/21695392-big-firms-united-states-have-never-had-it-so-good-time-more-competition-problem.
29. Anaele Pelisson and Graham Rapier, "This Chart Shows the 17 US Companies with the Biggest Piles of Cash," *Business Insider*, 4 December 2017, accessed on 2 February 2018 at www.businessinsider.com/chart-us-companies-with-largest-cash-reserves-2017-8.

30. *Nikkei Asian Review,* "Asia's Multinationals are Hoarding Cash Like Never Before," 28 September 2017, accessed on 15 April 2019 at https://asia.nikkei.com/Economy/Asia-s-multinationals-are-hoarding-cash-like-never-before2.

31. William I. Robinson, "Accumulation Crisis and Global Police State," *Critical Sociology,* March 2018, online edition available here: http://journals.sagepub.com/doi/abs/10.1177/0896920518757054.

32. U.S. General Accounting Office (GAO), "Federal Reserve System: Opportunities Exist to Strengthen Policies and Processes for Managing Emergency Assistance" (Washington, DC: GAO-11-696, July 2011).

33. The nuts and bolts of the new financial system and all its "instruments" are well explained by William K. Tabb, *The Restructuring of Capitalism in Our Time* (New York: Columbia University Press, 2012).

34. This is not the place to go into detail, but this comment must be tempered. In one sense, credit does contribute to the generation of new wealth. For instance, a bank may issue a mortgage that the customer uses to contract a construction firm and finance the building of a house. But this scenario is light years removed from the current global casino in which trillions of dollars are moved about independent of original wealth creation, and in which speculation in derivatives is often secondary, meaning that it is speculating on speculation.

35. Christian Marazzi, *The Violence of Financial Capital* (Bellinzona, Switzerland: Edizioni Casagrande, 2011); original emphasis.

36. Securities Industry and Financial Markets Association (SIMFA), *Simfa Fact Book 2018,* p. 51, table on "Global Bond Market Outstanding—Value," accessed on 15 April 2019 at www.sifma.org/wp-content/uploads/2017/08/US-Fact-Book-2018-SIFMA.pdf. See also "$100 Trillion Global Bond Bubble Poses 'Systemic Risk' to Financial System," *GoldCore,* 31 March 2015, accessed 17 March 2018 at www.goldcore.com/us/gold-blog/100-trillion-global-bond-bubble-poses-systemic-risk-to-financial-system/. The OECD has pointed to widespread growth of central government debt in OECD countries as a percentage of GDP. See Saskia Sassen, *Expulsions: Brutality and Complexity in the Global Economy* (Cambridge, MA: Harvard University Press, 2014), p. 21.

37. There are numerous works on dispossession through the new financial processes associated with the global economy. See, inter alia, my earlier work, William I. Robinson, *Global Capitalism and the Crisis of Humanity,* Saskia Sassen, *Expulsions: Brutality and Complexity in the Global Economy* (Cambridge, MA: Harvard University Press, 2014). David Harvey popularized his notion of "accumulation by dispossession" (which in turn is but an updating of the arguments of Rosa Luxemburg) in his two books, *The New Imperialism* (New York: Oxford University Press, 2003) and *A Brief History of Neoliberalism* (New York: Oxford University Press, 2005).

38. Akin Oyedele, "Americans Have $12.58 Trillion in Debt—Here's What it Looks Like," *Business Insider,* 17 February 2017, accessed on 2 February 2018 at www.businessinsider.com/us-household-debt-credit-ny-fed-q4-2016-2017-2.

39. Susan Soederberg, *Debtfare States and the Poverty Industry* (New York: Routledge, 2014).

40. On the $1 trillion credit-card debt figure, see Jennifer Surane, "U.S. Credit-Card Debt Surpasses Record Set at Brink of Crisis," *Bloomberg*, 7 August 2017, accessed 2 February 2018 at www.bloomberg.com/news/articles/2017-08-07/u-s-credit-card-debt-surpasses-record-set-at-brink-of-crisis. On delinquencies, see Pedro Nicolaci da Costa, "Americans are Having Trouble Paying Off Their Credit Cards—And it Could Spell Trouble for the Economy," *Business Insider*, 21 November 2017, accessed on 2 February 2018 at www.businessinsider.com/credit-card-delinquencies-a-red-flag-on-consumer-spending-2017-11.

41. For figures, see "Household Debt" chart at the OECD website, accessed on 2 February 2018 at https://data.oecd.org/hha/household-debt.htm, and for discussion see the recently unclassified OECD report, Christophe André, "Household Debt in OECD Countries: Stylized Facts and Policy Issues," OECD, Economics Department Working Papers No. 1277, 1 February 2016, accessed on 2 February 2018 at www.oecd.org/officialdocuments/publicdisplaydocumentpdf/?cote=ECO/WKP(2016)1&docLanguage=En.

42. Tom Hancock and Wang Xueqlao, "China's Millenials' Love of Credit Cards Raises Debt Fears," *Financial Times*, 5 August 2018, accessed on 12 April 2019 at www.ft.com/content/bb3166ea-8b1f-11e8-b18d-0181731a0340. In the 2010s, Chinese households became the largest credit-card users in the world, with over seven billion credit cards issued in that country. See Leanne Whalen and Gerry Shih, "Beijing's Blockade of U.S. Credit Card Companies May Finally End—Now That Chinese Companies Dominate," *Washington Post*, 21 January 2019, accessed on 12 April 2019 at www.washingtonpost.com/business/economy/beijings-blockade-of-us-credit-card-companies-may-finally-end--now-that-chinese-companies-dominate/2019/01/20/d52d8ad4-1354-11e9-803c-4ef28312c8b9_story.html?utm_term=.a0b9593a0a9.

43. Sameer Bhardwaj, "Indian Households' Debt Doubles in FY17–18," *Economic Times*, 28 January 2019, https://economictimes.indiatimes.com/wealth/borrow/indian-households-debt-doubles-in-fy17-18-what-are-we-borrowing-for-and-how-much/articleshow/67700374.cms?from=mdr.

44. David Scutt, "Global Debt Has Hit an Eye-Watering $215 Trillion," *Business Insider*, 4 April 2017, accessed on 2 February 2018 at www.businessinsider.com/global-debt-staggering-trillions-2017-4?&platform=bi-androidapp.

45. Doug Henwood, *Wall Street* (London: Verso, 1998), p. 36.

46. Although this is a notional (rather than actual) value (and moreover the vast majority of derivatives "cancel" each other out because they are "bets" on an event occurring that are offset by a comparative derivate "bet" on the event not occurring).

47. World Bank, World Development Indicators data base, 15 December 2017, p. 1, accessed on 2 February 2018 at http://databank.worldbank.org/data/download/GDP.pdf.

48. Gregory McLeod, "Forex Market Size: A Traders Advantage," *DailyFX*, 23 January 2014, accessed on 2 February 2018 at www.dailyfx.com/forex/ education/trading_tips/daily_lesson/2014/01/24/FX_Market_Size.html.

49. J.B. Maverick, "How Big is the Derivatives Market," *Investopedia*, 22 January 2018, accessed on 2 February 2018 at www.investopedia.com/ask/ answers/052715/how-big-derivatives-market.asp.

50. Larry Summers, "The Age of Secular Stagnation," *Foreign Affairs*, 15 February 2016, accessed on 2 February 2018 at http://larrysummers. com/2016/02/17/the-age-of-secular-stagnation/.

51. Manuel Castells, *The Rise of the Network Society*, Vol. I (New York: Blackwell, 1996), pp. 101–102.

52. United Nations Conference on Trade and Development (UNCTAD*)*, *Information Economy Report, 2017* (UNCTAD: Geneva, 2017), p. 17.

53. *The Economist*, "The Global List," 26 January 2019, p. 20.

54. Thomas Marois, "TiSA and the Threat to Public Banks," Transnational Institute (Amsterdam), April 2017, accessed on 2 February 2018 at www. tni.org/files/publication-downloads/tisa_and_the_threat_to_public_banks. pdf.

55. *The Economist*, "The Global List," 26 January 2019, p. 21.

56. Literature on the Fourth Industrial Revolution is considerable and is rapidly expanding. See, inter alia: Klaus Schwab, *The Fourth Industrial Revolution* (Geneva: World Economic Forum, 2016); Ford, *The Rise of the Robots*.

57. Patrick Foulis, "An Age of Giants," *The Economist*, 17 November 2018, special report insert, p. 7

58. Nick Srnicek, *Platform Capitalism* (Cambridge: Polity, 2017), p. 6. For more theoretical treatment on how digital capitalism has produced Internet (online) surveillance in the spheres of production, circulation, and consumption, see Thomas Allmer, *Toward a Critical Theory of Surveillance in Information Capitalism* (Frankfurt: Peter Lang GmbH, 2012).

59. Nick Srnicek, *Platform Capitalism* (Cambridge: Polity, 2017), p. 40.

60. Yasar Levine, *Surveillance Valley: The Secret Military History of the Internet* (New York: Public Affairs, 2018), p. 103.

61. Federal Reserve Bank of St. Louis, "Private Fixed Investment in Information Processing Equipment and Software" (graph compiled from U.S. Bureau of Economic Analysis), 2018, accessed on 15 April 2019 at https://fred. stlouisfed.org/series/A679RC1Q027SBEA.

62. *The Economist*, "Briefing: Business Under Trump," 26 May 2018, p. 24.

63. Pelisson and Rapier, "This Chart Shows the 17 US Companies with the Biggest Piles of Cash."

64. Nikkei Asian Review, "Asia's Multinationals are Hoarding Cash Like Never Before," 28 September 2017, accessed on 15 April 2019 at https:// asia.nikkei.com/Economy/Asia-s-multinationals-are-hoarding-cash-like-never-before2.

65. Melissa Parietti, "The Top 10 Technology Companies," *Investopedia*, 8 November 2018, accessed on 15 April 2019 at www.investopedia.com/

articles/markets/030816/worlds-top-10-technology-companies-aapl-googl.asp.

66. Kenneth Kiesnoski, *CNBC*, 8 March 2017, accessed on 2 September 2017 at www.cnbc.com/2017/03/08/the-top-10-us-companies-by-market-capitalization.html#slide=10. *The Economist* notes that "the titans"—the term it uses for the handful of tech companies that control the world market—"are the market itself, providing the infrastructure (or 'platforms') for much of the digital economy. Many of their services appear to be free, but users 'pay' for them by giving away their data. Powerful though they already are, their huge stock market valuations suggest that investors are counting on them to double or even triple in size in the next decade," *The Economist*, 20 January 2018, "Taming the Titans," p. 11.

67. *The Economist*, "The Global List," 26 January 2019, p. 20.

Chapter 2   Savage Inequalities: The Imperative of Social Control

1. Transcript of interview by *Real News Network*, 9 May 2018, accessed on 17 June 2018 at https://therealnews.com/stories/the-rich-have-escape-plan.

2. Adam Withnall, "Cartier Boss with \$7.5bn Fortune Says Prospect of the Poor Rising Up 'Keeps Him Awake at Night'," *Independent*, 10 June 2015, accessed on 12 June 2018 at www.independent.co.uk/news/business/cartier-boss-with-75bn-fortune-says-prospect-poor-rising-up-keeps-him-awake-at-night-10307485.html.

3. Oxfam (London), *Wealth: Having It All and Wanting More*, online report accessed on 4 March 2018 at the Oxfam website, http://policy-practice.oxfam.org.uk/publications/wealth-having-it-all-and-wanting-more-338125.

4. Oxfam, "Billionaire Fortunes Grew by \$2.4 Billion a Day Last Year as Poorest Saw Their Wealth Fall," Oxfam International, 21 January 2019, accessed on 14 March 2019 at www.oxfam.org/en/pressroom/pressreleases/2019-01-18/billionaire-fortunes-grew-25-billion-day-last-year-poorest-saw.

5. Michael Savage, "Richest 1% on Target to Own Two-Thirds of All Wealth by 2030," *The Guardian*, 7 April 2018, retrieved on 9 April 2018 at www.theguardian.com/business/2018/apr/07/global-inequality-tipping-point-2030.

6. Rupert Neate, "World's Billionaires Became 20% Richer in 2017, Report Reveals," *The Guardian*, 26 October 2018, accessed on 9 April 2019 at www.theguardian.com/news/2018/oct/26/worlds-billionaires-became-20-richer-in-2017-report-reveals.

7. Karl Marx, "Wage Labor and Capital," in Robert C. Tucker, *The Marx-Engels Reader* (New York: W.W. Norton, 1978), pp. 209–210.

8. Two overlapping schools of research into the historic determination of the capital-labor relation—known as the Regulation School and the Social Structures of Accumulation approach—have given us important theoretical schools for understanding how capital-labor relations have been shaped in particular historical circumstances. For an overview of Social Structures of Accumulation, see David M. Kotz, Terrence McDonough, and Michael

Reich, *Social Structures of Accumulation: The Political Economy of Growth and Crisis* (New York: Cambridge University Press, 1994). On the Regulation School, see, inter alia, Alain Lipietz, *Mirages and Miracles: Crisis in Global Fordism* (London: Verso Books, 1987). Both these schools emphasize waves of expansion and crisis in the world economy as the backdrop to how these relations are forged yet they typically focus on particular countries or regions, whereas here I focus on global capitalism as a whole.

9. A summary of these changes can be found in William I. Robinson, *A Theory of Global Capitalism: Production, Class, and State in a Transnational World* (Baltimore, MD: Johns Hopkins University Press, 2004), Chapter 1. More detailed exposition can be found in Peter Dicken, *Global Shift: Mapping the Changing Contours of the World Economy* (New York: Gilford, 2015, seventh edition).

10. Among the many studies on precarious labor, see Adrián Sotelo Valencia, *The Future of Work: Super-Exploitation and Social Precariousness in the 21ˢᵗ Century* (Chicago, IL: Haymarket, 2018, reprint edition).

11. Guy Standing, *The Precariat: The New Dangerous Class* (New York: Bloomsbury, 2011) popularized but did not coin this term. Standing's social democratic conception is seriously flawed. He suggests that the precariat is "a new class" rather than part of the working class experiencing a condition faced by expanding sectors of the working class. He does not conceive of this condition as an instance of the capital-labor relation. He takes a First World/Eurocentric view of the global precariat—what we could call "methodological Westernism"—and appears unable to combine class with racial, ethnic, and cultural analysis. His liberal orientation does not critique *capital* as a relation causal to the rise of the precariat as much as the state as an inadequate regulator of the market and its social consequences. For discussion, see inter alia, "Roundtable on the Precariat," *Great Transition Initiative*, October 2018, www.greattransition.org/publication/roundtable-precariat.

12. Karl Marx, *Capital*, Vol. I, in Robert C. Tucker, *The Marx-Engels Reader* (New York: W.W. Norton, 1978), pp. 431, 433–434.

13. Richard Freeman, "The Great Doubling: The Challenge of the New Global Labor Market," *The Globalist* online magazine, March 5, 2010, www.theglobalist.com/StoryId.aspx?StoryId=4542. The ILO placed the global working class in 2017 at 3.2 billion. International Labor Organization, *World Employment and Social Outlook 2017: Sustainable Enterprises and Jobs: Formal Enterprises and Decent Work* (Geneva: ILO, 2017), accessed on 29 May 2019 at https://ilo.org/wcmsp5/groups/public/---dgreports/---dcomm/---publ/documents/publication/wcms_579893.pdf.

14. International Labor Organization, "World Employment and Social Outlook: Trends 2019" (Geneva: ILO, 2019), p. 5, accessed on 10 October 2019 at https://www.ilo.org/wcmsp5/groups/public/---dgreports/---dcomm/---publ/documents/publication/wcms_670542.pdf.

15. See, for example, Dawn Paley, *Drug War Capitalism* (Oakland, CA: AK Press, 2014).

16. There is a vast literature on these modern-day processes of primitive accumulation around the world. See, inter alia: Mike Davis, *Planet of Slums* (London: Verso, 2006); Garry Leech, *Capitalism: A Structural Genocide* (London: Zed, 2012); Jan Breman, Kevan Harris, Ching Kwan Lee, and Marcel van der Linden (eds.), *The Social Question in the Twenty-First Century: A Global View* (Berkeley: University of California Press, 2019); Saskia Sassen, *Expulsions: Brutality and Complexity in the Global Economy* (Cambridge, MA: Harvard University Press, 2014). The 200-million-acre figure is from Sassen, pp. 80. The story of farmers' suicides in India can be found in Leech.

17. Mike Davis, *Planet of Slums*, p. 1.

18. *National Geographic*, "Why Cities are Leading the Way," February 2018, p. 5.

19. Samir Amin, "World Poverty, Pauperization and Capital Accumulation," *Monthly Review* (online), 1 October 2003, accessed on 10 April 2019 at https://monthlyreview.org/2003/10/01/world-poverty-pauperization-capital-accumulation/?utm_source=Tricontinental+English&utm_campaign=8c9cb1b47e-EMAIL_CAMPAIGN_2019_02_01_02_25&utm_medium=email&utm_term=0_9fbe436b65-8c9cb1b47e-190488593.

20. *World Migration Report 2015* (Geneva: IOM, 2015), p. 2.

21. International Labor Organization, *Global Employment Trends 2011: The Challenge of Job Recovery* (Geneva: ILO, 2011).

22. International Labor Organization, "World Employment and Social Outlook: Trends 2019" (Geneva: ILO, 2019), p. 2, accessed on 10 October 2019 at www.ilo.org/wcmsp5/groups/public/---dgreports/---dcomm/---publ/documents/publication/wcms_670542.pdf.

23. International Labor Organization, *World Employment Report 1996–97* (Geneva: ILO/United Nations, 1997).

24. As cited in Mike Davis, *Planet of Slums*, p. 199.

25. See, inter alia, Jeremy Rivkin, *The End of Work: The Decline of the Global Labor Force and the Dawn of the Post-Market Era* (New York: Putnam, 2004, updated edition); Stanley Aronowitz and William DiFazio, *The Jobless Future*, Second Edition (Minneapolis: University of Minnesota Press, 2010); Martin Ford, *The Rise of the Robots* (New York: Basic Books, 2015); and most recently, Nick Srnicek, *Inventing the Future: Postcapitalism and a World Without Work* (London: Verso, 2016).

26. Russ Mitchell and Tracey Lien, "Rides in Uber Robot Vehicles at Hand," *Los Angeles Times*, 19 August 2016, p. A1.

27. Natalie Kitroeff, "An Acceleration in Automation," *Los Angeles Times*, 25 September 2016, pp. A1, A14, A15.

28. Tom Huddleston Jr., "Walmart Will Soon Use Hundreds of A.I. Robot Janitors to Scrub the Floors of US Stores," *CNBC*, 5 December 2018, accessed on 19 April 2019 at www.cnbc.com/2018/12/05/walmart-will-use-hundreds-of-ai-robot-janitors-to-scrub-store-floors.html.

29. Daron Acemoglu and Pascual Restrepo, "Robots and Jobs: Evidence from US Labor Markets," *NBER Working Paper Series*, Working Paper 23285,

National Bureau of Economic Research, March 2017, accessed on 17 April 2019 at www.nber.org/papers/w23285.pdf.
30. "A Giant Problem," *The Economist*, 17 September 2016, p. 9.
31. This is *not* hyperbole. Reports of the renewed spread of slave labor around the world are now numerous. For the Brazilian case, see for example, Thais Lazzeri, "Investigation Reveals Slave Labor Conditions in Brazil's Timber Industry," *Mongabay*, 13 March 2017, accessed on 16 April 2017 at https://news.mongabay.com/2017/03/investigation-reveals-slave-labor-conditions-in-brazils-timber-industry/. On seafood slaves in Asia, see Robin McDowell, Margie Mason, and Martha Mendoza, "Stranded and Enslaved," *Associated Press* (online), 25 March 2015, accessed on 16 April 2019 at https://interactives.ap.org/2015/seafood-from-slaves/. See also the entire book by Kevin Bales, *Disposable People: New Slavery in the Global Economy* (Berkeley: University of California Press, revised edition, 2004). On women trafficked and enslaved for the global sex trade, see the award-winning documentary *Nefarious: Merchant of Souls*, directed by Benjamin Nolot, although one would want to dismiss the documentary's conclusion that salvation from this slavery lies in Christ (rather than a global mobilization against it).
32. Karl Marx, *Capital, Volume I*, in Tucker (ed.), *The Marx-Engels Reader*, pp. 423, 425.
33. Karl Marx, *Capital, Vol. III* (excerpt), in Tucker (ed.), *The Marx-Engels Reader*.
34. Karl Marx, *Capital, Volume I*, in Tucker, (ed.), *The Marx-Engels Reader*, pp. 422, 424, 429–430; original emphasis.
35. Karl Marx, *The Eighteenth Brumaire of Louis Napoleon*, 1952, p. 38, pdf of Internet edition from Marxist Internet Archive, available here: www.marxists.org/archive/marx/works/download/pdf/18th-Brumaire.pdf.
36. Franz Fanon, *The Wretched of the Earth* (New York: Grove Press, 1963). Fanon writes: "So the pimps, the hooligans, the unemployed, and the petty criminals throw themselves into the struggle like stout working men … The prostitutes too, and the maids who are paid two pounds a month, all who turn in circles between suicide and madness, will recover their balance, once more go forward, and march proudly in the great procession of the awakened nation" (p. 130).
37. See Chris Booker, "Lumpenization: A Critical Error of the Black Panther Party," in Charles E. Jones, *The Black Panther Party Reconsidered* (Baltimore, MD: Black Classic Press, 2005), pp. 337–362.
38. Joff P.N. Bradley and Alex Taek-Gwan, "On the Lumpen-Precariat-To-Come," *TripleC*, 16(2), 2018: 639–646, quote from p. 641.
39. It is important to note that surplus humanity, the precariat, and the lumpenprecariat are contingent categories. Those whose labor is surplus may later become formally employed, and vice-versa. There is no real categorical separation of surplus and precarious labor. Marx's very concept of stagnant labor as long-term surplus labor outside of the capital circuit faces this problem. Unless this labor simply lies down to die, it must do something, formal or informal, licit or otherwise, to survive day to day, and in one way or

another this activity makes the individual not "excluded" in the strict sense. In part, Marx resolved the problem with the (unsatisfactory) category of the lumpenproletariat. These are not stable categories; they are slippery. More than anything, they are heuristic concepts that help us make sense of the restructuring of global capital and global labor.

40. See, inter alia, Emmanuel Ness, *Southern Insurgency: The Coming of the Global Working Class* (London: Pluto, 2015).

41. Aronowitz, *How Class Works*, p. 58.

42. ILO, *World Employment and Social Outlook 2017: Sustainable Enterprises and Jobs: Formal Enterprises and Decent Work*.

43. See, inter alia, discussion in Manuel Castells and Alejandro Portes (eds.), *The Informal Economy: Studies in Advanced and Less Developed Countries* (Baltimore, MD: Johns Hopkins University Press, 1989).

44. Eva Swidler, "Invisible Exploitation: How Capital Extracts Value Beyond Wage Labor," *Monthly Review*, 1 March 2018, https://monthlyreview. org/2018/03/01/invisible-exploitation/.

45. Susan Soederberg, *Debtfare States and the Poverty Industry* (New York: Routledge, 2014).

46. See, e.g., "The Corporate Landlord: The Institutionalization of the Single-Family Rental Market and Potential Impact on Renters," report by Homes for All Campaign of Right to the City Alliance, July 2014, accessed on 7 May 2019 at https://homesforall.org/wp-content/uploads/2014/07/corp-landlord-report-web.pdf.

47. Soederberg, *Debtfare States*, p. 27.

48. Soederberg, *Debtfare States*, p. 1.

49. Soederberg, *Debtfare States*, p. 78.

50. Soederberg, *Debtfare States*, p. 92.

51. The number of payday loan outlets in the United States grew from 10,000 in 2000 to 21,000 in 2004. By the second decade of the century, some 12 million people found themselves forced to take out payday loans to get through each month. Seventy percent of these borrowers used the loans to pay utility and credit-card bills, rent or mortgage payments, or to buy food, while another 15 percent turned to them to cover unexpected emergency expenses. Users often paid an effective annual percentage rate (APR) in excess of 300 percent. For these details, see Nick Bourke, Alex Horowitz, and Tara Roche, "Payday Lending in America: Who Borrows, Where They Borrow, and Why," PEW Charitable Trusts, July 2012, accessed on 15 April 2019 at www.pewtrusts.org/~/media/legacy/uploadedfiles/pcs_assets/2012/pewpaydaylendingreportpdf.pdf.

52. Marx, as cited in Soederberg, *Debtfare States*, pp. 33–34.

53. Soederberg, *Debtfare States*, p. 171.

54. For details, see William I. Robinson, "Sadistic Capitalism: Six Urgent Matters for Humanity in Global Crisis," *Truthout*, 12 April 2016, accessed on 9 May 2019 at https://truthout.org/articles/sadistic-capitalism-six-urgent-matters-for-humanity-in-global-crisis/.

55. This data from an IMF report was cited in Sassen, *Expulsions*, p. 24.

56. Robert Reich, *The Work of Nations: Preparing Ourselves for 21st Century Capitalism* (New York: Vintage, 1992); Michael Hardt and Antonio Negri, *Empire* (Cambridge, MA: Harvard University Press, 2001); Stanley Aronowitz, *How Class Works: Power and Social Movement* ((New Haven, CT: Yale University Press, 2003).

57. See "The Trials of Generation Y," *The Guardian*, series published in March and April 2016, multi-authored, accessed on June 17 2018 at www.theguardian.com/world/series/millennials-the-trials-of-generation-y. Note that the letter designation of generations is confusing as there are multiple letters in circulation for the same generation. In another article, those born after 1995 are referred to as "Generation Z." See Trévon Austin, "New Poll Shows American Youth are Increasingly Supportive of Socialism," World Socialist Website, 13 March 2019, accessed on 8 April 2019 at www.wsws.org/en/articles/2019/03/13/yout-m13.html.

58. Kristin Lord, "Here Come the Young," *Foreign Policy*, 12 August 2016, accessed on 16 June 2018 at http://foreignpolicy.com/2016/08/12/here-comes-the-young-youth-bulge-demographics/.

59. For these details, see "Digital Labor: The Human Cumulus," *The Economist*, 26 August 2017, p. 5.

60. *The Economist*, "The Changing Labor Market," 6 October 2018, p. 65.

61. Maresi Starzmann, "Academic Alienation: Freeing Cognitive Labor from the Grip of Capitalism," *ROAR Magazine*, 2 June 2018, accessed on 15 June 2018 from https://roarmag.org/essays/academic-alienation-cognitive-labor-capitalism/.

62. Bradley and Taek-Gwan, "On the Lumpen-Precariat-To-Come," p. 642.

63. Pierre Bourdieu, *Outline of a Theory of Practice* (Cambridge: Cambridge University Press, 1977), p. 95. There is a burgeoning literature on work, social organization, culture, and consciousness in the digital era that we cannot discuss here. But see, inter alia: Michael Betancourt's very important study, *The Critique of Digital Capitalism: An Analysis of the Political Economy of Digital Culture and Technology* (New York: Punctum Books, 2016); Bernard Stiegler, *Automatic Society: The Future of Work*, Vol. I (Cambridge: Polity, 2017).

64. For a excellent theoretical treatment of these matters, see Thomas Allmer, *Critical Theory and Social Media: Between Emancipation and Commodification* (New York: Routledge, 2017).

65. Martin Ford, *The Rise of the Robots* (New York: Basic Books, 2015).

66. For this data, see Maresi Starzmann, "Academic Alienation: Freeing Cognitive Labor from the Grip of Capitalism," *ROAR Magazine*, 2 June 2018, accessed on 15 June 2018 from https://roarmag.org/essays/academic-alienation-cognitive-labor-capitalism/.

67. Zack Friedman, "Student Loan Debt Statistics in 2019: A $1.5 Trillion Crisis," *Forbes*, 25 February 2019, accessed on 9 April 2019 at www.forbes.com/sites/zackfriedman/2019/02/25/student-loan-debt-statistics-2019/#4623941133fb.

68. Tom Petruno, "Corporate Giants Awash in Cash as Economy Picks Up," *Los Angeles Times*, 24 March 2010, pp. A1, A8.

69. Klaus Schwab, *The Fourth Industrial Revolution* (Geneva: World Economic Forum, 2016), p. 38. Schwab reiterates what many have already observed: About one-half of total employment in the U.S. is a risk of being automated, characterized by a more sweeping scope of job destruction at a much faster pace than such shifts experienced during earlier industrial/technological revolutions under capitalism.

70. Tracy Lien, "Serving Pizzas Made by Robots," *Los Angeles Times*, 6 July 2017, pp. C1, C5.

71. See, e.g., Dave Jamieson, "The Life and Death of an Amazon Warehouse Temp," *Huffington Post*, 21 October 2015, accessed on 2 September 2017 at http://highline.huffingtonpost.com/articles/en/life-and-death-amazon-temp/; Jim Edwards "Brutal Conditions in Amazon's Warehouses Threaten to Ruin the Company's Image," *Business Insider*, 5 August 2013, accessed on 2 September 2017 at www.businessinsider.com/brutal-conditions-in-amazons-warehouses-2013-8.

72. As cited in Ford, *The Rise of the Robots*, p. 12.

73. Nick Srnicek, *Platform Capitalism* (Cambridge: Polity, 2017), p. 79.

74. Ford, *The Rise of the Robots*, p. 107.

75. Schwab, *The Fourth Industrial Revolution*, p. 38.

76. Adrian Chen, "The Laborers Who Keep Dick Pics and Beheadings Out of Your Facebook Feed," *Wired*, 23 October 2014, accessed on 2 September 2017 at www.wired.com/2014/10/content-moderation/.

77. An UNCTAD reported estimated (p. 62) that more than 85 percent of all retail and service workers in Indonesia and the Philippines were at risk of losing their jobs to digital automation: United Nations Conference on Trade and Development (UNCTAD*), Information Economy Report, 2017* (UNCTAD: Geneva, 2017).

78. UNCTAD, *Information Economy Report, 2017*, p. 62.

79. Ford, *The Rise of the Robots*, p. 26.

80. Geoffrey Mohan, "A New Generation of Farmworkers: Robots," *Los Angeles Times*, 25 July 2017, pp. A1, A10.

81. Christian Parenti, *Tropic of Chaos: Climate Change and the New Geography of Violence* (New York: Nation Books, 2012), p. 47.

82. "World faces 'climate apartheid' risk, 120 more million in poverty: UN expert," *UN News*, 25 June 2019, accessed here on 26 June 2019: https://news.un.org/en/story/2019/06/1041261.

83. Emmie Martin, "The Government Shutdown Spotlights a Bigger Issue: 78% of US Workers Live Paycheck to Paycheck," *CNBC*, 9 January 2019, accessed on 16 April 2019 at www.msn.com/en-us/money/markets/the-government-shutdown-spotlights-a-bigger-issue-78percent-of-us-workers-live-paycheck-to-paycheck/ar-BBS1cbe.

84. Eurostat (the EU statistical agency), "People at Risk of Poverty or Social Inclusion," January 2019 news release, accessed on 29 April 2019 at

https://ec.europa.eu/eurostat/statistics-explained/index.php/People_
at_risk_of_poverty_or_social_exclusion.

85. On hunger and food insecurity, see Food and Agricultural Organization
(FAO) of the United Nations, "The State of Food Security and Nutrition
in the World," 2019, Rome, accessed on 20 June 2019 at www.fao.org/3/
ca5162en/ca5162en.pdf. For discussion on the global land grabs, see Julie
de los Reyes and Katie Sandwell (eds.), *Flexicrops: A Primer* (Amsterdam:
Transnational Institute, April 2018), accessed on 30 April 2019 at www.
tni.org/files/publication-downloads/flexcrops06.pdf. Also see: Phillips, *The
Global Power Elite*, pp. 31–32; Sassen, *Expulsion*, Chapter 2, "The New
Global Market for Land." I calculated the figure of several hundred billion
dollars and half a billion acres based on data provided in these three sources.
The extent to which the recent land grabs has turned land into an often-
speculative commodity is brought home by data that shows the percentage of
a country's total land that has been snatched up by TCC investors. Some of
the most affected countries are the Philippines, with 17.24 percent, Liberia,
with 5.83 percent, Indonesia with 3.75 percent, Sierra Leone with 6.88
percent, and so on. For the data on world hunger and poverty, see Philipps,
various sections, and United Nations Development Program. "Sustaining
Human Progress: Reducing Vulnerabilities and Building Resilience,"
Human Development Report, 2014, accessed on April 15, 2019, at http://hdr.
undp.org/sites/default/files/hdr14-report-en-1.pdf.

86. Alvin So, *Class and Class Conflict in Post-Socialist China* (Singapore: World
Scientific Printers, 2013), pp. 4–5.

87. So, *Class and Class Conflict in Post-Socialist China*, p. vii.

88. Even absent "total wars," we may note that at the start of the twentieth
century only 10–20 percent of war casualties were civilians, whereas this
number jumped to 50 percent in World War II and then to 80 percent at
the turn of the twenty-first century. As cited in Jeff Halper, *War Against the
People: Israel, the Palestinians and Global Pacification* (London: Pluto, 2015),
p. 21.

89. Davis, *Planet of Slums*, p. 119.

90. Cedric Johnson, "Who's Afraid on Left Populism?", *New Politics*, XVII(2),
Winter 2019, accessed on 7 May 2019 at https://newpol.org/issue_post/
whos-afraid-of-left-populism/.

91. Michelle Quinn, "Silicon Valley Grows Up (Sort of)," *National Geographic*,
February 2019, p. 125.

92. Stephen Graham, *Cities Under Siege: The New Military Urbanism* (London:
Verso, 2011), p. 96.

93. See Radley Balko, *Rise of the Warrior Cop: The Militarization of America's
Police Forces* (New York: Public Affairs, 2013).

94. As cited in Halper, *War Against the People*, p. 24.

95. Graham, *Cities Under Siege*, p. xxi.

96. Leigh Campoamor, "Lima's Wall(s) of Shame," *NACLA Report on the
Americas*, 51(1), 2019: 30.

97. Sassen, *Expulsions*, p. 36.

98. Antonio Gramsci, *Selections from Prison Notebooks* (New York: International Publishers, 1971), p. 263.
99. Human Rights Watch, "Global: 140 Countries Pass Counterterror Laws Since 9/11," 29 June 2012, accessed on 9 May 2019 at www.hrw.org/news/2012/06/29/global-140-countries-pass-counterterror-laws-9/11.
100. Zygmunt Bauman, *Globalization: The Human Consequences* (Cambridge: Polity Press, 1998, pp. 111–112).
101. Mark Jay, "Cages and Crises: A Marxist Analysis of Mass Incarceration," *Historical Materialism*, 27, 2019. The quote is on p. 17 and the figure of two-thirds is on p. 1.
102. As quoted in Jay, "Cages and Crises," p. 21.
103. "Denmark Plans Double Punishment for Ghetto Crime" *BBC News*, 27 February 2018, accessed on 16 June 2018 at www.bbc.com/news/world-europe-43214596.
104. "Statement on Visit to USA, by Professor Philip Alston, United Nations Special Rapporteur on Extreme Poverty and Human Rights," *United Nations Human Rights, Office of the High Commissioner*, 15 December 2017, accessed on 15 June 2018 at www.ohchr.org/EN/NewsEvents/Pages/DisplayNews.aspx?NewsID=22533.
105. Caitlin Yoshiko Kandil, "Anti-Homeless Laws Crop Up in Santa Ana, in Line with a Statewide Trend," *California Health Report*, 25 January 2018, accessed on 19 April 2019 at www.calhealthreport.org/2018/01/25/anti-homeless-laws-crop-santa-ana-line-statewide-trend/.

Chapter 3   Militarized Accumulation and Accumulation by Repression

1. Jeff Halper, *War Against the People: Israel, the Palestinians and Global Pacification* (London: Pluto, 2015), p. 231.
2. The executive, Naemeka Achebe, was Shell's general manager in Nigeria, as cited in Daniel Faber, "The Unfair Trade-Off: Globalization and the Export of Ecological Hazards," in Leslie King and Deborah McCarthy (eds.), *Environmental Sociology: From Analysis to Action* (Lanham, MD: Rowman and Littlefield, 2009), p. 186.
3. Paul A. Baran and Paul M. Sweezy, *Monopoly Capitalism: An Essay on the American Economic and Social Order* (New York: Monthly Review Press, 1966), p. 213.
4. Dwight D. Eisenhower, "Farewell Address—January 17, 1961," retrieved on 19 April 2019 from the database of U.S. presidential speeches, "American History from Revolution to Reconstruction," at www.let.rug.nl/usa/presidents/dwight-david-eisenhower/farewell-address-january-17-1961.php.
5. Van Le, "Private Prisons Are Making Millions By Helping to Deport Longtime Immigrant-Americans—And They're Positively Gleeful About it," *America's Voice*, 9 August 2017, accessed on October 26, 2017 at https://americasvoice.org/blog/private-prisons-see-future-profits/.

6. David S. Cloud and Noah Bierman, "Lobby Effort Ignited Space Force," *Los Angeles Times*, 19 August 2018, pp. A1, A14–15.

7. Joseph A. Schumpeter, *Capitalism, Socialism and Democracy* (New York: Harper and Row, 1943).

8. For the above details and figures, see William I. Robinson, "Global Capitalist Crisis and Trump's War Drive," *Truthout*, 19 April 2017, accessed on 14 April 2019 at www.truth-out.org/opinion/item/40266-global-capitalist-crisis-and-trump-s-war-drive. It is hard to understate just how unprecedented is the escalation of U.S. military spending after 9/11. The Project on Defense Alternatives noted in 2010: "When divided by the number of full-time military personnel, DoD budget authority appears remarkably stable throughout the 25-year period 1983–1998. It begins to rise in 1998, accelerating sharply with the onset of the Iraq War. For 2007–2010, it averaged $459,000 per full-time person in uniform. This is 78% higher than the Reagan peak, 95% higher than in 1989, and nearly three times the inflation-adjusted peak during the Vietnam era." See its report, "An Undisciplined Defense: Understanding the $2 Trillion Surge in US Defense Spending," Project on Defense Alternatives, 18 January 2010, p. 2.

9. For instance, in his study *Spies for Hire: The Secret World of Intelligence Outsourcing* (New York: Simon and Schuster, 2008), Tim Shorrock places the non-reported budget for 16 intelligence and covert operations agencies in the United States at $60 billion annually.

10. CISION PR Newswire, "Global Homeland Security and Public Safety Market Report 2019—Market is Expected to Grow from $431 Billion in 2018 to $606 Billion in 2014," 6 February 2019, accessed on 2 May 2019 at www.prnewswire.com/news-releases/global-homeland-security--public-safety-market-report-2019---market-is-expected-to-grow-from-431-billion-in-2018-to-606-billion-in-2024-at-a-cagr-of-5-8-300790827.html.

11. P.W. Singer, *Corporate Warriors: The Rise of the Privatized Military Industry* (Ithaca, NY: Cornell University Press, 2003), p. 232.

12. For the above details and figures, see Robinson, "Global Capitalist Crisis and Trump's War Drive."

13. Tim O'Connor, "U.S. Has Spent Six Trillion Dollars on Wars that Killed Half a Million People Since 9/11, Report Says," *Newsweek*, 14 November 2018, accessed on 9 April 2019 at www.newsweek.com/us-spent-six-trillion-wars-killed-half-million-1215588. The *Newsweek* article cites a report released by Brown University's Watson Institute for International Relations and Public Affairs.

14. Nafeez Ahmed, "Unworthy Victims: Western Wars Have Killed Four Million Muslims Since 1990," *Middle East Eye*, 8 April 2015, accessed on 22 April 2019 at https://www.middleeasteye.net/opinion/unworthy-victims-western-wars-have-killed-four-million-muslims-1990.

15. David Vine, "Where in the World is the U.S. Military?," *Politico Magazine*, July/August 2015, accessed on 3 February 2018 at www.politico.com/magazine/story/2015/06/us-military-bases-around-the-world-119321.

16. See in particular Chapter 3, "Beyond the Theory of Imperialism," in William I. Robinson, *Global Capitalism and the Crisis of Humanity* (New York: Cambridge University Press, 2014). An abridged version of this essay is to be found in Robinson, *Into the Tempest: Essays on the New Global Capitalism* (Chicago, IL: Haymarket, 2018).
17. Robert D. Blackwill, "Defending Vital U.S. Interests: Policy Prescriptions for Trump," *Foreign Policy*, 25 January 2017, accessed on 17 April 2019 at https://foreignpolicy.com/2017/01/25/defending-vital-u-s-interests-policy-prescriptions-for-trump/. Blackwill was National Security Advisor to U.S. President George W. Bush and wrote the article as a senior fellow at the Council on Foreign Relations. Pentagon analysts are quite clear on the role of U.S. military intervention around the world as creating the conditions necessary for global capitalism to function unimpeded. One of the clearest statements in this regard is Thomas P.M. Barnett, *The Pentagon's New Map: War and Peace in the Twenty-First Century* (Berkeley, CA: Berkeley Publishers, 2005). Barnett is a "military geostrategist" at the U.S. Naval War College.
18. Zi Yang, "Privatizing China's Defense Industry," *The Diplomat*, 7 June 2017, accessed on 17 April 2019 at https://thediplomat.com/2017/06/privatizing-chinas-defense-industry/.
19. For these details, see Peter Phillips, *Giants: The Global Power Elite* (New York: Seven Stories Press, 2018), Chapters 2 and 5.
20. Phillips, *Giants: The Global Power Elite*, p. 228.
21. Madeline K. Albright and Stephen J. Hadley, "Middle East Strategy Task Force: Final Report of the Co-Chairs" (New York: Atlantic Council, 2016), p. 5. The report recommended for 2020–25 the deployment of more forces overseas, units trained in urban operations, overseas staging areas, and counter-drone systems. For 2040 and beyond, it called for independent small mobile fighting companies in the military and through private military companies, as well as training with virtual reality, battlefield robotics, and artificial intelligence.
22. This estimate is from Neta C. Crawford, "The Iraq War: Ten Years in Ten Numbers," *Foreign Policy*, 20 March 2013, accessed on 23 April 2019 at https://foreignpolicy.com/2013/03/20/the-iraq-war-ten-years-in-ten-numbers/.
23. Frank Slijper, "Guns, Debt and Corruption: Military Spending and the EU Crisis," Transnational Institute (Amsterdam), April 2013, p. 2, accessed on 24 April 2019 at www.tni.org/files/download/eu_milspending_crisis.pdf.
24. Andrew Rettman, "EU Figures Show Crisis-Busting Arms Sales to Greece," *EU Observer*, 7 March 2012, accessed on 14 April 2019 at https://euobserver.com/foreign/115513.
25. "What Percentage of the Global Economy Consists of the Oil and Gas Drilling Sector?," *Investopedia*, 20 September 2018, accessed on 20 June 2019 at www.investopedia.com/ask/answers/030915/what-percentage-global-economy-comprised-oil-gas-drilling-sector.asp.
26. See, for example, on just how central oil has been to the U.S. in recent years and how integrated it is to the global police state as I have laid it out here.

27. Javier E. David, "US-Saudi Arabia Seal Weapons Deal Worth Nearly $110 Billion Immediately, $350 Billion Over 10 Years," *CNBC*, 22 May 2017, accessed on 14 April 2018 at www.cnbc.com/2017/05/20/us-saudi-arabia-seal-weapons-deal-worth-nearly-110-billion-as-trump-begins-visit.html.

28. For all this data, see Aude Fleurant, Alexandra Kuimova, Nan Tian, Pieter D. Wezeman, and Seimon T. Wezeman, "The SIPRI Top 100 Arms-Producing and Military Services Companies," 2017 annual report of the Stockholm International Peace Research Institute (SIPRI), p. 1 and compiled from pp. 2–5, Table 1, accessed on 3 February 2018 at www.sipri.org/sites/default/files/2017-12/fs_arms_industry_2016.pdf. Note that information on the earnings for 26 of these 100 companies were unavailable and therefore the actual figure would be higher, perhaps substantially higher. The half-trillion-dollar figure for developing country arms purchases comes from Halper, *War Against the People*, p. 193.

29. Jeremy Scahill, *Blackwater: The Rise of the World's Most Powerful Mercenary Army* (New York: Nation Books, 2007). Blackwater later changed its name to Academi.

30. Leo Shane III, "Contractors Outnumber U.S. Troops in Afghanistan 3-to-1," *Military Times*, 17 August 2016, accessed on 10 April 2019 at www.militarytimes.com/2016/08/17/report-contractors-outnumber-u-s-troops-in-afghanistan-3-to-1/. In Iraq, the low-end estimate [because it did not include private military contractors stationed to protect installations] of 180,000 private military and related service contractors in Iraq exceeded the number of U.S. combat troops, which in 2007 numbered 160,000 soldiers. T. Christian Miller, "Contractors Outnumber Troops in Iraq," *Los Angeles Times*, 4 July 2007, accessed on 10 April 2019 at www.latimes.com/archives/la-xpm-2007-jul-04-na-private4-story.html.

31. Mark Landler, Eric Schmitt, and Michael R. Gordon, "Trump Aides Recruited Businessmen to Devise Options for Afghanistan," *New York Times*, 10 July 2017, accessed on 18 April 2019 at www.nytimes.com/2017/07/10/world/asia/trump-afghanistan-policy-erik-prince-stephen-feinberg.html?module=inline.

32. Singer, *Corporate Warriors*.

33. Singer, *Corporate Warriors*, p. 9.

34. Singer, *Corporate Warriors*, p. 18.

35. Singer, *Corporate Warriors*, pp. 15–16.

36. Moshe Schwartz and Joyprada Swain, "Department of Defense Contractors in Afghanistan and Iraq: Background and Analysis," *Congressional Research Service*, 13 May 2011, accessed on 10 April 2019 at www.fas.org/sgp/crs/natsec/R40764.pdf.

37. Shawn Engbrecht, *America's Covert Warriors: Inside the World of Private Military Contractors* (Washington, DC: Potomac Books, 2011), p. 18.

38. Gareth Porter, "America's Permanent-War Complex," *The American Conservative*, 15 November 2018, accessed on 7 May 2019 at www.theamericanconservative.com/articles/americas-permanent-war-complex/.

39. William Langewiesche, "The Chaos Company," *Vanity Fair*, 18 March 2014, accessed on 10 April 2019 at www. vanityfair.com/news/ business/2014/04/g4s-global-security-company. P.W. Singer, *Corporate Warriors: The Rise of the Privatized Military Industry* (Ithaca, NY: Cornell University Press, 2007).
40. Phillips, *Giants*, p. 260.
41. Phillips documents these connections at considerable length in Chapter 5 of *Giants*. See pp. 228–239.
42. As cited in Porter, "America's Permanent-War Complex." The familiar "revolving door" between the Pentagon and arms contractors sped up in the wake of the 2001 attacks. The percentage of three- and four-star generals who left the Pentagon to take jobs as consultants or executives with military contractors, which was already at 45 percent in 1993, climbed to 80 percent by 2005.
43. For these details, see Shorrock, *Spies for Hire*, pp. 12–14, 23.
44. For these details, see Tim Shorrock, "5 Corporations Now Dominate Our Privatized Intelligence Industry," *The Nation*, 8 September 2016, accessed on 24 April 2019 at www.thenation.com/article/five-corporations-now-dominate-our-privatized-intelligence-industry/.
45. Singer, *Corporate Warriors*, p. 69.
46. IBT Staff Reporter, "The Largest Company You've Never Heard Of: G4S and the London Olympics," *International Business Times*, 8 June 2012, accessed on 17 April 2019 at www.ibtimes.com/largest-company-youve-never-heard-g4s-london-olympics-739232.
47. Niall McCarthy, "Private Security Outnumbers the Police in Most Countries Worldwide," *Forbes*, 31 August 2017, accessed on 10 April 2019 at www.forbes.com/sites/niallmccarthy/2017/08/31/private-security-outnumbers-the-police-in-most-countries-worldwide-infographic/#46a7d34a210f.
48. "People in Detroit are Hiring Paramilitary Guards Because They've Lost Faith in the Government," *Vice News*, 2 May 2019, accessed on 3 May 2019 at https://news.vice.com/en_ca/article/43jw33/people-in-detroit-are-hiring-paramilitary-guards-because-theyve-lost-faith-in-government.
49. For these details, see, inter alia, Graham, *Cities Under Siege*; Halper, *War Against the People*.
50. The rise of the doctrine of "full spectrum dominance" is discussed, inter alia, in F. William Engdahl, *Full Spectrum Dominance: Totalitarian Democracy in the New World Order* (Boxboro, MA: Third Millennium Press, 2009).
51. Report by National Immigration Project, Immigrant Defense Project, and Mijente, "Who's Behind ICE? The Tech and Data Companies Fueling Deportations," October 2018, p. 58, accessed on 22 April 2019 at www.nationalimmigrationproject.org/PDFs/community/2018_23Oct_whos-behind-ice.pdf.
52. Yasar Levine, *Surveillance Valley: The Secret Military History of the Internet* (New York: Public Affairs, 2018).
53. Levine notes how in the 1960s radicals saw the development of computers and early information technology, including the Internet, as military and

corporate tools of surveillance and social control. The industry "would spin this mythology [of corporate and military-controlled CIT as tools of liberation] through the 1980s and 1990s, helping obfuscate the military origins of computer and networking technologies by dressing them up in the language of 1960s acid-dropping counterculture. In this rebranded world, computers were the new communes: a digital frontier," that would herald the creation of a better world and personal empowerment. See p. 113. He also identifies the important role in this propaganda campaign played by the magazine *Wired*, which was as much a corporate tool of the emerging tech sector as *Forbes* and *Fortune* is for the TCC as a whole: "Among the pantheon of techno-heroes promoted by the magazine's pages were right-wing politicians and pundits, telecom tycoons, and corporate lobbyists who swirled around Washington to whip up excitement and push for a privatized corporate-dominated Internet and telecommunications infrastructure," p. 135.

54. Levine, *Surveillance Valley*, p. 5.

55. Levine, *Surveillance Valley*, pp. 171–172.

56. In 1986, only 1 percent of the world's information was digitalized and 25 percent in 2000. By 2012, notes Zuboff, "the progress of digitalization and datafication (the application of software that allows computers and algorithms to process and analyze raw data) with new and cheaper storage technologies had translated 98 percent of the world's information into a digital format": Shoshona Zuboff, *The Age of Surveillance Capitalism: The Fight for a Human Future at the New Frontier of Power* (New York: Public Affairs, 2019), pp. 187–188.

57. Zuboff, *The Age of Surveillance Capitalism*, pp. 53. Zuboff's liberal analysis suffers from a fundamental flaw. She is on to something in seeing "surveillance capitalism" as unprecedented in the development of capitalism. Yet she falls back into the illusion that surveillance has undermined a happier era of "democratic capitalism" and "market democracy." She lashes out against "raw surveillance capitalism" because she sees it "as a threat to capitalism itself" (p. 194). Surveillance capitalism in this narrative is simply a rogue form that has undermined the "democratic capitalism" of an earlier era.

58. Andrea Peterson, "Former NSA and CIA Director Says Terrorists Love Using Gmail," *Washington Post*, 15 September 2013, accessed on 18 May 2019 at www.washingtonpost.com/news/the-switch/wp/2013/09/15/former-nsa-and-cia-director-says-terrorists-love-using-gmail/?utm_term=.e10fe2c6374b.

59. Levine, *Surveillance Valley*, pp. 178, 180.

60. Eugene Kim, "Amazon CEO Jeff Bezos Joins a Group led by ex-Google CEO Eric Schmidt to Advise the Pentagon," *Business Insider*, 1 August 2016, accessed on 27 April 2019 at www.businessinsider.com/amazon-ceo-jeff-bezos-joins-pentagon-defense-advisory-board-2016-8.

61. Frank Konkel, "The Details About the CIA's Deal with Amazon," *The Atlantic*, 17 July 2014, accessed on 27 April 2019 at www.theatlantic.com/

technology/archive/2014/07/the-details-about-the-cias-deal-with-amazon/374632/.

62. Levine, *Surveillance Valley*, p. 189.

63. Lee Artz, *Global Entertainment Media: A Critical Introduction* (Chichester, UK: Wiley Blackwell, 2015), p. 71. The phrase "media monopoly" was made popular by media scholar Ben Bagdikian's classic study, *The Media Monopoly* (New York: Beacon, 2000, updated edition). Global corporate consolidation has led to just a handful of global media behemoths and takes place so quickly that any study of the global oligopoly is in need of constant update.

64. Peter Dreier and Daniel Flaming, "Disneyland's Workers Aren't Paid a Living Wage," *Los Angeles Times*, 1 March 2018, p. A13.

65. For the details in this paragraph, see Phillips, *Giants*, pp. 266–272.

66. Phillips, *Giants*, p. 263.

67. Phillips, *Giants*, p. 264. Phillips provides details on the principal global PRP firms, global corporate behemoths in themselves, and so thoroughly cross-invested with the banks, media corporations, and so on, that they appear to be simply another branch of the integrated mass of global capital. See pp. 273–300.

68. Tom Secker and Matthew Alford, "Documents Expose How Hollywood Promotes War on Behalf of the Pentagon, CIA and NSA," *GlobalResearch*, 4 July 2017, accessed on 5 February 2018 at www.globalresearch.ca/documents-expose-how-hollywood-promotes-war-on-behalf-of-the-pentagon-cia-and-nsa/5597891.

69. Ford, *The Rise of the Robots*, p. 93.

70. This was pointed out to me by Steve Miller and Rosemary Lee, "Criminalization—A Fascist Tool to Reorganize Society," May 2017, unpublished commentary provided to the authors.

71. Dawn Paley, *Drug War Capitalism* (Oakland, CA: AK Press, 2014), p. 125.

72. Roy Walmsley, "World Prison Population List," 12th edition, Institute for Criminal Policy Research, 2018, accessed on 29 April 2019 at www.prisonstudies.org/sites/default/files/resources/downloads/wppl_12.pdf.

73. Ruth Wilson Gilmore, *Golden Gulag: Prisons, Surplus, Crisis, and Opposition in Globalizing California* (Berkeley, University of California Press, 2007).

74. Wendy Sawyer and Peter Wagner, "Mass Incarceration: The Whole Pie 2019," Prison Policy Initiative, 19 March 2019, accessed on 29 April 2019 at www.prisonpolicy.org/reports/pie2019.html. The 900 percent figure is from Mark Jay, "Cages and Crises: A Marxist Analysis of Mass Incarceration," *Historical Materialism*, 27(2019): 1–43, see p. 1.

75. Sawyer and Wagner, "Mass Incarceration: The Whole Pie 2019."

76. For these details, see Cody Mason, "International Growth Trends in Prison Privatization," The Sentencing Project, August 2013, accessed on 29 April 2019 at https://sentencingproject.org/wp-content/uploads/2015/12/International-Growth-Trends-in-Prison-Privatization.pdf; Saskia Sassen, *Expulsions: Brutality and Complexity in the Global Economy* (Cambridge, MA: Harvard University Press, 2014), pp. 68–69.

77. Samantha Michaels, "Leaked Memo Reveals Trump's Gift to Private Prison Companies," *Mother Jones*, 30 January 2018, accessed on 19 April 2019 at www.motherjones.com/crime-justice/2018/01/leaked-memo-reveals-trumps-gift-to-private-prison-companies/.

78. For these details, see The Sentencing Project, "Private Prisons in the United States," 2 August 2018, accessed on 29 April 2019 at www.sentencingproject.org/publications/private-prisons-united-states/.

79. For an important discussion on how corporations, corporate-funded foundations, and state agencies in the United States are attempting to coopt the movement against mass incarceration, see William I. Robinson and Oscar Fabian Soto, "Passive Revolution and the Movement Against Mass Incarceration: From Prison Abolition to Redemption Script," *Social Justice Blog*, 9 May 2019, accessed on 19 December 2019 at www.socialjusticejournal.org/from-prison-abolition-to-redemption-script/.

80. James Kilgore, "Electronic Monitors: How Companies Dream of Locking Us in Our Homes," *In These Times*, 23 April 2018, accessed on 29 April 2019 at http://inthesetimes.com/article/21084/electronic-monitors-GEO-Group_CoreCivic-mass-incarceration-prisons-jails. Geo Group in particular stands to benefit. In 2011, the global carceral conglomerate bought BI Incorporated, one of the largest providers of electronic monitoring devices.

81. As cited in Carl Takei, "From Mass Incarceration to Mass Control, and Back Again: How Bipartisan Criminal Justice Reform May Lead to a For-Profit Nightmare," *University of Pennsylvania Journal of Law and Social Change*, 20(2) (2017): 125–183, accessed 19 December 2019 at https://scholarship.law.upenn.edu/jlasc/vol20/iss2/3.

82. For these details, see Christoph Scherrer and Anil Shah, "The Return of Commercial Prison Labor," *Monthly Review Online*, 18 April 2017, accessed on 22 April 2019 at https://mronline.org/2017/04/18/the-return-of-commercial-prison-labor/.

83. Linda Evans and Eve Goldberg, *The Prison-Industrial Complex and the Global Economy* (San Francisco, CA: PM Press, 2012), p. 13.

84. American Civil Liberties Union, "In For a Penny: The Rise of America's New Debtors' Prison," October 2010, accessed on 19 April 2019 at www.aclu.org/sites/default/files/field_document/InForAPenny_web.pdf.

85. American Civil Liberties Union (ACLU), "A Pound of Flesh: The Criminalization of Private Debt," 2018. I accessed the full report on 12 April 2019, available here: www.aclu.org/sites/default/files/field_document/022318-debtreport_0.pdf. A summary is available here: www.aclu.org/issues/smart-justice/mass-incarceration/criminalization-private-debt.

86. Kayla James, "How the Bail Bond Industry Became a $2 Billion Business," *Global Citizen*, 31 January 2019, accessed on 19 April 2019 at www.globalcitizen.org/en/content/bail-bond-industry-2-billion-poverty/.

87. See, e.g., Jazmine Ulloa, 20 November 2018, "Bail Bond Industry Moves to Block Sweeping California Law," *Los Angeles Times*, online edition, accessed on 19 April 2019 at www.latimes.com/politics/la-pol-ca-bail-referendum-signatures-20181120-story.html.

88. "$elling Off Our Freedom: How Insurance Corporations Have Taken Over Our Bail System," *American Civil Liberties Union*, May 2017, pp. 3, 6, accessed on 19 April 2019 at www.aclu.org/sites/default/files/field_document/059_bail_report_2_1.pdf.

89. Parts of this section draw significantly from Robinson, *Into the Tempest*, Chapter 6, "Global Capitalism, Migrant Labor, and the Struggle for Social Justice."

90. International Labor Organization (ILO), data posted at ILO web page and accessed 19 December 2019: www.ilo.org/global/topics/labour-migration/lang--en/index.htm.

91. See "Figures at a Glance" at the website for the United Nations High Commission on Refugees (UNHCR) from the 2017 report, accessed on 19 April 2019 at www.unhcr.org/ph/figures-at-a-glance. It must be stressed that these varied figures for migrants and refugees worldwide are at best tentative as there are variations depending on the reporting agency and on methodology (e.g., how many refugees as counted by the UNHCR are counted by the ILO as migrant workers?).

92. See, e.g., Kam Wing Chan, "China: Internal Migration," in Immanuel Ness and Peter Bellwood (eds.), *The Encyclopedia of Global Human Migration* (Hoboken, NJ: Wiley-Blackwell, 2013).

93. Graham, *Cities Under Siege*, p. 132.

94. As cited in Reece Jones, "From Violent Borders: Refugees and the Right to Move," *NACLA Report on the Americas*, 51(1), 2019: 37.

95. Michelle Chen, "The US Border Security Industry Could be Worth $740 Billion by 2023," *Truthout*, 6 October 2019, accessed on 10 October 2019 at https://truthout.org/articles/the-us-border-security-industry-could-be-worth-740-billion-by-2023/.

96. Chen, "The US Border Security Industry Could be Worth $740 Billion by 2023." See also Todd Miller, "More Than a Wall: Corporate Profiteering and the Militarization of US Borders," *Transnational Institute*, 16 September 2019, accessed on 10 October 2019 at www.tni.org/en/morethanawall.

97. Esther Yu Shi Lee, "Private Prison CEO's 'Pleased' Their Earnings Soared from Keeping Immigrant Kids in Detention," *ThinkProgress*, 10 May 2016, accessed on 5 February 2018 at https://thinkprogress.org/private-prison-ceos-pleased-their-earnings-soared-from-keeping-immigrant-kids-in-detention-2425dc11532/.

98. Van Le, "Private Prisons Are Making Millions By Helping to Deport Longtime Immigrant-Americans—And They're Positively Gleeful About it," *America's Voice*, 9 August 2017, accessed on October 26, 2017 at https://americasvoice.org/blog/private-prisons-see-future-profits/.

99. *The Economist*, "Profiting from the Wall," 25 March 2017, p. 59.

100. For details, see, inter alia, Joseph Nevins, *Operation Gatekeeper: The Rise of the "Illegal Alien" and the Making of the U.S.-Mexico Boundary* (New York: Routledge, 2002).

101. American Civil Liberties Union, "The Constitution in the 100-Mile Border Zone," undated post on ACLU webpage, accessed on 19 April 2019 at www.aclu.org/other/constitution-100-mile-border-zone.

102. Juan Manuel Sandoval Palacios, "U.S.-Mexico Border States the U.S. Military-Industrial Complex," *Regions and Cohesion*, 7(1), Spring 2017: 87–121, quote from p. 93. See also his more detailed study in Spanish, *La Frontera Mexico Estados Unidos* (Mexico City: National Institute of Anthropology and History, 2017).

103. For an excellent brief documentary on ALEC, anti-immigrant legislation, and the vested corporate interest in the war on immigrants, see "Immigrants for Sale," accessed on 14 July 2017 at www.youtube.com/watch?v=vuGE1 VxVsYo (viewed on 1 January 2013). The documentary was produced by Brave New Foundation (www.bravenewfoundation.org/). See also www.mycuentame.org/immigrantsforsale.

104. For these details, see a 28 October 2010 report by National Public Radio (NPR), and reported at the NPR website, accessed on 14 July 2017, www.npr.org/2010/10/28/130833741/prison-economics-help-drive-ariz-immigration-law. Also see Ian Gordon, "The Immigration Hardliner Family Tree," *Mother Jones*, April 2012, accessed on 19 April 2019 at www.motherjones.com/politics/2012/03/john-tanton-anti-immigration-laws.

105. See Ian Gordon, "The Immigration Hardliner Family Tree," *Mother Jones*, April 2012, accessed on 19 April 2019 at www.motherjones.com/politics/2012/03/john-tanton-anti-immigration-laws.

106. See, inter alia, "Immigrant Detention Map and Statistics," *CIVIC*, accessed on 6 October 2017 at www.endisolation.org/resources/immigration-detention/.

107. Michelle Alexander, *The New Jim Crow* (New York: The New Press, 2012), p. 231.

108. Alene Tchekmedyian, "Prison Firm Sued by Immigrants," *Los Angeles Times*, 5 March 2017, p. A20.

109. For these varied details, see Aviva Shen, "The Corporation that Deports Immigrants Has a Major Stake in Trump's Presidency," *ThinkProgress*, 1 December 2016, accessed on 22 April 2019 at https://thinkprogress.org/trump-immigration-corporations-3ff5a3de7af/.

110. Report by National Immigration Project, Immigrant Defense Project, and Mijente, "Who's Behind ICE? The Tech and Data Companies Fueling Deportations," October 2018, p. 1, accessed on 22 April 2019 at www.nationalimmigrationproject.org/PDFs/community/2018_23Oct_whos-behind-ice.pdf.

111. Chen, "The US Border Security Industry Could be Worth $740 Billion by 2023."

112. Mark Akkerman, "Border Wars: The Arms Dealers Profiting from Europe's Refugee Tragedy" (Amsterdam: Transnational Institute, 2016), accessed on 23 April 2019 at www.tni.org/files/publication-downloads/border-wars-report-web1207.pdf. All the information in these two paragraphs is from the Executive Summary, pp. 1–2. I converted euro figures into dollars using the

April 2019 exchange rate. But this rate is subject to constant swings so these figures are shifting estimates.

113. The investigative reporting by *San Jose Mercury News* journalist Gary Webb first broke this story, as later memorialized in the 2014 Oliver Stone film, *Kill the Messenger*. See Gary Webb and Maxine Waters, *Dark Alliance* (New York: Seven Stories Press, 2014, reprint edition). See also, Peter Dale Scott, *Cocaine Politics: Drugs, Armies, and the CIA in Central America* (Berkeley: University of California Press, 1998).

114. Alexander, *The New Jim Crow*. Alexander's analysis, however, is seriously flawed. She explicitly rejects linking her analysis of the rise of mass incarceration to the larger issues of political economy, class, and capitalism, and writes off white prisoners, who make up roughly half of all prisoners and who share the same socioeconomic and class conditions as their black and Latino counterparts, as "collateral damage" of racist policies. See the critique by Jay, "Cages and Crises."

115. See, inter alia, Michael Woodiwiss, *Gangster Capitalism: The United States and the Globalization of Organized Crime* (New York: Basic Books, 2005).

116. John Gilber, *To Die In Mexico* (San Francisco, CA: City Lights, 2011).

117. Holly Ellyatt, "Global Drugs Trade 'As Strong as Ever' as Fight Fails," *CNBC*, 13 August 2013, accessed on 10 October 2019 at www.cnbc.com/id/100957882. For more detailed data and discussion, see the World Drug Report issued annually by the United Nations Office of Drugs and Crime (UNODC), home page here: https://wdr.unodc.org/wdr2019/index.html.

118. Of course, violent gangs and drug trafficking and the expanded social violence it rains down *is* a problem of crisis proportions. The point here is that these problems are themselves the fallout from capitalist globalization and the problems themselves are major sources of profit making.

119. Among the many works on the drugs wars in the Americas, see: Paley, *Drug War Capitalism*; William Aviles, *The Drug Wars in Latin America* (New York: Routledge, 2018); Jasmin Hristov, *Paramilitarism & Neoliberalism* (London: Pluto, 2014); Gilber, *To Die In Mexico*.

120. Paley, *Drug War Capitalism*, p. 16.

121. Paley, *Drug War Capitalism*, p.76.

122. See, inter alia, William I. Robinson, *Global Capitalism and Latin America* (Baltimore, MD: Johns Hopkins University Press, 2008).

123. Christy Thornton, "Ending U.S. Support for Mexican Repression Starts at Home," *NACLA Report on the Americas*, 18(4), 2016: 322–323.

124. Jorge Beinstein, "Las Nuevas Dictaduras Latinoamericanas," *Agencia Latinoamericana de Informacion*, 16 March 2018, accessed on 9 April 2018 at www.alainet.org/fr/node/191654.

125. See, inter alia, Charles Hale, Pamela Calla, and Leith Mullings, "Race Matters in Dangerous Times," *NACLA Report on the Americas*, 49(1): 81–89.

126. Andrea Germanos, "US Special Ops Training in Latin America Tripled, Docs Reveal," *Common Dreams*, 31 August 2016, accessed on 14 April 2014 atwww.commondreams.org/news/2016/08/31/us-special-ops-training-latin-america-tripled-docs-reveal.

127. Sarah Kinosian and James Bosworth, "Security for Sale: Challenges and Good Practices in Regulating Private Military and Security Companies in Latin America," report by the Inter-American Dialogue (Washington, DC), March 2018, accessed on 10 April 2019 at www.thedialogue.org/wp-content/uploads/2018/03/Security-for-Sale-FINAL-ENGLISH.pdf. The 16,000 figure is on p. 3, the "interwoven" quote from p. 2, the Brazil figures from p. 5.

128. Brett J. Kyle and Andrew G. Reiter, "A New Dawn for Latin American Militaries," *NACLA Report on the Americas*, 51(1), 2019: 19.

129. See, e.g., for Central America, William I. Robinson, "The Second Implosion of Central America," *NACLA* blog, 28 January 2019, accessed on 30 April 2019 at https://nacla.org/news/2019/01/28/second-implosion-central-america.

130. Kyle and Reiter, "A New Dawn for Latin American Militaries," p. 26.

131. Kinosian and Bosworth, "Security for Sale," pp. 10–11.

132. Halper, *War Against the People*, p. 69.

133. Max M. Mutschler and Marius Bales, "Global Militarization Index 2018," Bonn International Center for Conversion, 2018 annual report, pp. 14, accessed on 2 May 2019 at www.bicc.de/uploads/tx_bicctools/BICC_GMI_2018_e.pdf. Israel spend \$15 billion a year on its military, between 6.5–8.5 percent of its GDP, compared to about 4.3 percent spent by the United States, according to Halper, *War Against the People*, p. 37.

134. Halper, *War Against the People*, provides a long bibliographic list (pp. 43–44) of books on Israel's export of arms and military advisors and its doctrines and tactics of counterinsurgency and summarizes this cumulative research.

135. For these details, see Halper, *War Against the People*, pp. 65, 92.

136. Halper, *War Against the People*, p. 4.

137. Halper, *War Against the People*, p. 143.

138. See various sections in Halper, *War Against the People*.

139. Dennis J. Blasko, "Chinese Special Operations Forces: Not Like 'Back at Braff'," *War on the Rocks*, 1 January 2015, accessed on 18 April 2019 at https://warontherocks.com/2015/01/chinese-special-operations-forces-not-like-back-at-bragg/.

140. Alvin So, *Class and Class Conflict in Post-Socialist China* (Singapore: World Scientific Printers, 2013), p. 3.

141. Frank Hersey, "China to Have 626 Million Surveillance Cameras Within 3 Years," *Technode*, 22 November 2017, accessed on 4 May 2019 at https://technode.com/2017/11/22/china-to-have-626-million-surveillance-cameras-within-3-years/. According to the article, the Chinese facial and gait recognition market is the fastest growing program in the world. The market was worth in 2017 \$6.4 billion and was expected to have a growth rate of over 12 percent through to 2021, compared to the U.S. market worth \$2.9 percent.

142. See: Stephen Chen, "China to Build Facial Recognition Database to Identify Any Citizen Within Seconds," *South China Morning Post*, 12 October 2017, accessed on 4 May 2019 at www.scmp.com/news/china/society/

article/2115094/china-build-giant-facial-recognition-database-identify-any; Hersey, "China to Have 626 Million Surveillance Cameras Within 3 Years."

143. Hersey, "China to Have 626 Million Surveillance Cameras Within 3 Years."

144. Hersey, "China to Have 626 Million Surveillance Cameras Within 3 Years."

145. Ana Swanson and Edward Wong, "Trump Administration Could Blacklist China's Hikvision, a Surveillance Firm," *New York Times*, 21 May 2019, accessed on 22 May 2019 at www.nytimes.com/2019/05/21/us/politics/hikvision-trump.html.

146. For these details, see Alexandra Ma, "China is Building a Vast Civilian Surveillance Network," *Business Insider*, 29 April 2018, accessed on 4 May 2019 at www.businessinsider.com.au/how-china-is-watching-its-citizens-in-a-modern-surveillance-state-2018-4; Anna Mitchell and Larry Diamond, "China's Surveillance State Should Scare Everyone," *The Atlantic*, 2 February 2018, accessed on 4 May 2019 at www.theatlantic.com/international/archive/2018/02/china-surveillance/552203/; Eamon Barret, "In China, Facial Recognition Tech is Watching You," *Fortune*, 28 October 2018, accessed on 4 May 2019 at http://fortune.com/2018/10/28/in-china-facial-recognition-tech-is-watching-you/.

147. Alexandra Stevenson and Chris Buckley, "Blackwater Founder's New Company Strikes a Deal in China. He says He Had No Idea," *New York Times*, 1 February 2019, accessed on 18 April 2019 at www.nytimes.com/2019/02/01/business/erik-prince-xinjiang-china-fsg-blackwater.html.

148. *The Intercept* revealed the counterinsurgency operation. See Alleen Brown, Will Parrish, and Alice Speri, "Leaked Documents Reveal Counterterrorism Tactics Used at Standing Rock to 'Defeat Pipeline Insurgencies'," *The Intercept*, 27 May 2017.

149. Zoe Carpenter and Tracie Williams, "Since Standing Rock, 56 Bills Have Been Introduced in 30 States to Restrict Protests," *The Nation*, 16 February 2018, accessed on 30 April 2019 at www.thenation.com/article/photos-since-standing-rock-56-bills-have-been-introduced-in-30-states-to-restrict-protests/.

150. See, inter alia, Graham, *Cities Under Siege*.

151. Henry Wilkinson, "Political Violence Contagion: A Framework for Understanding the Emergence and Spread of Civil Unrest," *Lloyd's Emerging Risk Report, 2016*, accessed on 18 May 2019 at www.lloyds.com/~/media/files/news%20and%20insight/risk%20insight/2016/political%20violence%20contagion.pdf. Wilkinson was commissioned by Lloyd's to prepare the report. He is the director of The Risk Advisory Group, a private consulting firm.

152. The details in this paragraph are discussed by Nafeez Ahmed, "Defence Industry Poised for Billion Dollar Profits from Global Riot 'Contagion'," *Insurgent Intelligence*, 6 May 2016, accessed on 18 May 2019 at https://medium.com/insurge-intelligence/defence-industry-poised-for-billion-dollar-profits-from-global-riot-contagion-8fa38829348c.

Chapter 4 The Battle for the Future

1. Eric Hobsbawm, *The Age of Extremes* (New York: Vintage Books, 1996), pp. 584–585.

2. Apart from my own writings on the totalitarian nature of global capitalism, discussion on this characterization can be found in George Liodakis, *Totalitarian Capitalism and Beyond* (Burlington, VT: Ashgate, 2010); Sheldon S. Wolin, *Democracy Inc.: Managed Democracy and the Specter of Inverted Totalitarianism* (Princeton, NJ: Princeton University Press, 2008).

3. Antonio Gramsci, *Selections from the Prison Notebooks* (New York: International Publishers, 1973), pp. 275–276.

4. See, for example, the response of 14 academics, researchers, political thinkers, and activists, myself included, to the question "is fascism making a comeback?" put forward by *State of Nature: Conversations on Social and Political Theory* ("a blog entirely dedicated to interviews with leading thinkers in social and political theory"), 3 December 2017, accessed on 20 March 2018 at https://stateofnatureblog.com/one-question-fascism-part-one/.

5. I have been writing about the rise of twenty-first-century fascist projects since 2008. Much of my analysis was summarized in William I. Robinson, "Global Capitalist Crisis and Twenty-First Century Fascism," *Science and Society*, 83(2): 481–509. This section draws broadly from that article.

6. On the rise of neo-fascist movements in many of these countries at the turn of the century in Europe, see, inter alia, Robert O. Paxon's study *The Anatomy of Fascism* (New York: Vintage Books, 2004). In the second decade of the twenty-first century and especially concurrent with Trump's election in the United States, these and new far-right and neo-fascist movements experienced an upsurge, often winning seats in national legislatures. These include the Freedom Party in Austria, the National Front in France, Golden Dawn in Greece, Alternative for Germany in Germany, the Jobbik Party (Movement for a Better Hungary) and also the Fidesz party of Prime Minister Viktor Orbán in Hungary, Slovakia's People's Party-Our Slovakia, Holland's Party for Freedom, Forza Nuova in Italy (although the Northern League is far right but could not, I believe, be characterized as extreme right/neo-fascist). See, e.g., Tancredi Marini, "Neo-Fascist and Far-Right: Conquering Europe," *BlogActiv/EU-Logos*, 12 April 2017, accessed on 21 May 2019 at https://eulogos.blogactiv.eu/2017/12/04/neo-fascists-and-far-right-conquering-europe/. Very useful also is Nick Robins-Early and Willa Frej, "A Guide to the Far-Right Power Players Tearing Europe Apart," *Huffington Post*, 25 August 2018, accessed on 29 May 2019 at www.huffpost.com/entry/guide-far-right-players-europe_n_5b7bf18ee4boa5b1febee47a.

7. Gramsci, *Selections from the Prison Notebooks*, p. 182; emphasis added.

8. Gramsci, *Selections from the Prison Notebooks*, p. 221.

9. Gramsci, *Selections from the Prison Notebooks* p. 210.

10. See, inter alia, Paxon, *The Anatomy of Fascism*; Umberto Eco, "Ur-Fascism," *New York Review of Books*, 22 June 1995, accessed on 21 May 2018 at www.nybooks.com/articles/1995/06/22/ur-fascism/.

11. Rosengarten observes: "The appeal of Fascism hinged on … its ability to attract disaffected members of the rural petit-bourgeois class and even of disaffected artisans and agricultural workers … [Fascism] won the loyalty of thousands of declassed, embittered individuals who lacked a secure political identity. Fascism gave these people a new lease on life, a new sense of being recognized above and beyond their strictly class affiliations." See Frank Rosengarten, *The Revolutionary Marxism of Antonio Gramsci* (Chicago, IL: Haymarket, 2014), p. 55.

12. See Umberto Eco, "Ur-Fascism."

13. Benedict Anderson, *Imagined Communities* (London: Verso, 1983), pp. 15–16.

14. Alex Callinicos, *Race and Class* (London: Bookmarks, 1983), p. 38.

15. Trumpism, for instance, represents just such a mediation. Here there is a great deal of insight to be had from the fact that the presidential campaigns of both Bernie Sanders and Donald Trump in the 2016 U.S. presidential elections appealed to the same social base of disaffected workers, one with a left interpretation of the crisis and the other with a far-right populist and openly racist interpretation. While I cannot take up these issues here, only part of the story of the Trump electoral triumph was the racist mobilization of white workers and petty-bourgeoisie. The flip side of this mobilization was widespread voter suppression and disenfranchisement of voters from racially oppressed communities.

16. RSS stands for Rashtriya Swayamsevak Sangh (National Patriotic Organization), founded in 1925 as a right-wing Hindu nationalist paramilitary organization that drew its inspiration from Mussolini in Italy and other fascist movements in Europe.

17. Joah Bierman, "A Sales Pitch for Davos Globalists," *Los Angeles Times*, 26 January 2018, p. A3.

18. Robinson, "Global Capitalism and 21st Century Fascism." See also other sources in endnote 2.

19. As cited in Antonio A. Santucci, *Antonio Gramsci* (New York: Monthly Review Press, 2010), p. 85.

20. To be sure, fascist movements go back to the 1930s, and before that in a very different historical context, to the post-Reconstruction terror unleashed on the Black population.

21. Trump's decade-long reality television show, *The Apprentice*, and the concomitant false image as a successful businessman who "gets things done," helped to cultivate his charismatic status for those who would be susceptible to his subsequent political manipulation. I want to thank my copy and style editor, Jeanne Brady, for pointing this out. The larger observation is that a fascist project generally requires a charismatic figure that can be seen to embody repressed aspirations, frustration over powerlessness in the face of larger social forces, or to assuage psycho-social anxieties.

22. "Active Antigovernment Groups in the United States," *Southern Poverty Law Center*, no date given on report, but the report's data suggests it was

posted in early 2018; accessed on 14 April 2018 at www.splcenter.org/active-antigovernment-groups-united-states.

23. American Civil Liberties Union (ACLU), Press Release, New Mexico chapter, 18 April 2019, accessed on 22 April 2019 at www.aclu-nm.org/en/press-releases/aclu-new-mexico-asks-governor-and-attorney-general-investigate-armed-vigilantes.

24. The anti-government figure is from the ACLU, Press Release, as is the quote. The hate group figure is from Heidi Beirich and Susy Buchanan, "2017: The Year in Hate and Extremism," *Southern Poverty Law Center*, 11 February 2018, retrieved on 14 April 2018 at www.splcenter.org/fighting-hate/intelligence-report/2018/2017-year-hate-and-extremism.

25. Witness, anecdotally, the cover page of the 26 May 2018 edition of *The Economist*: "The Affair: Why Corporate America Loves Donald Trump."

26. See inter alia, William I. Robinson, "The Battle Against Trumpism and the Specter of 21st Century Fascism, *Telesur*, 21 January 2017, www.telesurtv.net/english/opinion/The-Battle-Against-Trumpism-and-Specter-of-21st-Century-Fascism-20170121-0022; "Trumpism, 21st Century Fascism, and the Dictatorship of the Transnational Capitalist Class," *Social Justice*, 20 January 2017, www.socialjusticejournal.org/trumpism-21st-century-fascism-and-the-dictatorship-of-the-transnational-capitalist-class/ (all accessed 19 December 2019); William I. Robinson, "What is Behind the Renegotiation of NAFTA? Trumpism and the New Global Economy," *Truthout*, 24 July 2017, accessed on 9 March 2018 at www.truth-out.org/news/item/41365-what-is-behind-the-renegotiation-of-nafta-trumpism-and-the-new-global-economy.

27. Pierre Bourdieu, *Distinction: A Social Critique of the Judgement of Taste* (Cambridge, MA: Harvard University Press, 1984).

28. Even the far-right billionaire Koch brothers, who had bankrolled Trump's 2016 presidential campaign and for years financed far-right movements in U.S. civil society, launched a multimillion-dollar campaign against the tariffs and against Trump's economic nationalism. See Brian Schwartz, "Billionaire Koch Brothers Network Unveils Phase One of Multimillion-Dollar Ad Campaign Against Trump's Tariffs," *CNBC*, 20 June 2018, accessed on 20 May 2019 at www.cnbc.com/2018/06/20/koch-brothers-unveil-first-ads-from-campaign-against-trumps-tariffs.html.

29. *Telesur*, "Brazil: Steve Bannon to Advise Bolsonaro Presidential Campaign," 15 August 2018, accessed on 10 November 2018 at www.telesurenglish.net/news/Brazil-Steve-Bannon-to-Advise-Bolsonaro-Presidential-Campaign-20180815-0003.html.

30. *The Guardian*, "Trump Joy over Bolsonaro Suggests New Rightwing Axis in Americas and Beyond," 29 October 2018, accessed on 10 November 2018 at www.theguardian.com/world/2018/oct/29/jair-bolsonaro-brazil-trump-rightwing-axis.

31. Jake Johnson, "After Win by Brazilian Fascist Jair Bolsonaro, World's Capitalists Salivate Over 'New Investment Opportunities'," *Common Dreams*, 29 October 2018, retrieved on 10 November 2018 at www.

commondreams.org/news/2018/10/29/after-win-brazilianfascist-jair-bolsonaro-worlds-capitalists-salivate-over-new.

32. Clifton Leaf, "Aetna CEO: 'Doing Nothing in the Current Model of Capitalism, Will Destroy Capitalism'," *Fortune*, 27 October 2017, accessed on 15 June 2018 at http://fortune.com/2017/10/27/cvs-aetna-mark-bertolini-capitalism/.

33. Antonio Gramsci, as cited in Marco Fonseca, *Gramsci's Critique of Civil Society* (New York: Routledge, 2016), pp. 23–24.

34. Karl Marx and Frederick Engels, *The Communist Manifesto*, 1848, in Robert C. Tucker (ed.), *The Marx-Engels Reader* (New York: Norton and Norton, 1978), p. 496.

35. Thomas Piketty, *Capital in the Twenty-First Century* (Cambridge, MA: Harvard University Press, 2014 [2013]).

36. My analysis of the reformist project is laid out in William I. Robinson, "Capitalism in the Twenty-First Century: Global Inequality, Piketty, and the Transnational Capitalist Class," in Lauren Langman and David A. Smith (eds.), *Piketty, Inequality and 21st Century Capitalism* (Boston, MA: Brill, 2018), pp. 238–254.

37. Organization for Economic Cooperation and Development (OECD), "In It Together: Why Less Inequality Benefits All," *OECD Publishing*, 2015. Accessed on 22 May 2019 at www.keepeek.com/Digital-Asset-Management/oecd/employment/in-it-together-why-less-inequality-benefits-all_9789264235120-en#page1. Notably, the report called for greater gender inequality, not as a matter of justice but because gender equality is shown to decrease income inequality.

38. George Soros, *The Crisis of Global Capitalism* (New York: Public Affairs, 1998).

39. The memo was widely published in the press at the time and is reproduced on hundreds of websites, among them Wikipedia at https://en.wikipedia.org/wiki/Summers_memo. Particularly useful is the discussion by John Bellamy Foster on the memo ("'Let Them Eat Pollution': Capitalism and the World Environment," *Monthly Review*, 44(8), 1993: 10–20). Following his work as Treasury Secretary in the second Clinton administration, Summers went on to become president of Harvard University, a post from which he resigned in disgrace for declaring that women are biologically less capable of learning math than men. It is worth recalling more of his infamous 1991 memo: "The measurements of the costs of health impairing pollution depends on the foregone earnings from increased morbidity and mortality. From this point of view a given amount of health impairing pollution should be done in the country with the lowest cost, which will be the country with the lowest wages. I think the economic logic behind dumping a load of toxic waste in the lowest wage country is impeccable and we should face up to that … The demand for a clean environment for aesthetic and health reasons is likely to have very high income elasticity. The concern over an agent that causes a one in a million change in the odds of prostate cancer is obviously going to be much higher in a country where people survive to get prostate

cancer than in a country where under 5 mortality is 200 per thousand. Also, much of the concern over industrial atmosphere discharge is about visibility impairing particulates. These discharges may have very little direct health impact. Clearly trade in goods that embody aesthetic pollution concerns could be welfare enhancing. While production is mobile the consumption of pretty air [*sic*] is a non-tradable. The problem with the arguments against all of these proposals for more pollution in LDCs (intrinsic rights to certain goods, moral reasons, social concerns, lack of adequate markets, etc.) could be turned around and used more or less effectively against every Bank proposal for liberalization."

40. "Why Isn't Capitalism Working?" *Reuters*, 9 January 2012, accessed on 22 May 2019 at http://blogs.reuters.com/lawrencesummers/2012/01/09/why-isnt-capitalism-working/.

41. See, for example, Kenneth Lehman, *Bolivia and the United States: A Limited Partnership* (Athens: University of Georgia Press, 1999).

42. See, for example, Jeffrey D. Sachs, *The End of Poverty* (London: Penguin, 2005); Joseph Stiglitz, *Globalization and Its Discontents* (New York: W.W. Norton, 2003).

43. Jerry Harris, "The Future of Globalization: Neo-Fascism or the Green New Deal," *Race and Class*, in press.

44. I place "green capitalism" in quotation marks precisely because it is in my view an oxymoron. I concur fully with Richard Smith's argument in *Green Capitalism: The God that Failed* (London: College Publications, 2016) that the only alternative to a market-driven environmental collapse is a largely planned and publicly owned economy.

45. Moreover, solar panel, battery and other "green capitalist" production circuits are linked backward to the extractive industries and are interlocked with the Silicon Valley-Wall Street-military-industrial-security nexus discussed in the previous chapter.

46. Trévon Austin, "New Poll Shows American Youth are Increasingly Supportive of Socialism," *World Socialist Website*, 13 March 2019, accessed on 8 April 2019 at www.wsws.org/en/articles/2019/03/13/yout-m13.html.

47. Austin, "New Poll Shows American Youth are Increasingly Supportive of Socialism."

48. *The Guardian*, "Billionaire JP Morgan Chief Attacks Socialism as 'a Disaster'," 4 April 2019, accessed on 8 April 2019 at www.theguardian.com/business/2019/apr/04/jamie-dimon-socialism-jp-morgan-banker-disaster.

49. Among the many, here are three that I have found worth the read: Paul Mason, *Postcapitalism: A Guide to Our Future* (New York: Farrar, Straus and Giroux, 2017); Bhaskar Sunkara, *The Socialist Manifesto: The Case for Radical Politics in an Era of Extreme Inequality* (New York: Basic Books, 2019), and Nick Srnicek and Alex Williams, *Inventing the Future: Postcapitalism and a World Without Work* (London: Verso, 2016).

50. See Samir Amin, "Letter of Intent for an Inaugural Meeting of of the Internationale of Workers and Peoples," *Pambazuka News*, 23 August 2018,

accessed on 2 January 20202 at www.pambazuka.org/global-south/letter-intent-inaugural-meeting-international-workers-and-peoples.

51. On the rise of the Pink Tide in the context of global capitalism, see William I. Robinson, *Latin America and Global Capitalism* (Baltimore, MD: Johns Hopkins University Press, 2008). On the decline of the Pink Tide, see Steven Ellner (ed.), *Latin America's Pink Tide: Breakthroughs and Shortcomings* (Lanham, MD: Rowman and Littlefield, 2019).

52. Adolf Reed, *Class Notes* (New York: The New Press, 2000).

53. Srnicek and Williams, *Inventing the Future*, pp. 3, 10.

54. Ronaldo Munck, "Workers of the World Unite (At Last)," *Great Transition Initiative*, April 2019, p. 3, accessed on 29 May 2019 at www.greattransition.org/publication/workers-of-the-world-unite.

55. The 207-million figure is from Munck, "Workers of the World Unite (At Last)," p. 5. The 50-million figure is from the webpage for the IndustriALL global union, www.industriall-union.org/. On the new transnational unionism, see also Peter Evans, "National Labor Movements and Transnational Connections: Global Labor's Evolving Architecture Under Neoliberalism," Institute for Research on Labor and Employment (University of California at Berkeley), IRLE Working Paper #116-14, September 2014, accessed on 29 May 2019 at http://irle.berkeley.edu/files/2014/National-Labor-Movements-and-Transnational-Connections.pdf. For discussion of the debate regarding trade union revitalization, see Cristian Ibsen and Maite Tapia, "Trade Union Revitalization: Where Are We Now? Where to Next?", *Journal of Industrial Relations* 59(1) 2017: 170–191.

56. See, inter alia: Alexia Fernández Campbell, "The Worldwide Uber Strike is a Key Test for the Gig Economy," *Vox*, 8 May 2019, accessed on 25 May 2019 at www.vox.com/2019/5/8/18535367/uber-drivers-strike-2019-cities; Sarah Jones, "Global Drivers' Strike Shows Tide May be Shifting for Uber and Lyft," *Intelligencer*, 8 May 2019, accessed on 25 May 2019 at http://nymag.com/intelligencer/2019/05/drivers-strike-shows-tide-may-be-shifting-for-uber-and-lyft.html.

57. Michael Lowy, *Ecosocialism: A Radical Alternative to Capitalism* (Chicago, IL: Haymarket Books, 2015).

58. See, for instance, Heikki Patomaki, "A World Political Party: The Time Has Come," published by *Great Transition Initiative*, February 2019, at www.greattransition.org/publication/world-political-party, together with a roundtable discussion (including a commentary by myself) at www.greattransition.org/publication/roundtable-world-party, both accessed on 24 May 2019). The Great Transition Initiative is (from its website): "an online forum on ideas and an international network for the critical exploration of concepts strategies, and visions to a future of enriched lives, human solidarity, and a resilient biosphere. By enhancing scholarly discourse and public awareness of possibilities arising from converging social, economic, and environmental crises, and by fostering a broad network of thinkers and doers, it aims to contribute to a new praxis for global

transformation." Its home page is https://greattransition.org/about/aims-and-background.

59. Samir Amin, "Letter of Intent for an Inaugural Meeting of the International of Workers and Peoples," published by the International Development Economics Associates on 3 July 2018 at its website, www.networkideas.org/featured-articles/2018/07/it-is-imperative-to-reconstruct-the-internationale-of-workers-and-peoples/, and accessed on 24 May 2019.

60. Max Elbaum, *Revolution in the Air: Sixties Radicals Turn to Lenin, Mao and Che* (London: Verso, 2002).

Index

currency speculation 33
currency swaps 32

Dakota Access Pipeline 109–10
data mining 1, 36–7, 58, 86–7, 89–90,
  99–100, 108–9, 149n66
Davis, Mike 45, 64
Davos *see* WEF
debt
  commodification of 28–9, 93
  to control working classes 31–2
  discipline of debtors 52–3, 58, 93
  government 28, 31, 54–5, 76–7
  growth, as basis of 32
  household 26, 32, 51–5
  student 29, 58, 93
"debtfare state" 52–3, 93
defense spending *see* military
  spending
deficits (fiscal) 31, 54–5, 76–7
"deglobalization" rhetoric 20, 119–20
Denmark 69
deregulation
  of financial industry 28, 30
  of labor markets 43
  limited rollback of 127–8
  of markets in general 25, 126, 129
  of transnational capital flows 25,
  26–7
  under Trump 120
derivatives 29, 32–3
deskilling 39, 55, 59
detention centers 95–6, 98–9, 109
Detroit 83
development 129–30
DHS *see* Homeland Security, Dept. of
dictatorships
  corporate support for 71, 109
  in Latin America 104–6
  support for corporations by 104
  see also authoritarianism
digitalization
  mass media and 120–1
  policing and 63–4, 66, 99–101
  repression and warfare and 84–90,
  99–100, 107–9

surplus humanity and 38–9, 46–7,
  49, 55–8
working class unity and 137–8
Dimon, Jamie 132
dispossession
  for agribusiness 45–6, 62
  enclosures 16, 45–6, 64–9, 129–30
  financial sector and 31–2, 62
  historic enclosures 16–17
  for Millennium Development Goals
  129–30
  for resource extraction 103, 105,
  109–10
  see also primitive accumulation
downward mobility 117–20
Driscoll's 61
drugs, war on 68, 73–4, 90, 102–3
DynCorp 79
dystopian future 1–2, 6

e-commerce 35–6
East Timor 56
eBay 87
eco-socialism 133, 138–9
economic data 67
The Economist 35–6, 149n66
Ecuador 105
education 58
Egypt 56, 65
Einstein, Albert 112
Eisenhower, Dwight D. 71–2
elections 139–40, 171n15
electronic monitoring 91, 92, 99,
  164n80
elites *see* transnational capitalist class
  (TCC)
Elliott, Liza 1–2
empathy vs contempt 118–20
enclosures 16, 45–6, 64–9, 129–30 *see
  also* dispossession; primitive
  accumulation
Energy Transfer Partners 109–10
Engels, Frederick 33, 127
environmental catastrophe 17–18
environmental justice movement 18,
  105–6
escape plans 40, 61

as goal of repression and warfare 3,
   5–6, 72–5, 80–1, 84–7, 90–9;
   Middle East warfare for 73–5,
   76–7, 79, 80–1, 101, 106–7
   increasing 27–8, 143n8
   levels of 143n8, 145n21
   limited restraint of 127–8
   of tech sector 37–8
proletarianization 44–5, 55–7, 117
propaganda 85, 87–9
property ownership 52, 64–5
protectionism 20, 124, 125, 172n28
protesters, repression of 105–6, 107–11
public services *see* social protections
PV (political violence) pandemics 110

racism
   environmental refugees and 18
   lumpenproletariat and 49–50
   mass incarceration and 69, 102
   in neo-fascism 118–19
   racial profiling 97
   of Trump 123
Raytheon 73, 87, 100
real subsumption of labor 55–8
recessions *see* crises; financial crisis
   (2008)
redistribution
   under Fordism-Keynesianism 24–5,
   41
   mild, under reformism 127–8, 129,
   134–5
   of power 41–51
   requirement for 129, 130
   upwards 13, 26–7, 28, 30–2, 51–5,
   76–7, 129
redistributive nation-state capitalism
   25, 27
refugee crisis 101 *see also* migrants
rehabilitation 92
Reich, Robert 55
Reiter, Andrew G. 105
rents 37–8, 52
repression and warfare
   capitalist hegemony's breakdown
   and 112–17

to contain surplus humanity 3,
   63–70
   inequality and 3, 31, 41, 63, 68–70,
   83
   against migrants 95–101, 118
   against most vulnerable 118–19
   normalization of 68, 118
   permanent war 74–5
   privatization of 5–6, 78–87, 160n30
   for profit 3, 5–6, 72–5, 80–1, 84–7,
   90–9; Middle East warfare for
   73–5, 76–7, 79, 80–1, 101, 106–7
   against protesters 18, 105–6, 109–11,
   126–7
   to redistribute upwards 54–5
   technological change and 84–90,
   99–100, 107–9
   worldwide examples 102–11
Republican Party (U.S.) 123, 125
resource extraction 104–6, 109–10,
   126, 134–5, 174n45
revolt 133–5
Revolution in Military Affairs (RMA)
   84–90
revolutionary struggle 138–41
revolving doors 161n42
rich, the *see* transnational capitalist
   class (TCC)
"riot control systems" 110
RMA (Revolution in Military Affairs)
robots
   replacing workers 47, 59
   for warfare and repression 64, 84, 85
Rupert, Johann 40, 63
Russia 83, 129

Sachs, Jeffrey 129
Safran 101
SAIC (Science Applications
   International Corporation) 82
Salesforce 100
Salvini, Matteo 126
Samsung 38
Sanders, Bernie 171n15
Sandoval, Juan Manuel 96
Sassen, Saskia 67
Saudi Arabia 79

Thanks to our Patreon Subscribers:

Abdul Alkalimat
Andrew Perry

Who have shown their generosity and comradeship in difficult times.

The Pluto Press Newsletter

Hello friend of Pluto!

Want to stay on top of the best radical books
we publish?

Then sign up to be the first to hear about our
new books, as well as special events,
podcasts and videos.

You'll also get 50% off your first order with us
when you sign up.

Come and join us!

Go to bit.ly/PlutoNewsletter